Congress and the Great Issues

1945–1995

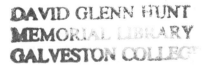

Congress and the Great Issues

1945–1995

Ronald D. Elving, Editor

Congressional Quarterly Inc.
Washington, D.C.

Cover design: Patt Chisholm
Book design: Patt Chisholm and Cyndi Smith

Library of Congress Cataloging-in-Publication Data

Congress and the great issues. 1945–1995 / Ronald D. Elving, editor
    p. cm.
  Includes index.
  ISBN: 1-56802-215-8 (pbk. : alk. paper)
  1. United States–Politics and government–1945–1989. 2. United
States–Politics and government–1989- 3. United States. Congress-
History–20th century. I. Elving, Ronald D.
E743.C615 1996
328.73'09'045–dc20   96-10595

Contents

Preface

It was not easy, in 1945, to obtain information about how one's member of Congress voted. House votes were often taken by aggregate shouts of "yea" or "nay" or recorded by individual "tellers" who reported only the total numbers to the Speaker—not the individuals who had voted each way. By such means, party leaders could keep their troops together while shielding individual members from the adverse consequences of their votes.

The public at large, and even the newspapers attempting to cover congressional decisions, sometimes found it impossible to identify the votes of the various members. It was in this environment that Nelson Poynter, a newspaperman from Indiana and Florida, endeavored to introduce a journalistic service that would break down House and Senate votes by individual.

Poynter and his wife, Henrietta, herself an accomplished reporter and writer, had begun providing information to newspapers as a government service during the war. Henrietta Poynter, in particular, had a passion for Congress and a keen awareness of how the institution shuttered itself from public view.

The Poynters wanted to provide not only the week-by-week vote scores but also a study of past voting records and capsule summaries of the issues facing Congress. The sum of these parts, called Congressional Quarterly, was to be bound and delivered to clients four times annually. It began publishing in the last year of the war and regularized its delivery thereafter. The various streams of information eventually were consolidated in a weekly publication called the *Congressional Quarterly Weekly Report.*

Fifty years after the founding of Congressional Quarterly, the *Weekly Report* marked its anniversary by publishing a series of articles looking back at significant episodes in the life of Congress over that half century. These biweekly articles were written by several *Weekly Report* editors and reporters under the direction of Executive Editor Robert W. Merry.

The episodes were chosen to illustrate how Congress and the country changed over that span of time. As in a picaresque novel, the articles reveal their characters by forcing them to work through various situations—some petty, some grand. Each episode was selected to capture the mood of a moment in American history as experienced within the institution of Congress.

A Changing Congress in a Turbulent World

The years following World War II brought great changes on the world stage, many of which had serious implications for Americans. For members of Congress, the challenge was to understand and respond to shifting global power relationships—military, economic, and cultural—while staying in touch with the local concerns of the voters who sent them to Washington. Their efforts to balance these demands, both in cooperation with the White House and in competition with it, shaped the nation we know at the end of the twentieth century.

In 1945 the United States was still at war in Europe and the Pacific, wearing down the weakened Axis powers of Germany and Japan. Victory seemed certain but was not yet in hand. Americans at home as well as overseas had altered the course of their lives. The degree of their personal sacrifices varied greatly, but nearly all Americans shared in some measure in this unprecedented national mission.

The year brought many milestones: Germany collapsed in May; the first atomic bomb was dropped on Hiroshima in August; and Japan surrendered in September. The United Nations was founded that summer, and the Soviet Union, back from the brink of extinction, established itself as one of two superpowers in the postwar world.

But before these resonating events took place, Americans said goodbye to their longest-serving president, Franklin D. Roosevelt, who died in April, just a few months into his fourth term in office. Roosevelt's death severed the symbolic connection between the prewar and postwar worlds.

The America of 1945 seems to us now irretrievably remote, a black-and-white movie of a memory. Half a century later, we marvel to think of homes without television and offices without computers. We can scarcely imagine travel without freeways or jet airplanes, much less summers without air conditioning.

Communications for home and business remained roughly what they had been two decades earlier. The telephone was common but far from ubiquitous. The great majority of households had radios, but television was still an experiment—political conventions were not televised until three years later, in 1948. Most Americans got their news from daily newspapers, of which the big cities still had several. It was typical for family members to spend the evening reading magazines. Many went to the movies as regularly as once a week, filling the large auditorium theaters to watch newsreels and cartoons as well as feature films.

There were just forty-eight states then, with a total population of less than 150 million. The federal government, once it shifted back to peacetime footing, spent an average of less than $43 billion annually from 1946 to 1950. The national debt stood at $259 billion. In 1995, by comparison, the federal budget was about $1.5 trillion, and the national debt nearly $5 trillion.

The U.S. economy of the mid-1940s was a war machine of unprecedented size and power, outproducing all the other combatant nations combined. In fact, the gross national product of the United States was roughly equal to the gross product of the rest of the world. Peace brought anxiety about maintaining prosperity, but the engines of growth persisted even after the war. Men mustering out of the service often had more trouble finding housing than finding a job. Despite some dislocation, the new economy continued to sustain total employment in excess of 60 million jobs (counting the armed forces) through the end of the decade. When Vice President Henry Wallace had mentioned 60 million jobs as a national policy goal in the prewar years, he had not been taken seriously.

The U.S. economy of that era was also remarkably self-contained. The nation produced its own food and used its own plentiful natural resources for fuel and raw materials. The automobiles, farm machines, factory tools, electric appliances, and household implements Americans purchased were, by and large, made in America. Even the great preponderance of the nation's wardrobe came from domestic fiber, mills, and clothing manufacturers.

The most disturbing aspect of the economy was the renewed warfare between labor and management. Forced to work and produce through the war for wages and prices set in Washington, union leaders and industrial managers were spoiling for a fight. Laws passed by Democratic Congresses in the 1930s had given labor most of the legal high ground, but some industries were prepared to shut down rather than yield to further wage demands. In the immediate postwar years, strikes would temporarily hobble transportation (then still primarily reliant on railroads) and the production of steel and automobiles.

At the war's end, the two political parties' identification with labor and management had become the main defining difference between them. Many other issues that had divided Democrats and Republicans over the generations had, in one sense or another, been resolved. Prohibition was dead; no one talked much about tariffs; and a bipartisan agreement had formed for an active American role in world affairs.

The new foreign policy consensus was composed of two strains of thought, both produced by the shock of Pearl Harbor. The first was a sense that the United States must never again be as vulnerable and naive in world affairs as it had been in 1941. The second was a new openness to the idea of collective security—treaties, alliances, and international organizations empowered to resist aggression and, to some degree, arbitrate disputes and order relationships between countries.

The latter idea was a direct reversal of the attitude following World War I when the Senate rejected President Woodrow Wilson's treaty establishing the League of Nations. But in 1945 the United Nations, the successor to the league, was born at a conference convened in San Francisco. The UN made its headquarters in New York City and became another symbol of U.S. leadership in the world.

But it was the first idea, the fear of vulnerability, that would inform U.S. foreign policy most profoundly. While the Axis powers lay vanquished, new enemies seemed to spring up almost immediately in the form of foreign governments and guerrilla movements. The U.S. interest in foreign affairs came to be defined by one principle above all: resistance to the advance of world communism.

By conjuring fearful images of the expanding communist bloc early in 1947, President Harry S. Truman would gain a respite from his declining political fortunes—he had lost control of Congress in the 1946 election. But the issue proved even more useful for a generation of Republicans. Later in the 1940s, the GOP capitalized on the fear of communism to instill distrust of Truman and the Democrats generally, helping the Republicans to win the White House and both chambers of Congress in the election of 1952.

Yet with all the foreign turmoil and labor unrest of the later 1940s, the compelling passions of the American populace in these years tended to be more personal. There was a great rush to make up for lost time. After years of deferral, the nation turned to having children with what seemed a sense of mission. Beginning in 1946 the "baby boom" continued for eighteen years, producing the spikes in the population curve that were the postwar period's defining demographic characteristic.

But if returning servicemen were eager to start their own families, they were less willing to settle back into their old jobs and neighborhoods. Veterans' benefits—the "G.I. Bill of Rights"—sent so many of them to college that enrollment in institutions of higher learning doubled after the war. This opportunity not only improved the education level of the workforce but also redefined the social idea of higher education, engendering an even wider presumption in the following generation that college was a middle-class right.

Also becoming more accessible in the postwar years was the dream of home ownership. Veterans' benefits, coupled with preexisting federal housing programs, made down payments and monthly mortgage bills manageable for average wage earners. Developers addressed the housing shortage by building new communities—sometimes almost overnight—on the outskirts of the big cities, within commuting distance of office buildings and factories. Partly as a consequence of these new living patterns, more Americans bought cars and fewer used mass transit.

Some veterans looked beyond the suburbs of their native cities to parts of the country they had seen while in uniform. The West Coast and the southern states began to experience an influx of new residents. The availability of practical air-conditioning machines accelerated the migration.

These changes, and others that followed, eventually transformed the political landscape as well. The dominance of the old urban political machines and the old southern courthouse gangs was broken. The farm vote shrank. Congressional seats added to the big industrial states of the Northeast and Midwest in the first half of the century would be reapportioned to the Sun Belt in the second half—to Florida, Texas, and especially California. At the same time, the postwar years brought a great surge of black migration northward to the urban economies generating jobs at high wages in states without Jim Crow laws.

With these population movements and the renewal of immigration as a major source of growth—the new arrivals coming mostly from Latin America and Asia—the United States was beginning a demographic transformation. For a time, the Democratic Party consolidated its position in Congress by holding nearly all the southern seats and adding clusters of seats from all the big cities. But as the end of the century neared, the Republicans finally restored their majorities of the 1920s, becoming the new party of the solid South while preserving their traditional strength in the suburban and rural districts.

If the country at large in 1945 was embarked on momentous social and economic changes, Congress was much the same institution it had been for decades. Power and influence followed strict hierarchies, largely based on tradition and seniority. Region mattered as much as party, if not more. The members were almost exclusively white males. The House had one African American member from

Chicago and one from Harlem, and no Hispanics or Asians. There were eight women in the House, none in the Senate.

When the 79th Congress convened in January 1945, it had thirty-three standing committees in the Senate and forty-eight in the House. Many of these committees had long since outlived their usefulness, and many more had overlapping jurisdiction with rival committees. But party leaders in both chambers were loath to extinguish any existing committees for fear of offending their chairmen or other senior members.

The biggest change in Congress during the Roosevelt era was its work schedule. In the 1930s Congress had been accustomed to meeting for a few months in the spring of the odd-numbered year and adjourning until the even-numbered year. But in the continuing crisis atmosphere of world war, Congress was in session most of the year. Here, too, the arrival of air conditioning, installed in the Capitol in the 1930s, made it possible for Congress to remain in session through the muggy Washington summer. In the postwar era, it became common practice for members of Congress from distant states to bring their families to Washington and buy homes in the area.

Even though the calendar had been altered, much of the congressional pattern of work stayed the same. Most members saw their jobs in the old-fashioned manner they had learned as members of state legislatures. They were party conscious and inclined to vote with the party. Exceptions were made for issues of regional sensitivity, the obvious example being Southern Democrats' refusal to countenance encroachments on states' rights—particularly regarding civil rights.

Congress had no budget process, preferring to authorize spending as each committee pleased and then sort out the priorities in the confines of the powerful Appropriations Committees—one each in the House and Senate—and the even more rarefied sessions of the conference committees that met to resolve differences between the two.

Congress emerged from the Great Depression and the war with something of an inferiority complex. President Roosevelt had dominated national affairs since his first election in 1932 and had vastly expanded the number and power of executive agencies. Congress had receded in importance and authority accordingly. Some of the older members could recall the primacy of Congress in the years before Roosevelt, and not a few members—older and younger and in both parties—were eager to regain that dominance.

To some degree, the post-Roosevelt sessions of Congress would rise in relation to the presidency, especially in setting domestic policy on fiscal matters and labor-management disputes. But subsequent presidents retained a special status and authority in the conduct of foreign affairs as well as a unique ability to focus the attention of the nation. Roosevelt had demonstrated the effectiveness of these powers, and there was little Congress could do to counteract either one.

The postwar Congress was unable to reclaim its central role in American government because in times of crisis the public tends to look to the executive leader rather than to the national legislature. It was not simply Roosevelt's personality that put Congress in eclipse but the trying times that elevated him to power and kept him there. Through the next half century, Congress battled to assert itself in relation to the presidency, having its best success when individual members had enough standing in the national consciousness to challenge the president.

By its nature, Congress is a diverse, reactive, and slow-moving institution, given to deliberation and obfuscation. Like a convoy of ships at sea, it must move at the pace of its slowest vessel—and many of its vessels are not built for speed. Congress was not immune to the forces shaping the national consciousness in the postwar years: it simply took longer for these forces to prevail in a system designed to resist and regulate change rather than foster it.

Congress was not without an impulse of its own for reform. For example, before the final adjournment of the 79th Congress in 1946, a major overhaul of the committee structure was cleared by both chambers and signed into law by President Truman. By reducing the number of standing committees by more than half, the Legislative Reorganization Act of 1946 was a watershed, even if there was less to it than met the eye.

The reform looked impressive on paper, but the practical effect was to telescope several related committees into one. The idea of abolishing fiefdoms for certain chairmen was only partially achieved—as many kept their privileges alive as chairmen of newly created subcommittees. In the years that followed, Congress returned to the habit of creating new committees when it saw fit. More radical notions of reform, including the election of committee chairmen and the limiting of their terms, were introduced in the 1970s and 1990s, respectively.

In the meantime, most of the change that occurred within Congress resulted from elections. Every two years, the cast of characters was at least somewhat rearranged, and occasionally the voters effected a change of ruling party. Throughout the half-century following World War II, a coalition of Democrats from the North and the South usually ruled both chambers. However, on certain issues—notably civil rights bills in the 1950s and 1960s, the Vietnam War in the 1970s, and the tax-and-spend issues of the early 1980s—Southern Democrats aligned themselves with minority Republicans.

Through the first two decades of the postwar era, the South remained a Democratic preserve. But the civil rights legislation of the mid-1960s moved the old Confederacy and the Border States into the Republican column in presidential elections and gradually eroded loyalty to the Democrats in congressional and state elections as well. By the mid-1990s the gradual, generational transformation of Southern Democrats into full-time Republicans had progressed to the point that most of the seats from the region were held by the party of Lincoln.

All these changes lay ahead of Congress when it convened in January 1945, still the creature of its own customs and peculiar isolation from the world. House members and most senators were accustomed to serving out their terms in relative obscurity, seldom seeing their names in the news and never hearing them on radio. The wise ones who were reelected regularly for long careers were not only content in this but also grateful for it, knowing that it insulated them from pressure and distraction and allowed them to do much as they pleased—for better or worse.

It seems fitting, then, to begin with the news of Roosevelt's death reaching the Capitol, where it was conveyed to Vice President Truman. A creature of Congress who felt out of place in Roosevelt's White House, Truman was still spending his days on Capitol Hill that April—presiding over the Senate and socializing with his cronies in the legislative branch.

Ronald D. Elving
April 1996

Congress and the Great Issues

1945–1995

For Congress and the nation, the postwar era began not with the formal ending of World War II but with the death of Franklin D. Roosevelt. Elected president four times, Roosevelt held the White House through a global depression and a worldwide war. He defined his party and his historical era as no other president had done since Abraham Lincoln, and his legacy would dominate national politics for the rest of the century.

Roosevelt's achievements were made possible by Democratic majorities in Congress far larger than any before or since. At their peak in the 75th Congress (1937-1938), the Democrats held more than 330 of the 435 seats in the House and 76 of the 96 in the Senate. Yet they were riven by the profound divisions of their history—between North and South, between urban and rural, between Roosevelt supporters and those who thought he went too far.

In his first term, Roosevelt saw the "Hundred Days" session of 1933 rush to embrace the New Deal. But as the decade wore on and the Depression persisted, Congress grew resistant. By 1938, an exasperated Roosevelt sought to purge certain senators and House figures, especially those who had scuttled his ill-fated plan to enlarge the Supreme Court. Nearly all of his targets triumphed in spite of him. In 1940, even as he neared his third electoral landslide, Roosevelt had to struggle mightily to win House approval for a peacetime draft.

When Pearl Harbor brought the United States into World War II, however, all other conflicts were at least temporarily submerged. Congress was subservient to the demands imposed by national crisis. Still, the internal struggles of the Democratic Party went on below the surface. Although Roosevelt was not challenged for renomination in 1944, party conservatives were strong enough to demand the removal of the vice president, Henry A. Wallace, a liberal reformer whom many considered to be a socialist.

The new Number Two, a compromise with the party's southern wing, was Harry S. Truman, a middle-rank second-term senator from the medium-sized border state of Missouri. Truman had been a farmer, an officer in World War I, and an unsuccessful haberdasher in his hometown of Independence, Missouri. He studied law in night school, won a judgeship, and moved up in state politics through his connections with powerful local politicians. In 1934 he was nominated and elected to the Senate. A decade later, Truman would be thrust into the role of national helmsman.

It was April 12, 1945, weeks before the surrender of Germany and months before that of Japan. Truman was vice president, but still spent much of his time at the Capitol. He was not too proud to preside over Senate sessions, performing the largely ceremonial function the Constitution accords the vice president. And so on the day of Roosevelt's passing, the news reached Truman in a private room hidden deep within the Capitol's labyrinthian halls.

The Death of a President

Robert W. Merry

The morning of April 12, 1945, dawned gray and rainy in the nation's capital, and nothing in the political agenda that Thursday suggested it had been reserved by history.

At the White House, presidential aides routinely assembled Franklin D. Roosevelt's daily correspondence and papers, to be air-shipped down to him at the "Little White House," his cozy cottage in Warm Springs, Georgia. Bad weather would delay the flight, so it would be well into the morning before the president could get down to his day's work.

On Capitol Hill, the calendar called for a light House schedule, and the chamber adjourned at mid-afternoon. As House Speaker Sam Rayburn of Texas descended from the rostrum he turned to Lewis Deschler, the parliamentarian, and invited him down for drinks in his private sanctum on the first floor of the Capitol.

"Be there about five," said the Speaker. "Harry Truman is coming over."

The Speaker's private room—Room 9 in the Capitol, now H-128—was a coveted place in those days. It wasn't particularly fancy. There were a few black leather easy chairs, old and well worn; a matching leather sofa; a fireplace; a big desk; and a refrigerator "camouflaged with veneer to more or less match the desk," as Truman biographer David McCullough described it.

To be invited there for drinks with Rayburn and the boys was a special privilege, conferred upon only a few well-chosen insiders on an occasional basis—and very few on a regular basis. Harry Truman was one of the regulars, and he enjoyed those afternoon sessions. They were special not only as a valued exchange of political information and gossip but also as a hallowed part of history.

The history began with Nicholas Longworth of Ohio when he was Speaker in the 1920s. Regularly, he would gather in an afternoon with his closest friend and greatest rival, John Nance Garner of Texas, to drink bourbon and trade tales. Almost always they would invite cronies in to enliven the discussion and expand the information pool.

Longworth, a Republican, and Garner, a Democrat, were as different as two politicians could be. Longworth was "an elegant Cincinnati dilettante with a gift for music and the small talk of elite salons," as congressional historian Neil MacNeil once put it. Garner, a product of the Texas sod, was aptly described by his nickname, "Cactus Jack."

But they were inseparable. Evenings the Speaker would drive his Texas friend home in the Speaker's official limousine, which both men referred to as "our car." Mornings he would stop by to pick Garner up for the trip back to the Capitol. And afternoons, at the dusk of the day's toil, they would "strike a blow for liberty," as they would call it when getting up to pour themselves yet another glass of bourbon and branch.

Servicemen in a New York canteen read newspaper reports about the sudden death of Franklin D. Roosevelt on April 12, 1945.

There was a name for these sessions—"Board of Education." It didn't have anything to do with educating young members in the fine points of parliamentary maneuvers. Rather it had to do with the leaders' use of the sessions to educate themselves on behind-the-scenes activities in the House.

"Well," Garner once explained, "you get a couple of drinks in a young Congressman, and then you know what he knows. . . . We pay the tuition by supplying the liquor."

When Garner became Speaker, he continued the tradition, and so did Rayburn, although Rayburn referred to the sanctum simply as "downstairs." And Rayburn was less interested in eliciting information from young members than in bringing into his circle the most savvy and well-informed politicos he could find. To be admitted into the Rayburn Sanctum was by definition to gain political leverage of immense value in the age-old art of political horse-trading.

That certainly wasn't lost on young Lyndon Johnson, who used his inner sanctum access to gain information of use to young, ambitious officials of the Roosevelt administration. As biographer Robert A. Caro describes it, Johnson ran errands for his New Deal friends, provided information, even landed a favor or two. "But what he got from them wasn't minor; it was, in fact, the largest thing in his political life during his first years in Congress"—the Marshall Ford Dam near Austin.

And so on this particular gray Thursday—April 12, 1945—Harry Truman looked forward

to joining Rayburn and his pals over in Room 9 at 5 p.m. It was a boring day in the Senate, where the conscientious vice president was presiding over a lackluster debate about a water treaty with Mexico. To while away the hours he wrote a letter to his mother and sister back in Independence, Missouri.

"I am trying to write you a letter today from the desk of the President of the Senate," he wrote, "while a windy Senator from Wisconsin is making a speech on a subject with which he is in no way familiar. . . ."

He adjured them to tune in their radio "tomorrow night at 9:30, your time," to hear his Jefferson Day address to the nation. "I think I'll be on all the networks so it ought not to be hard to get me," he wrote. "It will be followed by the President, whom I'll introduce."

When the Wisconsin senator, Republican Alexander Wiley, concluded his speech, Major-ity Leader Alben Barkley of Kentucky moved for a recess. The big clock over the main lobby entrance reported it was four minutes to five.

The vice president exited the Senate chamber through the swinging doors to his left and stepped briskly to his Capitol office across the lobby to tell assistant Harry Vaughan he would be with Rayburn. Then he made his way to the Speaker's sanctum, following a route through the Capitol later retraced by McCullough: eluding his Secret Service guard, he cut through the Senate Reception Room, went out past the eight-foot white marble statue of Benjamin Franklin, down the long, tiled corridor, around the columned well of the Senate Rotunda known as "Mark Twain's Cuspidor," on through the main rotunda under the dome, through Statuary Hall and briefly down another corridor to the stairway; he descended the stairs to the ground floor, went left down one hallway,

Roosevelt's body is borne toward the Capitol, where he had often tangled with conservatives in both parties during the previous twelve years.

then right down another. He reached the Board of Education a little past five.

Deschler had already arrived. Also there was James M. Barnes, a White House official who served on the congressional liaison team. It was growing dark in the room as the spring dusk gathered outside, but nobody had bothered to turn on the lights. Rayburn, Deschler, and Barnes had drinks in hand.

As pleasantries were exchanged the vice president poured himself a bourbon, then perched himself upon the big, overstuffed arm of the chair nearest Rayburn's desk. At this point Deschler recalled that a call had come in for Truman some time earlier from Stephen Early, a top White House official.

"Mr. Speaker," said the parliamentarian, "wasn't the vice president supposed to call the White House?"

"Oh, yeah, Harry," said Rayburn. "Steve Early wants you to call him right away. Want me to get him for you?"

"No, I'll get it," said Truman, taking the phone and dialing the White House number.

"This is the V.P.," he said.

The three cronies watched as the vice president's face suddenly turned grave. Early, clearly tense and sounding strangely nervous, instructed Truman to come to the White House "as quickly and as quietly as possible" and to enter via the North Portico on Pennsylvania Avenue. Visibly shaken, Truman hung up the phone.

"Jesus Christ and General Jackson!" he exclaimed. "Steve Early wants me at the White House immediately."

He stepped to the door and, with his hand still on the knob, turned to his solemn-faced friends.

"Boys," he said, "this is in the room. Something must have happened."

The vice president ran the length of the Capitol, his shoes pounding on the marble floor as he raced past the bronze and marble Civil War generals and state governors of the building's first floor, past the Senate barbershop, then up the side marble steps to his second floor office to get his hat. In minutes he was in the vice presidential Mercury being whisked to the White House by his driver, Tom Harty. At 5:25 the car pulled into the northwest entrance of the White House and deposited Truman at the North Portico.

Two ushers took him to the oak-paneled elevator that had served the mansion's residents since the days of Theodore Roosevelt. The slow, grinding contraption lifted him to the second floor, the president's private quarters.

There in her sitting room sat Eleanor Roosevelt. Steve Early was with her, along with Anna and John Boettiger, the Roosevelts' daughter and son-in-law. Mrs. Roosevelt stood up, stepped forward, and placed her arm on Truman's shoulder.

"Harry, the president is dead."

There ensued a long silence as Truman struggled for words.

"Is there anything I can do for you?" he asked finally.

"Is there anything we can do for you?" she replied. "For you are the one in trouble now."

White House officials summoned Chief Justice Harlan Fiske Stone, who rushed to the green-walled Cabinet Room with a Bible and administered the oath of office at 7:09. *Time* magazine reported that Harry Truman, sixty, "the neat, slim, spectacled man from Missouri," stood stiffly underneath Seymour Thomas's portrait of Woodrow Wilson. The magazine added: "The ceremony over, he lifted the Bible to his lips."

History moves in large currents and broad sweeps, but it chooses individual men and women as instruments of change. And hence the tale of Truman's day on April 12, 1945, represents more than just a slice of political life at a dramatic and momentous crossroads. After more than twelve years as president, Roosevelt had become something of an imperious leader, given to demanding—and getting—his way with the national legislature. His profound political successes had answered the nation's call for new national directions, but they had not bred humility in the president.

Truman, by contrast, was a man of fundamental humility, and that fact would transform the relationship between the White House and Congress, as least for a time. Almost from the beginning, as a stunned nation mourned the dead president amid collective sighs of disbelief and ritual expressions of respect and grief, Truman made clear in word and deed his intent to work with the legislative institution that had forged his political consciousness.

On his first full day in office, he broke precedent by going to the Hill for lunch. "To his friends in Congress," said *Time*, "President Truman said humbly and simply that he just wanted to assure them in person of his intense desire for cooperation." The point, according to *Time:* "Temporarily, at least, the days of Congressional-Executive fights are gone."

Three days later he was back to address a joint session of Congress, and the event served as testament to the grand scheme of peaceful succession crafted so brilliantly by the Founding Fathers a century and a half before. The applause was deafening as the new president entered the House chamber by the center door, and it increased as he mounted the rostrum. Fighting off an initial trace of nervousness as he read from a big, black book, the nation's new leader paid eloquent tribute to his predecessor and vowed fealty to his legacy. Then Harry Truman, a devout Baptist, reached back to the First Book of Kings for a prayer and simple statement of purpose:

" 'Give therefore thy servant an understanding heart to judge thy people, that I may discern between good and bad; for who is able to judge this thy so great a people?'

"I ask only to be a good and faithful servant of my Lord and my people."

Harry Truman's first months in the Oval Office were harrowing. President Roosevelt had done little to prepare his successor, excluding him from consultations and leaving him ignorant of vital developments. Truman was not privy to details of the Yalta Conference, where Roosevelt prearranged the postwar map with Winston Churchill, Joseph Stalin, and the other allied leaders. Truman barely knew about the Manhattan Project, then on the verge of testing the first atomic bomb. Yet it would be Truman who had to decide, within a few months of his swearing-in, whether to use that weapon on Japan.

No sooner had the war ended, however, than Truman was engulfed by another wave of problems on the domestic front. The demand for war goods had ended the Great Depression, and now that demand was at an end. Millions of men mustering out of the service discovered that jobs were in short supply, housing was hard to find, and food prices prohibitive.

The strains of the postwar adjustment were especially painful within the Democratic coalition. Truman was committed to the prolabor policies and politics of the 1930s. But in 1946, Truman's first full year in office, more workers were idled by strikes and more time was lost to strikes than in any other year in U.S. history. In April, 400,000 mine workers went out, and strikes threatened to shut down the railroads and the steel and auto industries. Truman's efforts to intervene pleased no one.

While he struggled with these domestic challenges, Truman was distracted by an array of equally compelling perils abroad. The United Nations Charter was signed in San Francisco in June 1946, but the ending of the war brought only a fragile peace. The Soviet army had occupied much of Germany, including Berlin, and most of Eastern and Central Europe as well. The cities and industries of Asia lay in ruins. The long-running civil war between communists and nationalists in China, suppressed for nearly a decade by the war with Japan, had resumed.

Truman's popularity, a powerful political reality when his Gallup Poll approval score hit 87 percent in mid-1945, was almost entirely dissipated by the summer of 1946. Republicans campaigning for Congress that fall could point to unemployment, inflation, labor unrest, and myriad tales of corruption in government. Millions of voters wanted the United States to do more to help Europe and China, while at least as many were distressed at continuing U.S. troop commitments in occupied Germany and Japan.

Even if Truman had been blessed with less trying circumstances, he would still face the swing of the political pendulum. The president's party usually loses ground in midterm elections. And by November 1946, the Democrats had held the White House and both chambers of Congress continuously for fourteen years. A change in Congress was overdue.

Republican Takeover of Congress

Ronald D. Elving

In the first week of January 1947, a House member from Ohio named George H. Bender presented a new broom to every fellow Republican arriving to be sworn in for the 80th Congress. The note attached to each read: "Here's yours. Let's do the job."

Bender needed a lot of brooms. In the elections held the previous November, voters had sent seventy-five Republican freshmen to the House and seventeen Republican freshmen to the Senate. Overall, the GOP gained a net of fifty-six seats in the House, thirteen in the Senate. It was the first time the party of Lincoln had controlled both chambers since the elections of 1930.

The Republican triumph had been national in character and scope, consistent on the issues and successful from New England through the Midwest to the West Coast. (The only exception was the Confederate South, which remained a Dixiecrat stronghold.)

"This was the greatest Republican victory in 18 years," wrote Joseph W. Martin Jr., the Massachusetts Republican who would become the new Speaker of the House. "It was the revival of the Republican Party, the ultimate proof that the party had survived the ordeal of the 1930s."

Indeed, the voters had decided the Republicans should not only survive but rule. After preferring Democrats at virtually all levels of power throughout the Depression and World War II, the electorate had delivered a message that was rare in its clarity and unmistakable in its significance. It was time, the voters said, for a change.

The victorious Republicans were certain the era of Franklin D. Roosevelt had been interred with its namesake. "For the first time in 14 years, the United States is not in a state of emergency," said Robert A. Taft, the Republican senator from Ohio, whom many considered Roosevelt's preeminent foe.

The Republican campaign had deftly exploited many different dissatisfactions, directing voter ire at the ruling party. Meat and housing were in historically short supply. When the Chicago *Sun* sponsored an election prediction contest that fall, a thirty-two-year-old housewife named June Shaw was among the top performers. "Simple," she explained. "I just listened to what the ladies were saying while I was standing in the meat line."

Veterans returning from the war in Europe and the Pacific found jobs scarce. Families wondered when the boys still overseas would be home. Union labor wanted wage increases; business wanted regulatory relief; everyone wanted lower taxes. "Had Enough?" the bumper stickers and billboards asked. "Vote Republican."

President Harry S. Truman was all but officially rendered a caretaker in the White House, easy pickings for the GOP nominee in 1948. The accidental president who had been sworn in when Roosevelt died in 1945 was widely held

Republican Joseph W. Martin Jr., right, and Democrat Sam Rayburn, left, passed the Speaker's gavel back and forth four times between 1947 and 1955.

responsible for the Democratic catastrophe. *Time* magazine referred almost casually to Truman as lost and forlorn in the "the office that had proved too much for him." Arkansas senator J. William Fulbright, a Democrat, suggested Truman appoint a Republican secretary of state (which was then the office first in line for the presidency) and resign, so as to "place the responsibility of running the government on one party and prevent a stalemate."

In the days after the election, Truman seemed to acknowledge some of the criticism by lifting government controls on everything but rents and rice and sugar (these areas of scarcity were deemed too likely to produce price shocks). But for the first time since Roosevelt's first election, the initiative in governing and the focus of attention had shifted undeniably from the White House to Capitol Hill—and from Democrats to Republicans.

On swearing-in day, January 3, outgoing Speaker Sam Rayburn of Texas showed genuine warmth in presenting Martin, sixty-two, as his successor. The two were close in age and had served together for more than twenty years, both single men who lived for their work and politics. They had maintained a friendly rivalry over the years despite Martin's status as Republican leader (beginning in 1939) and Rayburn's as Speaker (beginning in 1940). Once asked to campaign for Martin's Democratic opponent in Massachusetts, Rayburn replied: "Speak against Martin? Hell, if I lived up there I'd vote for him."

Martin was among the most approachable leaders in House history. Generally addressed as Joe both at home and on the Hill, he took phone calls from constituents at all hours. In November he had been up all night at the small newspaper he owned in North Attleboro, taking calls from victorious candidates around the country. In the wee hours, one surprise winner in Missouri kept Martin on the line while no fewer than fifty-seven well-wishers paraded to the phone.

Rayburn often had said he would not stand for party leader in the minority, but he was prevailed upon to accept that role in the 80th Congress. John W. McCormack of Massachusetts, the second-ranking Democrat, personally asked the Texan to stay in the saddle. The Democratic caucus was sharply divided between North and South. Rayburn was uniquely able to hold the halves together.

On the Senate side, the title of majority leader passed from Democrat Alben W. Barkley of Kentucky, who had held it for a decade, to Wallace H. White Jr. of Maine. Both men were sixty-nine and generally respected among their colleagues. But the real power in both parties was in the hands of others.

The Republicans were led in foreign affairs by Sen. Arthur H. Vandenberg of Michigan, who became Senate president pro tempore at the relatively youthful age of sixty-two (he had been in the Senate since 1928, surviving the New Deal elections that decimated the ranks of older colleagues). A former isolationist, Vandenberg had been part of the American delegation to the United Nations conference and had become something of an internationalist.

The real power among the Republicans, however, belonged to the man they looked to on domestic affairs, the distinguished but unpretentious Taft, son of President William H. Taft and a senator since 1939. Taft was about to become chairman of the Senate Labor and Public Welfare Committee as well as chairman of the Senate GOP's Steering Committee.

The arriving Republicans could not wait to pursue their broad-scale agenda of change. Federal spending, reported to be heading toward $42 billion for fiscal 1947 (busting a budget of $35.1 billion), would be sharply curtailed. Republicans routinely talked about cutting the budget by 10 percent or more. A balanced budget was assumed. The only question was how far spending had to be cut to achieve that balance while also reducing revenues.

The latter question arose immediately because the new majority's fiscal menu also featured a tax cut, and not a bashful one. Harold Knutson, the thirty-year veteran Republican from Minnesota who was about to take over the chairmanship of the Ways and Means Committee, announced he wanted to chop the personal income tax by 20 percent—retroactive to the first of the year—and Martin agreed to make it a priority.

Industrial unions, which had grown in size and power with the adoption of favorable organizing laws in the 1930s, were another Republican target. "Big labor" had slipped in public favor because of postwar strikes and wage demands.

And though the foreign policy of the day had been devised in bipartisan fashion (overwhelming votes had favored U.S. membership in the United Nations), the campaign had raised questions about foreign aid levels and the degree of U.S. involvement around the globe. In Massachusetts, for example, successful Republican Senate candidate Henry Cabot Lodge Jr. had made stump speeches against U.S. assistance to Marshal Tito in Yugoslavia.

The House freshman class of 1946 featured scores of World War II veterans, including John F. Kennedy, D-Mass., third from right, and Richard M. Nixon, R-Calif., far right.

The Republicans also were eager to control the apparatus of congressional investigations. "We shall open with a prayer and close with a probe," boasted Rep. Clarence J. Brown, R-Ohio, after the November voting.

The prospects for probing were varied and substantial. Republicans wanted to look for communists (or their sympathizers) in the government, the unions, and the entertainment industry. They wanted to investigate tales of wartime profiteers in league with well-placed politicians (Sen. Theodore G. Bilbo, D-Miss., would be denied his seat on swearing-in day due to such allegations against him).

Not least on the target list for investigation was the House itself. The new majority pledged a thorough scrubbing of the books kept by the Democrats through the previous eight Congresses, which in fact the General Accounting Office already had begun. A prime suspect was Sergeant at Arms Kenneth Romney, who had run the House bank and allowed members to cash their paychecks months before receiving them. Romney would soon be convicted on charges of making false statements and would be sent to prison.

Even as they were clearing the decks of such internal matters, the arriving Republicans of 1947 had the benefit of a major institutional reform bill having been enacted the previous year. The bill reduced the number of committees in the House and Senate by more than half, provided a retirement system (to encourage retirements), and modernized the system of hiring staff. It also restricted such practices as proxy voting in committee (which would make a comeback, even as the number of committees once again increased).

As a result, members of the Class of 1946 spent far less campaign and legislative energy on the mechanisms of Congress itself than would their successors in the mid-1990s. But the political dynamic of impatience with Washington was obvious in both years. Although the Class of 1946 had no shared manifesto as explicit as the 1994 Contract with America, they ran well-coordinated campaigns emphasizing antigovernment themes.

As individuals, the members of the two "revolution" classes were demographically different. In 1946 every Republican freshman was white, and only one, Katharine P. C. St. George of New York, was female. The class was also notable for its military experience. Sixty-nine members of the 80th Congress elected in 1946 had been on active duty in the armed services during World War II (1941-1945). All but a handful of these men had been in uniform within a year of their election.

Among these returning servicemen were several who would figure prominently in the politics of the postwar era. One was John F. Kennedy, just twenty-nine, who had returned to Boston from the South Pacific decorated for valor (he saved crew members' lives after their PT boat was sunk) and fated for politics. A safe Democratic district that included Cambridge came open in 1946, and Kennedy moved in to take 42 percent in a ten-candidate primary. His campaign blanketed the district with mailed reprints of a *Reader's Digest* article on Kennedy's war exploits.

Another was Republican Richard M. Nixon, who had mustered out of the Navy as a lieutenant commander and at thirty-three ousted a veteran Democrat in California's Twelfth Dis-

trict. Nixon distributed 25,000 white plastic thimbles that said, "Elect Nixon and needle the P.A.C." (a reference to the Political Action Committee, a predecessor of the AFL-CIO's Committee on Political Education). Once sworn in, Nixon headed for the House Un-American Activities Committee to begin hunting subversives.

The newly elected Senate class included Lodge, who had resigned his seat in the midst of his second term and served a tour with the Army. Lodge would be Nixon's vice presidential running mate in their unsuccessful 1960 campaign.

The Senate Class of 1946 also included Joseph R. McCarthy of Wisconsin, who had taken the party nomination away from twenty-two-year incumbent Robert M. La Follette Jr., son of the legendary progressive "Fighting Bob." The younger La Follette had been distracted by his efforts on behalf of the congressional reform package (which he co-authored with Rep. Mike Monroney, D-Okla.) prior to the September primary.

McCarthy, just thirty-seven on Election Day, had been an Army intelligence officer and a local judge. He ran an aggressive challenge on behalf of party conservatives who had never accepted the La Follettes, and he would soon burst upon the national consciousness as a leader in the hunt for communists in government.

In the first week of the new Republican majority, there seemed so much to do, so many avenues to explore, that the Republicans could hardly help but succeed. But the sheer weight of opportunity was daunting.

"The Republicans have promised more than they ever can accomplish," said Robert Lee "Muley" Doughton, the North Carolina Democrat who was giving up the gavel at the Ways and Means Committee. "Now that they have the opportunity we will see just how they do it."

In the parliamentary systems of Europe, national leaders whose parties lose their majorities are summarily ejected. Even Winston Churchill lost his job as prime minister when his party lost elections held the year after the end of World War II. But under the U.S. Constitution, the president and Congress are elected independently, and the president remains in office despite the worst disasters in midterm legislative elections. That was why, in 1947, Republicans were setting the agenda on Capitol Hill but Harry Truman remained very much alive and well in the Oval Office.

Despite the new leadership in Congress, Truman retained particular importance, and even primacy, in the arena of foreign affairs. Republicans' willingness to follow the president's lead overseas was, in part, a habit acquired in the war. But the GOP had also come to share some of the internationalist presumptions that Truman had inherited from Roosevelt—a fact that would make his postwar era profoundly different from the one after World War I.

After the 1914-1918 war, most Americans longed for disengagement from world problems. Panic over "Bolshevism" had infected the country in the so-called Red Scare of 1919 and 1920. But the Soviet Union of that time was isolated and weakened by civil war, and the fears were short-lived. In the same era, President Woodrow Wilson had tried to sell the nation on his own idealism and faith in international cooperation and peacekeeping. But in 1919 he physically collapsed in the midst of what may well have been a quixotic effort; and the following year, Senate Republicans defeated his League of Nations treaty.

In the next two decades, the sentiment for isolation ran strong. It influenced the passage of immigration restraints in the 1920s and the Smoot-Hawley restrictive tariff of 1930. Even as the totalitarian states of the Soviet Union, Nazi Germany, and imperial Japan armed for war in the 1930s, most Americans believed they could stay clear of the conflagration. The America First Committee came to symbolize what may have been the unspoken conviction of a majority of Americans, and almost surely of most Republicans, particularly in the Midwest and the Far West.

Thinking changed after the Japanese attack on Pearl Harbor, which taught a bitter lesson: America might prefer to be left out of world affairs, but the world would not always leave America alone.

But an equally important part of the change would come after the war was over. This time, the world struggle had not ended with the Soviet Union on its knees but on the march. The spectacle of the Red Army standing astride much of Europe focused the minds of nearly everyone, regardless of party. The rise of global communism had become a material threat to capitalism and democracy wherever they existed.

Truman and the Policy of Containment

Mark Willen

No reason was given for the White House summons, and the leaders in Congress who responded had no sense of impending crisis. "We hadn't a clue," Sen. Arthur H. Vandenberg of Michigan would later tell a colleague.

Flanked by Secretary of State George C. Marshall and Under Secretary Dean Acheson, President Harry S. Truman welcomed the congressional leaders to his executive office at 10 a.m. It was February 27, 1947, a chilly, damp, gray Thursday.

As soon as everyone was seated, Truman set the scene. Britain, in desperate financial straits, had informed the United States that it could no longer provide support for Greece and Turkey. Both were in grave danger of falling to communist insurgents—a fate the United States could not tolerate. The president told the members that he had decided on a major aid program and that he wanted their support in pushing it through Congress as quickly as possible. Truman was not asking for advice; he already had made up his mind.

Marshall came next. Although he had been secretary of state for only a month, Marshall's distinguished war record made him a hero, and he was revered by congressional leaders, who listened closely to him. With few dramatics and a plethora of detail, Marshall explained that British Ambassador Lord Inverchapel had told him personally February 24 that Britain's domestic woes would prevent it from providing further aid to Greece and Turkey. Without an infusion of aid from the United States, he said, the Greek economy would collapse, and the Greek government could not suppress the communist-led guerrillas. A civil war would be likely to end with Greece as a communist state under Soviet control. Then Turkey would almost surely fall as well.

"It is not alarmist to say that we are faced with the first crisis of a series which might extend Soviet domination to Europe, the Middle East and Asia," said Marshall. The choice for the United States was "acting with energy or losing by default."

The congressional leaders sat grim-faced. This was not what they wanted to hear. America was finally at peace, and Republicans had just won control of Congress with a mandate to address the nation's domestic problems.

Truman surveyed the room. The House delegation included Republican Speaker Joseph W. Martin Jr. of Massachusetts, Democratic Minority Leader Sam Rayburn of Texas, Foreign Affairs Chairman Charles A. Eaton of New Jersey, and New York's Sol Bloom, the ranking Democrat on Foreign Affairs. In addition to Vandenberg, the Senate delegation included Appropriations Chairman Styles Bridges of New Hampshire and Thomas T. Connally of Texas, the ranking Democrat on Foreign Relations. In an embarrassing oversight, no one had thought to invite Ohio Senator Robert A. Taft, chairman of the Republican Policy Com-

Participants at a February 27, 1947, White House meeting on Greece-Turkey aid gather to discuss up-coming Moscow peace talks (from left): Sens. Bridges and Barkley; Speaker Martin; Sens. Connally and Vandenberg; Rep. Eaton. (Barkley did not attend the Greece-Turkey meeting.)

mittee, a fact that Vandenberg brought to Truman's attention after the meeting.

Truman invited questions, and they came quickly, many tinged with skepticism. "Why do we have to pull British chestnuts out of the fire?" "How much is this going to cost ultimately?" "What are we letting ourselves in for?"

As Marshall responded, Acheson found himself growing increasingly agitated. He found the questions "rather trivial" and "adverse" and thought the answers took the discussion off track.

The Greek-Turkish challenge was close to Acheson's heart. In Marshall's State Depart-

ment, Acheson had been working nonstop to formulate the U.S. response to the British decision. He couldn't understand why these congressmen did not recognize that the United States stood at Armageddon.

Although most accounts, including Truman's and Vandenberg's, credit Marshall with a forceful and effective statement, Acheson was plainly disappointed. "My distinguished chief, most unusually and unhappily, flubbed his opening statement," Acheson wrote in his memoirs, *Present at the Creation.*

"This was my crisis," Acheson continued. "For a week I had nurtured it. These congressmen had no conception of what challenged them; it was my task to bring it home."

Acheson leaned over to Marshall and asked in a stage whisper: "Is this a private fight or can anyone get into it?" Truman gave Acheson the floor.

In the past eighteen months, Acheson began, the position of the democracies of the world had seriously deteriorated. While the United States had been busy trying to save Central Europe from Soviet control, Moscow had been busy elsewhere and with greater success than generally realized.

The Soviet Union had laid down any number of bets, said Acheson, and if it won just one of them, it won them all. If it seized control of Turkey, then Greece and Iran would fall. If it controlled Greece, then Turkey and Iran would fall.

Acheson spoke for close to fifteen minutes. Historian Robert J. Donovan reports that when he finished, everyone in the room knew that not since ancient times had the world seen such a stark polarization. There were now only two world powers: the United States and the Soviet Union.

Vandenberg responded first, saying he had been greatly impressed, even shaken, by what he had heard. It was clear that the situation went beyond the immediate question of Greece and Turkey.

Vandenberg told Truman that it was absolutely necessary that the request for aid be accompanied by an explanation to the American people of the entire grim situation just as it had been explained by Marshall and Acheson. "Mr. President," he declared, "if you will say that to the Congress and the country, I will support you, and I believe that most of its members will do the same."

Truman went around the room, inviting comments. Several members agreed with Vandenberg; no one spoke out in opposition to the aid

request. Truman agreed to Vandenberg's advice. As the conference broke up, Truman said, "Nobody knows where this will lead us."

Acheson moved quickly to steer newspaper coverage of the impending crisis to reflect the White House's perspective. Press accounts suggest he was largely successful.

But not all reaction was favorable. As word spread through Congress, many voiced concern. Florida's Democratic senator Claude Pepper said the whole matter should be turned over to the United Nations. Georgia's Democratic senator Richard B. Russell suggested that the United States might as well admit Britain as a state. "It would cost this country far less than the commitments now proposed as our obligations," he said. "The king could run for the Senate, as could Winston Churchill."

As preparations continued for Truman's address, the president began a long-scheduled trip to Mexico, and Marshall departed for a six-week conference in Moscow. This again left the crisis in the lap of Acheson, who by all accounts enjoyed his finest hour. Acheson and Marshall had each other's complete trust—as well as Truman's—and many historians believe the combination of their skills made them the strongest one-two team ever to control the State Department.

Drafters of Truman's speech followed Vandenberg's advice and put the problem in the context of saving the world from the Soviet menace. The speech went through several drafts, with Truman aide Clark Clifford suggesting changes on Truman's behalf. At one point, the speech was cabled to Marshall in Paris. Marshall thought it far too strong.

"It seemed to Gen. Marshall and to me that there was a little too much flamboyant anticommunism in the speech," wrote Marshall's aide, Charles Bohlen, who was traveling with the secretary. Washington's reply to Marshall stated that "in the considered opinion of the ex-

ASSOCIATED PRESS

President Truman, addressing a joint session of Congress on March 12, 1947, calls for aid to Greece and Turkey to block the advance of communism.

ecutive branch, including the president, the Senate would not approve the doctrine without the emphasis on the Communist danger," according to Bohlen.

Truman met again with congressional leaders—including Taft this time—on March 10 and outlined his plan in detail. He would ask for $400 million in aid to Greece and Turkey, and he would make his speech to a joint session of Congress that would be broadcast on radio and television.

The speech was set for 1 p.m. March 12, but the House chamber was full by 12:30. Joseph M. Jones, a State Department official who recounted the crisis in his book, *The Fifteen Weeks*, described the scene on the floor as chaotic. In addition to members, the Cabinet and invited guests, "dozens of ex-congressmen . . . loitered in conversation with old friends on the periphery of the chamber. Every clerk, secretary or functionary on Capitol Hill whose fa-

miliar face would get him past a guard at the door was also on the floor. One Democratic representative had planted himself, with his small daughter on his lap, in a seat on the center aisle."

Clifford accompanied the president on the drive to the Capitol. They went over the speech one last time, underlining sentences that needed emphasis. Then Truman spoke enthusiastically about the four-day Key West vacation he was to begin as soon as the speech was over.

At precisely 1 p.m. the doorkeeper announced the president, and everyone rose. Escorted by the traditional committee of senators and representatives and carrying his speech in a black folder under his arm, Truman strode down the aisle. He mounted the clerk's desk below the Speaker's rostrum, acknowledged the continuing ovation with a broad smile, opened his folder and began.

The speech lasted eighteen minutes. Truman, whose style was normally flat and unimpressive, spoke with considerable authority, "tripping only occasionally, speaking with a newly acquired forcefulness," as *Time* magazine put it. Throughout the speech, members looked unusually grave, but with one notable exception, according to *Time*. Midway through the speech, Taft "took off his glasses, rubbed his face and yawned prodigiously."

The address was simple and direct. Truman described a desperate situation in Greece but quickly moved on to meet Vandenberg's demand for a broader explanation. In the process, he defined the cold war that had already begun and set out what would come to be known as the Truman Doctrine of containment.

"At the present moment in world history, nearly every nation must choose between alternative ways of life. The choice is too often not a free one." One way of life, Truman continued, was based on the will of the majority and was characterized by free elections, individual liberty, and representative government. In the other, the will of a minority was imposed on the majority through terror and oppression, a controlled press, and rigged elections. Then Truman made the case for U.S. aid. "I believe that it must be the policy of the United States to support free peoples who are resisting attempted subjugation by armed minorities or outside pressure. I believe that we must assist free peoples to work out their own destinies in their own way."

The speech was met by a standing ovation. Truman acknowledged it with a fleeting smile. He looked up to where his wife was sitting and bowed to her, and then made his way out of the chamber. He was driven directly to the airport so he could begin his short vacation.

Vandenberg met with reporters later that afternoon and expressed support: "The president's message faces facts, and so must Congress." Vandenberg's role in the promulgation of the Truman Doctrine completed a process that turned him from isolationist to internationalist. By his own account, that transformation began with the Japanese attack on Pearl Harbor six years earlier. It can easily be argued that its culmination came at the White House meeting of February 27, when he literally demanded that Truman expound his doctrine as the price for congressional support for Greek-Turkish aid.

The speech dominated the next day's newspapers. The *New York Times* ran a three-line banner headline and put the text of the address on the front page, along with stories about the speech and congressional reaction. The *Times* noted that there would be opposition but said congressional approval was certain. While some papers spoke against U.S. involvement, most supported it.

Senate and House hearings began the next day. Concern focused on the breadth, scope, and cost of U.S. commitment. Specific objections were raised to bypassing the United Nations, which was still in its infancy and considered by many a repository of hope for world peace.

The UN issue was quickly seized by Vandenberg, who had developed a method of playing both partisan politician and bipartisan statesman. His technique was to find a relatively minor objection to a particular administration policy and then insist on a negotiated compromise that would ensure support for the broader policy objective. In this case, Vandenberg added an amendment to the Greek-Turkish aid bill that had little real effect other than to make it seem as though proper respect had been paid to the United Nations. When the amendment was adopted, passage of the aid plan was assured.

The Senate passed the bill April 22 by 67-23; Republicans split 35-16 and Democrats 32-7. The House followed two weeks later, voting 287-108, with Republicans split 127-94 and Democrats 160-13. (An American Labor Party member also voted no.) A short conference produced the final measure, which was cleared May 15 and which Truman signed May 22.

By then Marshall, Acheson, and the rest of the foreign policy team were nearly ready with a broad recovery plan designed to do nothing less than rebuild Europe so it could withstand Soviet pressure. Marshall outlined the plan June 5. It was quickly welcomed in Europe, and from it grew the big four-year Marshall Plan for European recovery.

Clifford later would look back on these months of 1947 and describe them in momentous terms. "I think it's one of the proudest moments in American history," Clifford told Truman biographer David McCullough. "What happened during that period was that Harry Truman and the United States saved the free world."

Following its decision to aid Greece and Turkey, Congress committed itself to rebuilding Europe under the Marshall Plan. The commitment grew to entail $12 billion over the next four years—a staggering sum for foreign aid at a time when the entire federal government spent less than $40 billion a year.

The Truman administration also continued to confront the Soviet threat in Europe more directly. When troops of the Warsaw Pact cut off access to the western zones of Berlin in April 1948, the air forces of the United States and Great Britain began the most massive airlift in history to relieve the city. Over the next eighteen months, more than 2.3 million tons of food and coal were flown in before the Soviets relented.

But while Truman's stand abroad earned him respect, his performance on domestic issues was less widely admired. The Republican Congress swiftly passed the Taft-Hartley Act in 1947, limiting unions' right to strike and outlawing the "closed shop" that required workers to join a union. Truman vetoed Taft-Hartley and saw his veto overridden by two-thirds majorities in both the House and Senate.

Many conservative Democrats voted to override, demonstrating not only the lack of party discipline among Democrats but also the downturn in public support for unions. The disruption caused by strikes and threatened strikes had begun to engender resentment, as had the government's perceived role in granting some union workers wage increases far in excess of what other workers were receiving.

The 80th Congress was busy on many fronts, seeking to reverse the process of enlarging government through ever greater regulation and bureaucracy. Stuck defending government in an era of rising antigovernment feeling, Truman compounded his political problems by tackling the issue of race. Weeks after the 1946 election, Truman had appointed a Civil Rights Commission, partly out of concern that blacks who had come North during and after the war were gravitating into the Republican Party. The commission's recommendations, issued in the fall of 1947, called not only for a federal antilynching law but also for voting rights for African Americans and an end to discrimination in hiring and schools. The report enraged many Southern Democrats, who had regarded the commission's very existence as an affront to states' rights.

Truman had roots in the southern tradition, but he had voted for antilynching laws in the past and believed in the fundamental claims of what was then called "the Negro cause." In the summer of 1948 he would issue orders integrating the military, a move that made it increasingly likely the southern states would bolt the coalition in November. It was generally assumed that, without the electoral votes of the old Confederacy, Truman could not hold the White House.

It appeared that Truman, diminished by his battles with Congress and leading a shattered party, would be no match for New York governor Thomas E. Dewey, the 1944 Republican nominee who had waited patiently for a second chance.

= 1948 =

The "Do-Nothing" Congress

Rhodes Cook

Jaunty, confident, and nattily dressed in a white linen suit, President Harry S. Truman seemed conspicuously out of place as he arrived to address a Democratic Convention one observer described as "the zaniest, worst-managed and most dispirited in American political annals."

The Democrats in July 1948 had much to be dispirited about. Since the last presidential election, President Franklin D. Roosevelt had died; Republicans had retaken both houses of Congress; the Democratic Party appeared to be unraveling on both the left and the right, and all of its leaders, including Truman, seemed powerless to stop it.

With Truman lagging badly in the polls, the nation's political pundits were just counting the days until the Republican nominee, Gov. Thomas E. Dewey of New York, would take over the White House.

Nothing about the Philadelphia convention hall served to shake the Democrats' mood of despondency. Delegates and guests sweltered inside the aging hall near the railyards. There was no air-conditioning, and hot klieg lights had been set up for a new communications medium called television.

The action on the floor was hot as well. There was a brawl over the platform's civil rights plank and a subsequent walkout by delegates from Alabama and Mississippi. On the final night, interminable nominating speeches had pushed the proceedings two hours past midnight before Truman and his running-mate, Senate Minority Leader Alben W. Barkley of Kentucky, rose to accept their nominations.

Nonetheless, Truman was able to rouse the delegates with a speech that was combative from the start. "Senator Barkley and I will win this election and make these Republicans like it, don't you forget that," he said defiantly.

It was the first time, said *Time* magazine, that the Democratic Convention had heard anyone say the word "win" as if he meant it.

Truman followed with a brief defense of the sixteen years of Democratic presidential rule before turning his attention to his prime target, the Republican 80th Congress. Truman called for repeal of the Taft-Hartley Act that banned closed union shops, criticized Congress for its failure to pass a housing bill, and described the tax reduction measure that Congress had approved as a "Republican richman's tax bill."

As cries of "Pour it on 'em, Harry!" rose from the crowd, Truman sprang a surprise: "On the 26th day of July, which out in Missouri they call Turnip Day, I'm going to call that Congress back," he announced, to make them tackle legislation their party platform said they favored.

Truman ticked off a laundry list of measures that he wanted the special session to address, from anti-inflation legislation to an overhaul of the recently enacted Displaced Persons Act. "They could do this job in fifteen days if they wanted to do it," Truman said. "What that worst

21

Harry Truman clasps hands with running mate Alben Barkley at the Democratic convention, where he used his acceptance speech to announce that he would force Congress into special session.

80th Congress does in its special session will be the test."

Twelve hours later, back in Washington, the president issued a proclamation for the first special session of Congress in a presidential election year since 1856 on the grounds, he said, that the "public interest requires it."

Republicans howled in protest that only Truman's sagging political interests required it. But it allowed Truman to regain the initiative on substance and generate political momentum.

It was not the first time that political commentators had written Truman off and then been required to take a second look at him. In terms of popular approval, his three-year presidency had been a roller-coaster ride.

From an approval rating of 87 percent upon succeeding FDR in the spring of 1945, Truman had fallen to 32 percent in the Gallup Poll by the fall of 1946. Labor disputes, meat shortages, and the Republican cry of "Had Enough?" had all taken a toll.

Through much of 1947, however, Truman's popularity rating had rebounded into the 55 percent to 60 percent range, as foreign policy initiatives such as the Marshall Plan, the Truman Doctrine (aid to Greece and Turkey), and the policy of containment won voter support. But by early 1948, Truman's approval rating had plummeted again to under 40 percent amid signs that the Democratic Party was coming apart.

In late 1947 FDR's former vice president, Agriculture and Commerce secretary, Henry A. Wallace (who was fired by Truman in 1946), formed a new third party on the left. In early 1948 a number of Southern Democrats, angered by Truman's advocacy of a far-ranging civil rights program as well as their diminishing influence within the party, began laying the groundwork for a southern-based "Dixiecrat" Party, which in July nominated South Carolina governor Strom Thurmond for president.

Some of the New Dealers who remained within the Democratic Party led an effort to draft Gen. Dwight D. Eisenhower to lead the Democratic ticket in 1948. The boomlet ultimately fizzled when Eisenhower shunned the nomination. But the anger of old New Dealers with an unelected president who was never part of their inner circle was slow to fade.

Typical was the reaction of FDR's interior secretary, Harold L. Ickes (father of President Clinton's deputy chief of staff), who at one point called Truman "stupid" and later wrote him: "You have the choice of retiring voluntarily and with dignity, or of being driven out of office by a disillusioned and indignant citizenry."

Publicly, Truman tended to ignore the criticism from fellow Democrats. More difficult to ignore was the 80th Congress, which was busily writing legislation that would govern domestic and foreign policy for years to come.

The Democratic president and the GOP Congress found common ground on a number of in-ternational issues. In May 1947 Congress approved the Greek-Turkish aid program requested by Truman. In April 1948 it passed the Marshall Plan for European recovery. In June 1948 Congress approved a peacetime draft law.

But in domestic affairs, Congress and the president were often at loggerheads. Truman's recommendations to extend New Deal social welfare concepts in the fields of education, housing, medical care, and social security were largely ignored by Congress.

In a slap at FDR's four terms, it sent to the states in March 1947 a constitutional amendment limiting the tenure of future presidents to two terms. In June it enacted the Taft-Hartley Labor-Management Relations Act over Truman's veto. And throughout the 80th Congress, Republicans zealously investigated charges of administration misbehavior.

Then Truman's "Turnip" session opened in late July 1948, Republicans were in no mood to cooperate. But they were divided on how to proceed. Sen. Robert A. Taft of Ohio, the GOP's congressional leader, was irritated by the whole idea of a special session and wanted to do nothing at all.

Dewey, who initially called the idea a "frightful imposition," was more ambivalent. While his campaign manager, Herbert Brownell Jr., described it as "a rump session called at a political convention for political purposes in the heat of a political campaign," Dewey also thought it advantageous for Republicans to show leadership by passing a plank or two of their platform into law.

In particular, Dewey suggested that the special session liberalize the restrictive immigration provisions of the Displaced Persons Act, which Truman had denounced in his acceptance speech as "anti-Semitic" and "anti-Catholic."

But there was no love lost between Dewey and Taft. Not only had the two been combat-

Truman arrives at Union Station in St. Louis on November 5, 1948, bearing a newspaper whose headline proclaims the outcome that most pollsters and journalists had predicted.

ants for the GOP presidential nomination in 1948, but also they led opposing wings of the Republican Party. Dewey championed the internationalist "Wall Street" crowd; Taft represented the more conservative Midwestern isolationists.

The special session adjourned August 7 after only eleven days of legislative business, without action on the Displaced Persons Act or much else. "Their theme song between now and November," scoffed Barkley, "should be 'I Got Plenty o' Nuttin'.'"

Truman quickly took up the cry. Barnstorming the country, he lambasted the "do-nothing Republican 80th Congress" at every opportunity. He accused the Republicans of trying to roll back vital New Deal programs that were the

only defense between many working-class Americans and another depression.

Republicans had "murdered" housing legislation, Truman argued. Farmers should oppose the Republicans because "this Republican Congress has already stuck a pitchfork into the farmer's back." And congressional Republicans, he warned, were "silent and cunning men, who have developed a dangerous lust for power and privilege."

Dewey complained about his rival's "mudslinging," "cheap wisecracking," and "ranting, boasting partisanship." But he abstained from mounting a defense of the 80th Congress. On occasion, he called it "one of the best" and complimented it for having done a "swell job." But he rarely defended its individual programs, even when they were under direct assault from Truman.

Privately, Dewey did not seem to have a much higher regard for the Republican Congress than Truman did. He told one reporter who fancied a House career that it would be best if he were not elected; he might become "one of those congressional bums." Besides, polls showed that Dewey's calm and confident high-road campaign was working.

As Election Day neared, the pundits agreed that Truman had put on an energetic and entertaining show. Criss-crossing the country by train, he had covered 31,500 miles, made 350 speeches, spoken some 560,000 words to an estimated 6 million listeners. Still, hardly anybody besides Truman believed he had any chance of winning.

The Roper Poll had suspended its surveying in early September, figuring that there was no way Truman could win. Gallup completed its final poll a week before the election, showing that while Dewey had lost much of his thirteen-point lead from late August, Truman still trailed by 5 percentage points. And *Newsweek* polled fifty Washington journalists on the eve of the election, most of them bureau chiefs, and all predicted a Dewey victory.

But as the first flurry of returns from the Northeast came in, Truman took a lead he never relinquished. GOP officials were still hopeful of victory well into the night. At 10:30 p.m., the chairman of the Republican National Committee, Rep. Hugh Scott of Pennsylvania, announced, "Now we have come to the Republican half of the evening."

But the Republican half never materialized. When Ohio conclusively went for Truman at 11 a.m. the next morning, Dewey conceded. Truman had won in the popular vote count by slightly more than 2 million votes out of 48.8 million cast. In the electoral vote, he had beaten Dewey, 303 to 189, with 39 votes for Thurmond.

Truman's victory was accompanied by a Democratic congressional sweep that reversed the Republican triumph of 1946. Democrats registered a net gain of 75 seats in the House, jumping from 188 seats to 263, and scored a net gain of 9 seats in the Senate, increasing their number from 45 seats to 54.

"There is only one question on which professional politicians, poll-takers, political reporters and other wiseacres and prognosticators can any longer speak with much authority. That is how they want their crow cooked," wrote national columnists Joe and Stewart Alsop, who ordered theirs "fricasseed."

It was hard to deny that Republicans had suffered from overconfidence or that Truman had run an appealing, feisty campaign. But, at bottom, it was still a Democratic era, and Truman was able to reassemble most of the New Deal coalition of urban ethnics, organized labor, conservative Southern Democrats, farmers, minorities, and liberal intellectuals.

Of the twenty-eight states that Truman carried, twenty-three had voted in each of the previous four elections for FDR. Thurmond won only the four southern states where he was able to wrest the Democratic ballot position from Truman. Wallace won nowhere.

"Harry Truman had made his campaign on the record of the 'worst Congress in history,'" said *Time* in its postelection issue. "Whether or not he accepted that indictment completely, the voter was ready to accept it in part."

Time complimented Truman for waging "a single-handed fight without parallel in U.S. history. . . . [He] was now the absolute boss of a resurgent Democratic Party. Republicans might not be able to stand it. But the Republic could."

President Truman's willingness to confront the specter of communism helped him right his political ship in 1947 and win reelection in 1948. But the tide of world events soon was to turn against the United States, converting international issues from an asset to a liability for the president and his party.

In the fall of 1949, Truman announced to the nation that the Soviets had tested their first atomic bomb. Soviet possession of the bomb meant that the United States could no longer count on trumping any military threat by resorting to an arsenal of unique, unanswerable power. Within weeks of that disturbing news, communists led by Mao Tse-tung completed their ouster of the Chiang Kai-shek government from the mainland of China. As the last of the Nationalist troops fled to the island of Formosa, one-fourth of the world's population was added to the communist bloc.

Even the formation of the North Atlantic Treaty Organization (NATO) that same year, providing for the common defense of Western Europe and North America, did not ring with reassurance so much as with renewed warning. It was now common to speak of the cold war, and some had begun to regard a third world war as inevitable.

The Soviets' nuclear breakthrough was widely assumed to have been achieved through espionage. But even before this, a new Red Scare had been in full cry in the United States. Sources, some responsible and some reckless, pointed to the presence of active, committed Soviet agents in government, academia, organized labor, and the entertainment industry. Truman himself had instituted a loyalty program in 1947 that reviewed the backgrounds and associations of federal officials and employees and resulted in thousands of dismissals and resignations.

The House Un-American Activities Committee was in its heyday, issuing subpoenas and trafficking in rumor. In August 1948, HUAC held hearings in which a former communist named Whittaker Chambers accused Alger Hiss, a State Department official, of being a Soviet agent. Hiss denied it and was charged with perjury when Chambers produced papers to document his version of the facts.

Late in 1949, as the boats left for Formosa, a jury in New York found eleven leaders of the U.S. Communist Party guilty of advocating the overthrow of the government by force. The judge handed out five-year prison terms for all the defendants but one who got three years. In another New York courtroom, Hiss was on trial for perjury for which he would be sentenced to five years.

Against this background, the junior senator from Wisconsin, Joseph R. McCarthy, was beginning to plan his campaign for reelection in 1952. The youngest member of the Senate when he took the oath in 1947, McCarthy had passed three years in relative obscurity. Now he was contemplating a series of speeches around the country that he hoped would raise his political profile. And he was in search of an issue that would give those speeches some bite.

= 1950 =

McCarthy and the Climate of Fear

Ronald D. Elving

Early in 1950, a first-term Republican senator from Wisconsin named Joseph R. McCarthy left Washington on a party-sponsored speaking tour of several small cities. He brought along two speeches on topics the party leadership was pushing at the time: housing policy and the existence of communists in the U.S. government.

At his first stop in Wheeling, West Virginia, on February 9, McCarthy decided to go with the speech about the communists. He gave copies to the local paper and radio station. That night, he delivered the speech for the Ohio County Republican Women's Club in a hotel meeting room, launching an episode of fear and loathing in the Senate and in the country at large that has had few parallels in American history.

According to several accounts, the senator spoke these words from his prepared text: "While I cannot take the time to name all the men in the State Department who have been named as active members of the Communist Party and members of a spy ring . . . I have here in my hand a list of 205, a list of names that were made known to the secretary of State. . . ."

The account the Wheeling *Intelligencer* reporter filed that evening included the number 205. When this reached the Associated Press, a bureau editor in Charleston called a part-time correspondent to confirm the number with McCarthy. Receiving confirmation, the editor put the story on the wire in the middle of the night.

Only a handful of newspapers carried the item the next day, February 10, but reporters were waiting to talk to McCarthy when he stopped at Stapleton Airport in Denver. McCarthy told them he had left his list in his suit bag still on the plane. But he said there were "207 bad risks" at State. Later that same evening he spoke on a radio program in Salt Lake City and said there were "57 card-carrying Communists" at State.

The numbers 205 and 57 had been derived from earlier reports to Congress by the State Department itself. In 1946, and again in 1948, department officials had responded to inquiries by describing the background checks done on employees. The reports had said that 285 cases had been set aside for further investigation as "bad risks" and 108 as presumed communists.

McCarthy and his speechwriters had taken these lists, subtracted the employees known to have left the department, and tagged the remainder as Reds still working at State.

On his way back to Washington, McCarthy stopped off in his home state and had lunch with three writers for the *Milwaukee Journal.* When it was suggested that McCarthy's failure to divulge any names meant he had none, the senator replied: "I'm not going to tell you bastards anything. I've got a pail full of shit and I'm going to use it where it'll do me the most good."

Though little-known nationally at the beginning of 1950, McCarthy had been making political waves in Wisconsin for a decade. He burst

Millard E. Tydings, left, and Joseph R. McCarthy face off on first day of Senate hearings on the latter's allegations of communist subversion in the federal government.

on the scene in 1939, becoming the youngest circuit judge in state history at age thirty. What made that early success all the more remarkable was that at twenty, McCarthy had been a bankrupt farmer with an eighth-grade education.

McCarthy's parents, devout Irish Catholics and Democrats, ran a small farm in the Fox River Valley of east-central Wisconsin. Joe, in his mid-teens, built up a chicken business that was fairly successful before an outbreak of disease wiped out his laying stock. He enrolled in high school at twenty, and a sympathetic prin-

cipal allowed him to complete courses by taking exams. He finished the four-year curriculum in a school year.

McCarthy worked and borrowed his way through Marquette University, studying engineering for two years, and then switching to law. His fellow students remembered him playing endless games of poker and his reputation as a fearless bettor and bluffer.

He got his law degree in 1935 and practiced small-town law for three years. He joined the Young Democrats, ran for county prosecutor, and lost. When a sixty-six-year-old judge came up for reelection, McCarthy challenged him on the basis of his age. Campaigning door to door, the upstart won by a handful of votes.

In 1942 the young judge enlisted in the Marines and served as an intelligence officer in the Pacific, primarily briefing pilots before and after bombing missions. In 1944, while still in the Pacific, McCarthy switched parties and filed for the Republican nomination for the Senate against the incumbent senator, Alexander Wiley. Running as "Tail Gunner Joe" and "the flying judge," McCarthy lost but got 80,000 votes.

Mustering out later that year, he began running against the state's other senator, Robert M. La Follette Jr., son of the legendary governor and senator, "Fighting Bob" La Follette, patron saint of the progressive faction in the state GOP.

McCarthy campaigned furiously from town to town, and La Follette got home from Washington too late to head off an upset in the September 1946 primary. McCarthy swept past an underfunded Democrat in November and at thirty-eight was the youngest member of the Senate taking the oath in January 1947.

Arriving back in Washington a week after his Wheeling speech, McCarthy found himself a sudden celebrity. The State Department had issued three separate denials of his charges within four days of the speech, helping convert initial curiosity into intense interest. And while some newspaper editorials had already begun to attack McCarthy as irresponsible, many papers (including the Hearst papers and the Chicago *Tribune*) were now devoting front page headlines to his charges.

The young senator had indeed tapped into an issue of great emotional power—greater perhaps than he knew. The United States in 1950 was at peace, but far from at ease. Americans had watched the Soviet Union devour Eastern Europe and get its own atomic bomb. Commu-

nists had seized power in China in 1949. At home the belief was widespread that "fifth column Communists" were infiltrating the academic, cultural, and political life of the nation. Many conservatives were especially exercised over China. The thinking was that communist sympathizers in the State Department had undermined U.S. support for Gen. Chiang Kai-shek and facilitated Mao Tse-tung's takeover.

McCarthy determined to make his next move within the confines of the Senate. Scott W. Lucas of Illinois, the Democratic majority leader, gave McCarthy such an opportunity February 20, but saw to it there would be no roll calls that afternoon, hoping to minimize attendance and attention. It was a vain hope.

On the floor, McCarthy began working his way through a list of cases derived from the investigative work of an FBI agent. The list had been seen much earlier by members on the House side, but McCarthy scrambled the order and purported to have received the names from patriotic individuals deep within the State Department.

The Democrats could soon see their plan to ignore McCarthy was foolish and tried instead to confront him. Lucas and a chorus of other Democrats baited McCarthy on the floor, expecting to shame him into retreat. But the rougher the Democrats became, the more recklessly McCarthy counterpunched. The battle dragged on into the night, with Lucas flailing for means to upstage the Republican.

In the end, the clumsy tactics of the majority greatly enhanced the news value of McCarthy's already sensational charges. It was suggested that the best way to deal with the dust-up was to hold a hearing before a special subcommittee of the Senate Foreign Relations Committee, and such a hearing was scheduled for March 8.

The Democrats named as chairman Millard E. Tydings of Maryland, an irreproachable conservative who was chairman of the Armed Ser-

McCarthy brandishes "evidence" of communist agents in government during his speech to the Catholic Press Association in Rochester in May 1950.

vices Committee. The other two Democrats on the committee were New Englanders—Theodore F. Green of Rhode Island and Brien McMahon of Connecticut, the latter known for his partisanship. The Republicans put up Henry Cabot Lodge of Massachusetts and Bourke B. Hickenlooper of Iowa.

The Tydings Committee (as it became known) met in the Senate Caucus Room in what is now the Russell Building. Tydings rudely interrupted McCarthy's opening statement and badgered the Republican throughout the hearing. It was soon apparent that, while McCarthy thought the panel was supposed to investigate whatever names he threw out, Tydings and the other Democrats were there to discredit him and his charges.

McCarthy indicated that he would submit eighty-one names, but the few he brought forward in the early committee sessions proved to be either false leads or cold trails. The Democrats on the panel treated him scornfully.

In the second week of hearings, McCarthy came forth with a list of eight, seven with connections to State, who had "pro-Communist proclivities" or had given "pro-Soviet" advice. On the list was Owen J. Lattimore, a Johns Hopkins professor who had been a White House adviser to Chiang Kai-shek during World War II. McCarthy would later describe Lattimore as "the architect of U.S. policy in the Far East" and as the Soviets' "top espionage agent in America."

Tydings obtained Lattimore's file and reported to the committee March 23 that the man had briefly worked for State and given a speech there but had no present connection to the department. McCarthy was unfazed. "I am willing to stand or fall on this one," he said.

McCarthy produced as a witness Louis F. Budenz, a former editor of the Communist *Daily Worker* who had implicated others as communists or sympathizers. Budenz testified that he had been told Lattimore was a communist (if not necessarily a spy). The Democrats and their committee counsel cut him up in cross-examination, but Budenz left a strong impression. *Time* magazine wrote that his testimony, while it proved nothing, could not be lightly dismissed.

Lattimore appeared before the committee in April, dismissing Budenz's accusation as "gossip and hearsay." (This faceoff would inform a dramatic scene in Allen Drury's 1959 novel *Advise and Consent*.) But Republican senators seized on Budenz as an indication that McCarthy was onto something after all. McCarthy already had been receiving thousands of telegrams from supporters, but with the Lattimore case he once again seemed to have captured the attention of the wider populace. The *New York Times'* Arthur Krock allowed as how "many fair-minded persons" were willing to hear McCarthy out.

McCarthy had been hammering at the Truman administration for keeping State's loyalty files closed. As the pressure of public opinion grew, Tydings asked President Truman to relent. The president had long opposed this step as violating privacy and damaging department morale. But under the circumstances, the files were opened to members of the committee.

The Tydings Committee held hearings over four months and compiled a record of some 2 million words. On July 17 it released a 347-page report scathingly critical of McCarthy, signed by the three Democrats. The report said all of McCarthy's targets had been investigated and cleared, in some cases repeatedly. The charges were "a fraud and a hoax . . . perhaps the most nefarious campaign of half truths and untruth in the history of this Republic."

Lodge filed a minority report; Hickenlooper did not. But both had already stated that the loyalty files had failed to prove or disprove charges against any of McCarthy's eighty-one names. That conclusion was largely lost, however, in the bitter recriminations over the majority report. The intemperate tone, aggravated by Tydings' equally harsh remarks in delivering the document on the Senate floor, marked the committee as partisan and diluted its effect.

McCarthy, for his part, declared the report "a signal to the traitors, Communists and fellow travelers in our government that they need have no fear of exposure from this administration."

The public at large might not have known quite what to make of the Tydings report. But they did know that North Korea had invaded South Korea the month before and that the United States had been engaged in the conflict. They knew that spies had been passing atomic secrets from the West to the East. And many of them felt dissatisfied with the answers they got from the Democrats in Washington.

Out on the campaign stump, candidates that year found communists in government a political mother lode. In Florida, Democratic senator Claude Pepper was defeated in his spring primary by a conservative who accused him of communist sympathies. (He would later return to Congress for a long career in the House.) That alarm bell was heard in Congress, which enacted (over Truman's veto) a law requiring the registration of communists, front groups, and internal subversives in time of war.

That fall, McCarthy campaigned against Tydings and had the satisfaction of seeing him beaten (along with Majority Leader Lucas, who lost to Everett McKinley Dirksen).

McCarthy had reached a rare plateau of influence, and he would remain there through the 82d Congress, helping his party to one of its greatest victories ever in the elections of 1952. But such controversy and anger already surrounded him that it was not hard to imagine him falling as rapidly as he had risen.

T he case that Sen. Joseph R. McCarthy sought to bring before Congress and the public in 1950 was immeasurably aided by the North Korean invasion of South Korea in late June. Whether the senator had found any actual communists in Washington, those streaming south across the 38th Parallel that summer were real enough.

President Truman ordered U.S. air and naval units to Korea and asked the United Nations to send troops. With the Soviet delegate absent, the Security Council gave its approval. The war went well at first, with Gen. Douglas MacArthur leading a surprise landing at Inchon—behind the North Korean lines. But when MacArthur's men reached the Yalu River—the Chinese frontier—hundreds of thousands of Chinese soldiers counterattacked. By late November, the American-led UN forces were forced into retreat.

The Wisconsin senator's stock was soaring. It scarcely mattered that he had yet to root out a single spy in government (as, indeed, he never would). What mattered was that voters saw in McCarthy's charges an explanation for adverse changes in the world—a way to resolve their own bewilderment.

Underlying much of McCarthy's talk about communist subversion was the implication that, had it not been for these alleged traitors, the United States might have escaped the complex postwar mess overseas. For some, the ultimate lesson was that Soviet agents had dragged the United States into fighting World War II in Europe. After Pearl Harbor, the Roosevelt administration decided that the first task was the defeat of fascism, a priority shared by many Republicans—particularly the party's northeastern establishment. But there was always an alternative view, more popular in the Midwest and West, that the first task should be to avenge the massacre in Hawaii. For some of these "Asia Firsters," the second task after the defeat of Japan would have been to take on the Chinese communists.

The Asia First contingent had some overlap with the old America First movement. If America had been forced out of isolation by the Japanese attack, it made sense simply to repel that invader and return to isolation. But both America First and Asia First counted among their adherents many conservatives whose fear and loathing of communism was now growing to overshadow all other considerations.

At the vortex of these three political streams stood Robert A. Taft, the Ohioan who had arrived in the Senate in 1938 and swiftly become the Republicans' intellectual and legislative leader. Taft was known as an opponent of overseas involvements—particularly those compelled by prearranged agreements. Yet he yielded to no man in his abhorrence of communism. He dealt cautiously with the hero of the "Europe Firsters," Gen. Dwight D. Eisenhower. But Ike took Taft on in the 1952 presidential primaries. Taft led the balloting at the GOP Convention until a shift of votes from the Northeast denied him the one political prize for which he had longed.

The Last Stand of Robert Taft

Robert W. Merry

In April 19, 1953, Sen. Robert A. Taft, majority leader in the Senate and the most powerful legislator in Congress, flew in a presidential airplane to Augusta, Georgia. He was the guest of the country's new Republican president, Dwight D. Eisenhower, for a weekend of relaxation and golf. Eisenhower had a purpose beyond camaraderie for this weekend. He knew he would need the Senate Republican leader if he was to get his program through Congress, and that required that he cement a sturdy personal association with this strong-willed Ohio an who personified his party's conservative wing.

Just the year before, the two men had been bitter rivals for their party's presidential nomination. It had been Taft's third try for that prize, and his people had worked furiously to outmaneuver the man known affectionately throughout the country as Ike. Eisenhower had been a political newcomer in 1952, but he brought powerful assets to the presidential game. The former general was famous as one of the country's greatest World War II heroes, and his infectious grin gave him an avuncular persona that seemed to soothe the nation's political anxieties.

But during the nomination battle his people had pummeled the Taft forces with allegations of political chicanery in Texas and other southern states, and the residues of bitterness left by that controversy stirred fears among Republicans that the party would not be able to unify for its new challenge of running the country.

And so this weekend was important not just for Eisenhower and Taft, but for the Republican Party and the nation as well. Political observers throughout the country were watching to see just how these two men would get along.

They got along very well. The weekend strengthened what was becoming a mutually enjoyable political alliance. But for Taft the visit was not as pleasant as he had anticipated. His golf game had been uncharacteristically dreadful, and he knew the cause. In fact, he was beginning to worry more and more about the cause.

A persistent pain in his left hip had become increasingly intense, and now it was spreading to his left thigh. In the days following the Augusta trip it would spread further to nearly all of his joints. He tired easily, and his characteristic political brusqueness turned to irritability. Two weeks after the golf outing he exploded during a White House meeting and cast his fury directly at Eisenhower. Taft wanted serious cuts in military spending, but the administration was holding back.

"With a program like this," Taft shouted at the president, "we'll never elect a Republican Congress in 1954!" Pounding his fist on the table, he added, "You're taking us down the same road Truman traveled. It's a repudiation of everything we promised in the campaign!"

The assembled congressional leaders and administration budget officials were shocked,

Taft was a picture of confidence as he hobbled to a meeting with President Eisenhower in June 1953, but he had less than two months to live.

and Eisenhower flushed visibly. Some of those present quickly injected small talk into the discussion to defuse the tensions. A few days later Taft apologized to the president.

But the outburst, like his golf game, was a product of the pain that now racked his body. Still, he didn't complain, and he resolved to ignore the discomfort as he went about his hectic political and legislative schedule. Bob Taft was a man of focus. He hated small talk, could not engage in banter, seldom abandoned his work for diversions of recreation or culture. Much of the power he had accumulated in the Senate over his fourteen years there was attributed to his intense concentration, his unrivaled mastery of the details of legislation, his refusal to be sidetracked by ancillary matters or personal digressions. When Taft spoke, everyone knew his words sprang from conviction, and the conviction gave his words added force. And he would not diminish that force now by letting on that he was in pain.

But by the end of April he knew he must see a doctor. He went to his wife's Washington physician, who promptly sent him to Walter Reed Hospital for tests. By now he was running a fever, and doctors could see that he was anemic. He underwent every test the doctors could think of. But they could not identify the problem. "I have acquired a most unpleasant disease," Taft wrote to an old Yale classmate, "and I am doing my best to try to find out how to cure it. Primarily, it is an anemic condition and a lack of red corpuscles."

When Taft left Walter Reed, he looked pale and limped badly. Clearly something was seriously wrong, but nobody knew precisely what it was. So he tried to ignore the problem and resume his work. He instructed a trusted staffer, I. Jack Martin, to issue a bland statement to the press reassuring the nation about his health. Then he headed to his hometown of Cincinnati to give a foreign policy speech that he expected to kick up some controversy.

When he got there it became clear that he could not deliver the speech. Weak and in pain, he entered Cincinnati's Holmes Hospital for more tests. His son Robert delivered the speech for him, before an audience of the National Conference of Christians and Jews.

It was vintage Taft, laced with traces of the isolationism for which he was famous. Taft despised diplomatic alliances and foreign entanglements—precisely the building blocks for the country's postwar policy of "containment."

Although he accepted in principle the importance of resisting the spread of communism, he didn't want the country to dilute its sovereignty or its freedom of action through tightly drawn treaties and relationships with other nations. Taft particularly disliked the alliance with Britain that President Harry S. Truman's foreign policy architects had forged after the war to foster international stability. And he disdained the United Nations and harbored deep suspicions about NATO.

All those sentiments were evident in his speech. He called for a "completely free hand" in Asia, challenging the bipartisan consensus that America must be a world leader and that world leadership required complex foreign alliances.

Even though Taft did not deliver the speech himself, the press gave it wide currency, and Eisenhower felt obliged to take issue with his Senate ally. As Taft biographer James T. Patterson would write, "It testified to Taft's extraordinary power and prestige that one speech, delivered by his son, could so disturb the columnists and unsettle the administration."

In the hospital Taft was administered cortisone and given X-ray therapy. The fever subsided, and so did the pain. He seemed cheerful and optimistic, despite the fact that he remained at Holmes for days. Then came the news. Doctors had discovered nodules in the skin of his abdomen and forehead. Tissue was removed for biopsies. The results were in. Taft had cancer. It was probably terminal.

Robert Alphonso Taft was born in Cincinnati on September 8, 1889, into a family of national prominence. During his childhood, his father, William Howard Taft, served as governor of the Philippines. When he was at Yale, his father became president of the United States. During his early adulthood, his father became chief justice. The Taft family was expected to excel, and young Taft did not disappoint his elders. He was first in his class at prep school, first in his class at Yale, first in his class at Harvard Law.

He was a product of the midwestern values of his home region—Republicanism, nationalism, self-reliance, frugality. The region's leading journalistic voice was Col. Robert McCormick's conservative and isolationist Chicago *Tribune*. The guiding political spirit was Abraham Lincoln, who had saved the Union, freed the slaves, and founded a political party that dominated the country's electoral landscape for the better part of six decades.

But by 1930, when Taft was elected to the Ohio Senate, the Great Depression had struck the nation and devastated the Republican Party. Taft would spend the rest of his life fighting the new political force shaped by Franklin D. Roosevelt. His nemesis would be liberalism in all its guises, the prevailing orthodoxy of the Northeast, in Taft's view the antithesis of all he held dear.

Taft was forty-nine when he arrived in the U.S. Senate in 1939. Roosevelt's New Deal was well entrenched, and the president dominated the political agenda. Democrats outnumbered Republicans in the Senate 69 to 23; in the House the margin was 262 to 169.

But Taft quickly saw political opportunity in two forms. One was the emergence of the so-called conservative coalition, the alliance of opposition Republicans and Southern Democrats disenchanted with the New Deal. The other was the GOP's leadership void. No Republican of legislative acumen had emerged to present a bold and consistent critique of the New Deal

New Senate Majority Leader Taft confers with Minority Leader Lyndon B. Johnson, D-Texas, on opening day of the GOP-controlled 83d Congress.

and offer imaginative and forceful leadership for the opposition. Taft moved to fill that void.

He gained a reputation as a sober-sided, hard-working, and brilliant legislator who knew more about more legislation than anyone else around. In Republican councils, as senators grappled with who should take the lead in yet another pressing issue, the call would go up, "Let Bob do it." They knew he would handle it with dispatch and thoroughness, and so they piled on responsibility. With responsibility came power.

And Democrats discovered that, once they got beyond the harsh rhetoric and fierce partisanship, there was a man of rare conviction who eschewed political gamesmanship, spoke straight from the shoulder, and delivered on his political promises. As Harry Lundeberg, head of the Seafarers International Union, put

it, Taft "doesn't give you a lot of sweet con like the others."

By the time the Republicans regained control of the Senate after the 1946 elections, Taft was the party's uncontested leader. But he turned down the job of Senate majority leader and let that title go to Maine's Wallace H. White Jr., an able but colorless man who gladly took his cues from Taft. Meanwhile, Taft wielded immense power as chairman of the GOP Policy Committee (which set party strategy) and chairman of the high-profile Labor and Public Welfare Committee. He also was second in line on Finance, behind his friend Eugene D. Milliken of Colorado.

As *Newsweek* said, "In the influence he wielded in his party's councils, Taft reigned supreme—the undisputed and dominant Republican figure not only in Congress but the nation as well." The magazine said Taft had "no glamour, no engaging hobbies, few close friends, and little of the personal magnetism that draws a popular following. . . . Taft's success stemmed rather from his amazing legislative know-how."

From his position of power Taft shepherded through Congress the famous Taft-Hartley Act, designed to restore what most Republicans considered a greater equilibrium in labor-management relations. When the Senate passed Taft's bill, *Time* magazine called it "a testimonial to Taft's conduct of (the) debate." *Time* predicted the conference committee product "would be pretty much Taft's." It was. And, when Truman vetoed the bill, Taft guided the Senate and his House allies to an override.

But Truman trumped Taft and his Republicans in the 1948 elections, and again the Ohio senator found himself in the minority. Angry and at times bitter, he flirted with the harsh anticommunist crusade of Wisconsin's Republican senator Joseph R. McCarthy and nursed his hopes for winning the GOP's 1952 presidential nomination and capturing the White House.

But his hopes were dashed at the Republicans' Chicago convention, and so, in 1953, he found himself drawing contentment in becoming majority leader in the new Republican-dominated Senate and helping (and guiding) the new GOP president.

Taft found the new role to his liking. He developed a deep respect for Eisenhower—"a man of good will," as he described the new president to a friend. To another he observed, "He is grasping things pretty well." For his part, Eisenhower relied heavily upon Taft, and some old Ike allies even complained that the president tilted toward Taft more than he did his old friends. Taft was facing a period of his greatest glory. He was dealing with a president he respected. He was at the vanguard of national

policy making. His dominance of the Senate was well established. He had reached a position of legislative power seldom matched before or after.

Then came that pain in his hip.

Taft took the news of his cancer with what the doctors considered remarkable calmness. He asked penetrating questions as if he were not involved in the matter. He received radiation treatment without complaint. Then he left the hospital and returned to Washington. Following a second diagnosis at New York Hospital—equally grim—he set about to dispose of major personal and political matters in Washington.

On June 10 Taft lumbered down the aisle of the Senate a few minutes before the bell was to ring in the day's session. He was pale and looked weak. His shirt collar hung loosely about his neck. He sat down at his customary desk, leaned his crutches against the desktop, and conversed quietly with California's William F. Knowland. Later, a statement from Jack Martin explained to quizzical reporters the nature of the situation. Taft, it said, was seriously ill and was relinquishing his majority leader duties to Knowland for the remainder of the session.

It was to be forever. On July 31 Robert Taft died at New York Hospital.

His rapid decline stunned his colleagues and the nation. He was eulogized far and wide as a giant among senators. Four years later the Senate itself confirmed that judgment, including Taft in a circle of its five greatest members—along with Henry Clay, Daniel Webster, John C. Calhoun, and Robert M. LaFollette. It was a fitting tribute to a man who had accumulated more power and wielded it more imaginatively and forcefully than anyone else that anyone could remember—who indeed may have been the greatest senator of the century.

In the four years following his speech at Wheeling, West Virginia, Sen. Joseph R. McCarthy came to symbolize the nation's obsession with the threat of communism at home and abroad. He also came to symbolize the ruthlessness with which some were willing to exploit the anxieties of the time. McCarthy had no intellectual pretensions and was an indifferent orator. But he had a gift for meeting people and binding them to him—allies, adversaries, even reporters. He would sometimes introduce the journalists covering his speeches to the audience, saying they were employees of the "New York Daily Worker" or the "Milwaukee Daily Worker." After finishing his speech, McCarthy would ask the same reporters to meet him later for a drink.

In 1952 McCarthy's career had to undergo an important test. In the midst of his high-profile crusade on the stage of national and world politics, the junior senator from Wisconsin had to go home and ask the voters to give him another term. The Democrats nominated the state's young attorney general, Thomas E. Fairchild, who was then his party's only statewide elected official. Far from being a radical, Fairchild was a partner in a Milwaukee establishment law firm and a descendant of some of the state's earliest Yankee settlers. He appealed to many Republicans, including progressives of the La Follette stripe and traditionalists who regarded McCarthy as a ruffian and an embarrassment.

But McCarthy, as an Irish Catholic and a fervent anticommunist, had crossover appeal of his own among the ethnic Democrats of Milwaukee and the factory towns around Wisconsin. The same dynamic was strong enough elsewhere that John F. Kennedy, running for the Senate that year in Massachusetts, carefully avoided criticizing McCarthy.

During the campaign, the anti-McCarthy forces produced a pamphlet that systematically refuted McCarthy's claims and exposed his distortions. It was largely the work of several newspaper journalists, some of whom were simultaneously writing news reports about the campaign. A minor classic in campaign propaganda, it was probably better read in Washington than in the blue-collar precincts of Kenosha, Janesville, or Stevens Point.

In November McCarthy won with 54 percent of the vote and swiftly claimed a mandate. But it was a Republican year almost everywhere, and McCarthy conspicuously trailed the rest of the GOP ticket in Wisconsin. Dwight D. Eisenhower carried the state with 61 percent of the vote, and the Republican governor was reelected with better than 62 percent.

The search for communists in government won McCarthy worldwide attention. It also made him one of the most familiar figures in American politics. But in the end, the need to take on more important targets and produce more impressive results would cause McCarthy to overreach.

McCarthyism's Self-Destruction

Robert W. Merry

In the fall of 1953 Sen. Joseph McCarthy cut short his Caribbean honeymoon and rushed back to Washington to open up a new battlefront in his four-year struggle against government subversives. The Wisconsin Republican announced that he had fresh information of communist infiltration into the Army Signal Corps Center at Fort Monmouth, New Jersey.

He assigned his Permanent Investigations Subcommittee to the case and called a procession of Army officers before the panel. In characteristic fashion, he badgered and bullied them, generating plenty of headlines in the process.

Over in the White House, President Dwight D. Eisenhower and his men watched this new development with growing alarm. When Eisenhower had taken office the previous January, his aim had been to neutralize McCarthy—and preserve Republican unity—by showing his own dedication to the communists-in-government issue.

Some administration officials, including Attorney General Herbert Brownell Jr., had considered the issue an effective weapon against Democrats in the forthcoming 1954 elections. Brownell, embracing elements of the McCarthy cause, had attacked former president Harry S. Truman on the issue, warning that the Communist Party had become "a greater menace now than at any time" in the past, and fostered the firing of some 2,200 government "security risks."

But now McCarthy was taking on the U.S. Army, the very institution that had nurtured Eisenhower's career. Was it possible, insiders were beginning to ask, that McCarthy's ultimate target was Ike himself?

"It is clear by now," wrote columnist Stewart Alsop, "that to underestimate McCarthy is folly, as the administration strategists who believed they could undercut him by 'fighting fire with fire' must surely have discovered." Alsop added that Eisenhower and McCarthy clearly were "in opposite corners"; a clash between them was "inevitable."

Stewart Alsop and his brother Joseph, partners in column writing, had gathered information on the immediate postwar period in occupied Germany, when Eisenhower was supreme commander. They learned that a communist fifth column had infiltrated the American command, controlling financial and manpower policy, fostering the communist takeover of numerous West German newspapers, and nearly gaining dominance over West German labor unions.

The Alsops concluded McCarthy was simply waiting for an opportunity, following an intraparty clash with the president, to spring this trap on Eisenhower. Joseph Alsop even sought a meeting with the White House chief of staff, Sherman Adams, to warn him of the danger. Casting aside journalistic propriety, the columnist urged the White House to take on McCarthy.

Army counsel Joseph Welch, left, excoriates Sen. Joseph McCarthy, right, as "reckless and cruel" at the climactic June 9, 1954, Senate hearing.

"Alsop, we'll fight," said Adams.

But Eisenhower had little zest for the fight. That became evident when Secretary of the Army Robert T. Stevens sought White House support in his effort to resist the indiscriminate subpoenas that McCarthy's committee had been issuing against Army officials. The White House declined to stand behind Stevens and told him to cut a deal with the committee.

The committee's hardline Republicans were in no mood for compromise, and Stevens ended up in capitulation. He essentially agreed to let McCarthy subpoena anyone he chose, so long as he promised to be polite. That got Stevens attacked and ridiculed by Washington's growing anti-McCarthy forces. The Alsops called the damage "irreparable."

And Eisenhower retreated from a direct assault on McCarthy that many Washington hands had expected at a March 3, 1954, news conference. Fully 256 reporters showed up, a record at the time, expecting hot news. They were disappointed. The president's comments turned out to be surprisingly mild; he didn't even refer to McCarthy by name.

Meanwhile, McCarthy was charging ahead with his hard-fisted Army hearings. Concluding he had a strong case involving an Army dentist named Irving Peress, he became more pugnacious than ever.

Peress had entered the service as a captain in early 1953. Asked to fill out a form concerning membership in groups deemed subversive by the attorney general, he had written, "federal constitutional privilege." Soon he came under investigation by Army intelligence and the FBI as a possible security risk. Even as the investigation proceeded, Peress was promoted to major, then offered an honorable discharge.

McCarthy blasted away, saying the case proved that the Army was filled with subversives bent on protecting and promoting their own. When he called Peress before his committee, the former officer, claiming Fifth Amendment protection, refused to answer any questions.

Then McCarthy called Brig. Gen. Ralph W. Zwicker, who had been Peress' commanding officer and who had alerted McCarthy to the Peress case. But, instead of praising the general for stepping forward in the anticommunist cause, he blamed Zwicker for allowing Peress' promotion to go through. In scandalous fashion, he berated and insulted the general.

"You should be removed from any command," declared the senator, adding he considered Zwicker unfit to wear the Army uniform.

When a transcript of the closed-door session leaked to the press, it caused a sensation. The *New York Times* published the entire document, and McCarthy quickly came under fiery attack, even from some of his erstwhile allies. The Chicago *Tribune*, once a strong McCarthy backer, abandoned the senator. Columnist David Lawrence, another McCarthy defender, called his behavior "a bad mistake." Republican senator Charles E. Potter of Michigan, a longtime McCarthy partisan, characterized his conduct as "a distorted, twisted, circus performance."

With McCarthy weakened, Eisenhower began his counterattack. The weapon of choice was a remarkable 15,000-word document produced by Army counsel John G. Adams. It rendered an unsavory portrait of McCarthy and Roy M. Cohn, his chief lieutenant, abusing their senatorial positions in seeking to intimidate the Army in behalf of an enlisted man named G. David Schine.

Intense, ambitious, and arrogant, Cohn was McCarthy's committee counsel. He was a brilliant lawyer with a passion for internal security issues and utter devotion to the interests of McCarthy. *Time* magazine said he showed "contempt for all but the top boss."

Schine, the son of a wealthy hotel magnate, was Cohn's closest friend. Schine was given to collecting fancy cars, hanging out in nightclubs, and chasing movie stars. After Schine's gradua-

tion from Harvard, Cohn got him a job at the committee.

When Schine received his draft notice, Cohn and McCarthy used their lofty Senate positions to try to get him a commission. When that failed they pressured Army officials to give him special treatment—exemption from guard duty and tough training exercises, as well as cushy assignments.

Cohn's pressure tactics, conducted with McCarthy's apparent sanction, became more and more blatant, and his behavior toward John Adams, the Army counsel, became more and more obnoxious. Soon administration officials learned an important fact bearing on the matter: the wealthy Schine had been supplementing Cohn's income.

All this was detailed in Adams' report, and on March 10 Defense Secretary Charles E. Wilson revealed the report's contents to McCarthy. He threatened to make the report public unless the senator fired Cohn. McCarthy refused.

Wilson promptly sent an abbreviated version of the report to all members of McCarthy's subcommittee and to the Armed Services Committee. It quickly hit the newspapers and caused a stir.

The *New York Times* published the report verbatim and announced in a front-page headline: "Army Charges McCarthy and Cohn Threatened It in Trying To Obtain Preferred Treatment for Schine." United Press called the report "sensational," adding that it hit the Senate "like a bombshell."

But Joseph Alsop noticed something interesting about the report. It was merely a third the length of the original document, which he had read some weeks earlier in John Adams' office. Adams had placed the matter "off the record" before allowing Alsop to read the report, and hence he couldn't report on it until after it had become public. Now he alone among Washington's journalists knew the full

McCarthy speaks to his committee counsel, Roy M. Cohn, seated, during Cohn's questioning of Secretary of the Army Robert T. Stevens.

story, and he and his brother promptly filed a column entitled "The Tale Half Told." In the column, they filled in the gaps.

First, they revealed that the original version detailed the "disgusting obscenities" that characterized Cohn's dealings with Army brass. The Alsops said Cohn's "Nazi-like sense of power" derived directly from his position as McCarthy's chief counsel.

Second, they provided new information on the unusual relationship between Cohn and McCarthy. When alone with Adams, McCarthy would protest that he sought no special treatment for Schine, and he would denigrate Cohn. At one point he actually told Adams that he wished to fire Cohn but couldn't, for some unspecified reason. But when Cohn, in McCarthy's presence, would berate Adams and demand special privileges for Schine, the senator would remain silent. The implication, the Alsops wrote, seemed to be that Cohn possessed a peculiar power over McCarthy.

Third, their column revealed that a leading member of the McCarthyite press, acting in McCarthy's behalf, had promised top Army officers that McCarthy would terminate his Army investigation if the Army in turn would give Schine a soft New York assignment.

The report was devastating, but McCarthy fought back. He produced a series of eleven memos that impugned the integrity and veracity of his Army accusers. In fact, the memos were bogus—manufactured in McCarthy's own back rooms and backdated as part of a desperate McCarthy attempt to turn the tables on his adversaries.

By that time the issue had become so confused and bizarre that members of McCarthy's subcommittee decided they must take control. They voted to bring in a new counsel to take over from Cohn and to initiate a fresh investigation into the allegations and counterallegations swirling around the committee. McCarthy would relinquish his chairmanship pending the outcome of the investigation, which would be directed by the panel's second-ranking Republican, Karl E. Mundt of South Dakota.

The Army-McCarthy hearings, held in the Caucus Room of the Old Senate Office Building, opened with great fanfare on April 22, 1954. The room was overflowing with nearly 400 spectators and more than 100 reporters. For weeks the nation's attention was riveted on that drama-drenched hearing room as charges and countercharges flew back and forth and McCarthy sought to maintain control through parliamentary maneuvers.

"Point of order, Mr. Chairman," he would intone in yet another effort to insert his commentary into the proceedings.

Then a new face and new persona emerged. They belonged to Joseph Nye Welch, an Iowa-born, Harvard-educated trial lawyer with a razor-edged tongue and a flair for the dramatic. As counsel for the Army, he quickly established himself as a deft and flamboyant presence—and more than a match for McCarthy.

The senator didn't know it, but his support was evaporating throughout the country. By now he had positioned himself as an enemy of the highly popular President Eisenhower, and polls indicated Americans were abandoning his cause by the millions. His performance during the hearings tattered his image further. As America watched on television, McCarthy projected himself as a mean-spirited, somewhat childish boor.

At one point, seeking to get Welch off balance, the senator opened up an attack on a young Boston lawyer named Fred Fisher, a law partner of Welch's in the Boston firm of Hale and Dorr. The man, McCarthy alleged, had once belonged to a communist-front group called the Lawyers Guild, but despite that Welch had sought to get him a job on the Permanent Investigations Subcommittee.

"I am not asking you at this time to explain why you tried to foist him on this committee," McCarthy shouted at Welch.". . . I get the impression that, while you are quite an actor, you play for a laugh. I don't think you have any conception of the danger of the Communist Party."

It was the moment that Welch had been waiting for. Directing his rhetoric and ire at McCarthy as rapt Americans watched in their living rooms, Welch explained that Fisher had belonged to the group for a mere six months in his youth; now he was a respected member of the Young Republicans. And, Welch revealed, when he had learned of Fisher's past affiliation he had counseled him to abandon his plans to help the committee and return to Boston—for his own sake. Then, in stentorian tones of accusation, he added: "Little did I dream you could be so reckless and so cruel as to do an injury to that lad. . . . Let us not assassinate this lad further, Senator. You have done enough. Have you no sense of decency, sir, at long last? Have you left no sense of decency?"

It was a fearsome blow, and McCarthy, unmasked as never before, couldn't recover. For weeks, the sequence was seen repeatedly on television and movie newsreels. It was the subject of endless editorials and commentary. It even became the focal point of an influential documentary called "Point of Order." The bottom quickly dropped out of what was left of the movement called McCarthyism. It ended with hardly a whimper.

Following the disastrous Army-McCarthy hearings in the spring of 1954, Sen. Joseph R. McCarthy's star descended as sharply as it had risen. The Gallup Poll had been registering a decline in his public support since March, and in June a motion was made for his censure. A committee approved the motion; in December the Senate condemned him by a 67-22 vote. Largely discredited, McCarthy faded from view. In 1956 he was admitted to a hospital for treatment of ailments related to alcoholism. He died there in May 1957 at the age of forty-eight.

McCarthy's downfall, preceded the year before by the death of Robert A. Taft, left the core conservatives of the Republican Party without a natural spokesman. They were dissatisfied with President Eisenhower, who seemed to them to be little more than a caretaker for the New Deal. Eisenhower's support of NATO symbolized a Europe-oriented foreign policy that appeared willing to let communism take its course in Asia. He had not only sought a negotiated settlement in Korea but also refused to answer Chinese provocations in the waters separating Formosa from the mainland. When the French were fighting to preserve their colonies in Indochina, Eisenhower offered substantial monetary aid but no troops. In 1954 Vietnam was partitioned—with the communists claiming the northern half.

On the domestic front, the president had appointed former California governor Earl Warren as the new chief justice of the United States in 1954. Although Warren was a Republican, he had been popular enough among Democrats that in 1946 he was nominated for reelection by both parties. The Supreme Court over which Warren presided soon found disfavor with conservatives. In its first year, the Warren Court ruled that "separate but equal" schools were inherently discriminatory against African American children and ordered the dismantling of segregation.

In 1955 a black woman named Rosa Parks in Montgomery, Alabama, refused to give up her seat on a public bus to a white man. Her arrest led to a citywide boycott of the bus system by blacks and a few sympathetic whites. The next year a federal court ruled that segregation on public transit was unconstitutional. In 1957 Congress would pass a compromise civil rights bill to protect voting rights, and Eisenhower would send troops to Little Rock, Arkansas, to enforce desegregation.

But Republicans disgruntled with Ike had no champion to challenge him in 1956 and so accepted his renomination. The president reprised his earlier victory over Adlai E. Stevenson that fall, but his second landslide did not restore his party to power on Capitol Hill, where Democrats had made a comeback in 1954. The confidence with which Republicans had come to power in 1953 had ebbed, and Eisenhower's reelection had done little to restore it. As the decade of the 1950s waned, the initiative in American politics was once again shifting back to the party of Roosevelt.

= 1958 =

Voters Punish Ike's Allies in Congress

Rhodes Cook

Many Americans in the late 1950s watched "Ozzie and Harriet," drove big-finned automobiles, and danced to rock 'n' roll. But it was hardly the age of innocence later depicted on television.

The nation's booming postwar economy had begun to slump. The tumultuous battle for civil rights was under way. And the cold war was entering a new stage, as the Soviets took the first step into space by launching the Sputnik satellite in 1957.

Confidence in the avuncular president, Dwight D. Eisenhower, had clearly been shaken. And in the midterm elections of 1958, his Republican Party suffered a stunning rebuke at the polls that would reverberate across the political landscape for years to come.

Republicans entered the 1958 election in a strong minority position in Congress: they were down just 49–47 in the Senate and 234–201 in the House. But after the voting that November, they held barely one-third of the seats in either chamber. So huge were the GOP's post–1958 deficiencies that the Democrats were able to live off the margin for a generation, retaining control of both House and Senate for the next twenty-two years.

Beyond raising the Democrats' numbers, the election of 1958 changed the nature of their majorities. The new Democrats included many from the North, the Midwest, and the Far West. The South's grip on the reins of power on Capitol Hill began to loosen.

This trend was not readily apparent in the last two years of the Eisenhower presidency. Texan Sam Rayburn continued to reign as House Speaker. Lyndon B. Johnson, another Texan, remained as Senate majority leader. What was more, southerners chaired most of the congressional committees.

But the decline in the South's influence within the party was set in motion, and by the mid-1960s it would erode significantly. It was then that Congress readily approved major initiatives on civil rights and other landmark pieces of LBJ's Great Society program.

Few were surprised by the Democrats' success in 1958. They had regained control of Congress in 1954 after two years in the minority (occasioned by Eisenhower's landslide election in 1952). The Democrats had maintained their grip in 1956 (despite Eisenhower's easy reelection win) and picked up momentum thereafter.

In August 1957 Democrat William Proxmire easily won the Senate seat of the late Joseph R. McCarthy, who had died in May of a liver ailment. That November, Democrats swept the governorships in New Jersey and Virginia. And in the state elections in Republican Maine in September 1958, Democrats won the governorship and two House seats to go along with Edmund S. Muskie's victory in the Senate race. "This is obviously not one of our good years," said GOP senator Norris Cotton of New Hampshire.

AP / WIDE WORLD PHOTOS

In the two years since President Dwight D. Eisenhower's landslide reelection, public confidence in him had eroded.

Alarmed by signs of widespread apathy within their ranks, the Republicans in early October 1958 held a White House strategy session that produced a manifesto. It declared that if a new Democratic Congress were elected, "we are certain to go down the left lane which leads inescapably to socialism."

The president also sharpened his rhetoric. Campaigning in Baltimore in late October, Eisenhower used terms such as "political free spenders," "radical," "gloomdoggler," and "extremist" to describe Democratic critics of his self-described moderate, middle-of-the-road government.

Eisenhower, Vice President Richard M. Nixon, and other GOP campaigners painted the picture of a Democratic Party so at odds with itself that it was incapable of governing. They lauded the fiscal responsibility of conservative Southern Democrats, such as Sens. Harry Flood Byrd of Virginia (chairman of the Finance Committee) and Richard B. Russell of Georgia (chairman of the Armed Services Committee), while depicting liberal Northern Democrats as "political radicals."

Yet while the high-pitched rhetoric aroused some of the GOP faithful, the mood of the year continued to work strongly in the Democrats' favor. A series of Gallup Polls summed up the unsettled tenor of the times. Fully one-third of Americans in late 1957 feared there would be another world war within five years. Nearly two-thirds in early 1958 thought business was in a recession. And nearly half of Americans in the fall of 1958 thought that race relations across the South were growing worse.

Recovery from the recession of 1957–1958 had begun, but voter confidence in Republican economic policy did not rebound accordingly. The Sputnik launching had weakened voter confidence in the administration's defense and space programs. And southern resentment of Eisenhower's decision to use troops in Arkansas in 1957 to enforce an integration order at a Little Rock high school had curtailed GOP hopes for gains in the South in 1958.

Moreover, Republicans backed "right to work" ballot measures that were bitterly opposed by organized labor in California, Ohio, and other important states. This inspired labor to get its members out to vote, and the aroused members voted against right-to-work and for the Democrats. *Time* magazine would call the GOP's identification with these proposals "indeed the stupidest of all Republican campaign stunts."

In November, Democrats scored their most decisive victory since the heyday of the New Deal. They picked up 15 Senate seats (up from 49 to 64) to reach their highest level in the chamber since 1940, and they gained 48 House seats (up from 235 to 283) to reach their highest total in that chamber since 1936.

Among the Democrats elected to the House for the first time that fall were Dan Rostenkowski of Illinois, John Brademas of Indiana, Neal E. Smith of Iowa, Quentin N. Burdick of North Dakota, and Robert W. Kastenmeier of Wisconsin.

The Senate class of 1958 included Thomas J. Dodd of Connecticut (father of Sen. Christopher J. Dodd), Muskie of Maine, Philip A. Hart of Michigan, Eugene J. McCarthy of Minnesota, and the forty-year-old Robert C. Byrd of West Virginia.

Democrats lost none of the seats that they had previously held in the Senate and lost only one in the House, that of Coya Knutson (1955–1959) of Minnesota. And her loss was something of a fluke. Knutson's husband, Andrew, publicly pleaded with her to abandon her political career because, he said, "our home life has deteriorated to the extent that it is practically non-existent." He endorsed his wife's primary opponent. Despite the embarrassment of this "come home Coya" campaign, she lost the seat by less than 1,500 votes.

Notable Republican victories in 1958 were few and far between. Nelson A. Rockefeller ousted Democratic governor Averell Harriman

in New York. Young Mark O. Hatfield unseated a Democratic incumbent to win the governorship in Oregon.

The handful of new Republican House members included Silvio O. Conte of Massachusetts and John V. Lindsay of New York. Barry M. Goldwater of Arizona was elected to a second term in the Senate, making him the de facto leader of the GOP's decimated conservative wing.

"This election can be regarded as remarkable only because some Republicans did well," wrote Raymond Moley of *Newsweek.*

It was not long before repercussions were felt on Capitol Hill. Chagrined by their showing at the polls, restive Republicans were in the mood for new leadership. And as the 86th Congress convened in January 1959, Rep. Charles A. Halleck of Indiana led a revolt against House Minority Leader Joseph W. Martin of Massachusetts.

The crusty seventy-four-year-old Martin had been the Republican House leader since 1939, serving as Speaker in the two Congresses when Republicans had a majority (the 80th and 83d) and as minority leader in the other eight.

The fifty-eight-year-old Halleck had been Martin's lieutenant, taking the majority leader's job when Martin was Speaker and functioning as an unofficial assistant minority leader under Martin since 1955. Although the two had few policy differences, their personal rivalry had long smoldered. Martin had privately complained that Halleck bypassed him to deal directly with the White House on legislative matters. Twice before, in 1953 and 1957, Halleck had talked about challenging Martin but decided not to.

As it was, Halleck's challenge in 1959 did not come into the open until the day before the vote. Martin's supporters offered a compromise that would have created a new post of assistant leader and would also have cleared the way for

Elizabeth Echford passes a hostile crowd outside a Little Rock high school on September 4, 1957. Eisenhower's use of troops to enforce integration hurt his party in the South.

another Republican to replace Martin in his dual role as chairman of the GOP Policy Committee. But the compromise was turned down, the call for a secret ballot was approved, and Halleck was chosen minority leader by a vote of 74–70 on the second ballot.

The contest had been less a liberal-conservative argument than a conflict between generations. Younger Republicans were largely in Halleck's camp. Martin also attributed his defeat to GOP election reverses, which, he said, "had the boys confused. They wanted a fall guy."

Victory created problems of its own for the Democrats. Southerners remained in most of the positions of power on Capitol Hill, but their share of seats within the majority party had been significantly reduced by the 1958 elections.

Democrats still controlled more than 90 percent of the House and Senate seats from the "Solid South." But all fifteen Senate seats and forty-seven of the forty-eight House seats that the party gained in 1958 were from outside the South. As a result, the Southern share of Democratic seats fell from nearly 50 percent in each chamber in the 85th Congress (1957–1958) to less than 40 percent in the 86th.

And many of the new Democratic members wanted a more activist agenda. During the 1954 campaign, Eisenhower had predicted in 1954 that the election of a Democratic Congress would produce a "cold war" of partisan politics. That did not happen either then or after the 1956 election, the first presidential election since 1848 in which the White House winner's party failed to carry either chamber of Congress.

To the chagrin of many liberal Democrats, Eisenhower and Democratic congressional leaders often operated on the same wavelength. "About 85 percent of the time Eisenhower's programs were just an extension of Democratic principles," Rayburn said on the eve of the 1958 vote. "We're not going to hate Eisenhower bad enough for us to change our principles."

Johnson tended to agree, boasting during the 1958 campaign: "Never in our history has a president received such responsible backing from an opposition party."

Eisenhower averaged fewer vetoes in the Democratic-controlled 84th and 85th Congresses than the Republican 83d (1953–1954). Only three times from 1955 to 1958 had the Democratic Congress even tried to override an Eisenhower veto, and none were overridden.

Johnson did let it be known the day after the 1958 elections that he would press for a twelve-point legislative program, which included action on housing, urban renewal, depressed areas, water resources, airports, and interest rates—all points of contention with the administration in 1958.

Yet Johnson's talk of a Democratic "mandate" was tempered with words of caution. When the 86th Congress convened in January, he told his Democratic colleagues there were limits on what they could do without control of the White House. "We have been given great strength, but not overriding strength," he said.

His approach was not popular with many in the party, including the liberal Democratic Advisory Council. Formed after the 1956 election by Democratic National Committee Chairman Paul M. Butler, the council included former president Harry S. Truman, Sen. Hubert H. Humphrey of Minnesota and former governor Adlai E. Stevenson of Illinois, the party's presidential standard-bearer in 1952 and 1956.

In the month before the 1958 election, both Butler and Truman railed against southern hegemony in Congress. Truman argued that "it might be good for the country" if some southerners lost their committee chairmanships, singling out Senator Byrd of the Finance Committee and Mississippi senator James O. Eastland of the Judiciary Committee.

After the election, the council unveiled its own legislative agenda, calling for stronger civil rights measures, curbs on Senate filibusters, liberalization of immigration laws, and a $1.25 per hour minimum wage. Rayburn quickly dismissed the document. The record of the 86th Congress turned out to be modest. The major accomplishments, statehood for Hawaii and a labor reform law, were just as much administration bills as Democratic.

The 86th Congress often found itself subsumed in 1960 presidential politics, with four Democratic senators in hot pursuit of their party's nomination. John F. Kennedy of Massachusetts won, beating out Johnson, Humphrey, and Stuart Symington of Missouri. And with Kennedy's election, Democrats would once again control both ends of Pennsylvania Avenue.

It was to be a long road back for the Republicans. But out of the ashes of their 1958 debacle, one of the GOP survivors was sure he saw the route to the party's redemption. "Quit copying the New Deal," said Goldwater. "The voters will come back when they find that the Republican Party stands a little to the right of center."

The Congress that convened in 1959 had more Democrats than any since the high-water mark of the New Deal in the late 1930s. But this numerical superiority brought little immediate change in national policy: the presidency was still held by Republican Dwight D. Eisenhower, who, in his final years in office, was at least as cautious as ever. Just as significant, the Democrats on Capitol Hill were as divided as ever into factions—especially regional factions.

In the 86th Congress (1959-1961), the Democrats had more than 280 seats in the House. The Senate, newly enlarged to include two new members from Hawaii and two from Alaska, had sixty-four Democrats. Even so, more than one-third of the Democrats in each chamber hailed from the South.

Nearly a century after the Civil War, the "party of Lincoln" had yet to establish a presence in the old Confederacy. Some southern states had voted for the Republican presidential candidate, Herbert Hoover, in 1928 (when the Democrats nominated Al Smith, a Catholic) or for Eisenhower in the 1950s. A few mountain districts preserved a Republican tradition stretching back to the Civil War, and there were small party organizations in each state that would distribute political appointments when the GOP held the White House.

But on the whole, Dixie sent Democrats to Washington, making southerners disproportionately numerous in the Democratic caucus. They were also likely to stand out in the caucus by reason of their views: the typical Southern Democrat in Congress was neither a liberal nor a populist but a product of the economic and social establishment that ran things in his home state or district.

"Dixiecrats" often voted together—especially on civil rights, military spending, and farm supports (peanuts, cotton, and tobacco have long been among the most subsidized crops in the United States). When Southern Democrats made common cause with Republicans, they constituted a working majority in either chamber. This ad hoc alliance was dubbed the "conservative coalition."

The Southern Democrats' other weapon was seniority, and it too was forged by the interaction of congressional rules and regional voting behavior. Through most of the twentieth century, committee chairmanships were awarded to majority party members almost entirely by seniority. In the one-party South, where members' reelection was all but assured, seniority accumulated undisturbed.

Once secured, a chairmanship could be highly effective in blocking legislation. This was especially important as the number of nonsouthern Democrats grew. Even if the new "national Democrats" could beat the conservative coalition on certain floor votes, they were powerless if a bill never reached the floor at all. It was still a relatively easy matter for a well-placed chairman to bottle up a bill. And no chairman was better placed to do so than Howard W. Smith of Virginia, chairman of the Rules Committee.

Smith and Rayburn: Power Struggle

Ronald D. Elving

In January 1961, the month John F. Kennedy was inaugurated as president, Democrat Sam Rayburn of Texas celebrated his seventy-ninth birthday. Nearing the half-century mark as a member of the House, Rayburn was also beginning his seventeenth year as Speaker. In June he would have presided over the House twice as long as Henry Clay. In September he would be diagnosed with the cancer that would take his life within two months.

But as the year began, the gruff and wily "Speaker Sam" was at the peak of his powers and committed to one mission: breaking the historic power of the Rules Committee so that his party's new president could succeed.

The battle to be joined might not engage the public, but the stakes for history were high. By taming the power of Rules, Rayburn would alter the feudal relationship between the Speaker and the autonomous baronage of committee chairmen. But beyond that lay a far larger struggle for control of the nation's agenda.

Kennedy had campaigned on a promise to reinvigorate the nation. And while few voters may have known precisely what that promise meant, Kennedy's admirers in Congress knew what it meant to them. An activist core had been pushing for more liberal legislation on federal aid to education and housing, civil rights, the minimum wage, and other labor issues. Rules had resisted at every turn, denying bills floor access on tie votes of 6–6 (with two Southern Democrats voting with the panel's four Republicans).

Although Rayburn's formal resolution merely sought to enlarge the Rules membership from twelve to fifteen, his intent was to add two more Democrats who would vote with the Democratic majority. Neil MacNeil, long the congressional correspondent for *Time*, wrote in his book *Forge of Democracy* that the procedural fight was hard to explain at the time. "Superficially, the representatives seemed to be quarreling about next to nothing: the membership of the committee. In reality, however, the question raised had grave import for the House and for the United States."

Without the power to move bills to the floor, the national Democratic leadership of the 1960s and 1970s never could have enacted the civil rights bills, Medicare, the War on Poverty, or the environmental legislation that became the era's landmarks.

The problem with Rules was personified in its Democratic chairman, Howard Worth Smith of Virginia. As chairman since 1955, Smith had been pleased to scuttle years' worth of legislation he did not favor. Sometimes the former jurist (known in the House as "Judge" Smith) granted rules that would ease a bill's defeat. Sometimes he refused to grant a rule at all. Just the previous August, he had cheerfully blocked a fistful of bills being pushed by Senator Kennedy and other liberals in both chambers.

Rayburn personally had his reservations about the liberal agenda, much as he had doubts about the later phases of Franklin D.

House Rules Committee Chairman Howard Smith, Democrat of Virginia.

Roosevelt's domestic program. He was, after all, a southerner representing a rural cotton-growing district. His father, like Smith's, had fought in the Confederate Army. And he had told constituents over the years that he saw racial conflict "working itself out" locally without interference from outsiders who "do not know what the racial question is."

Nonetheless, the Speaker was about to set all this aside for two reasons. One was the election of the first Democratic president in eight years. Rayburn had reversed his earlier estimation of Kennedy. The Speaker, bald and uncomfortable with cameras, had once discounted the telegenic Kennedy as shallow. The second reason was the growing perception that the Speakership itself was being diminished by the power of the Rules chairman.

At seventy-seven, Smith was a gentleman of the old school and a defender of the Old Dominion. He had a pale, almost spectral appearance highlighted by bushy, upswept eyebrows. He was devoted to states' rights, which meant the strict enforcement of Jim Crow laws. When confronted with a bill he saw as impinging on states' rights, he would return to his dairy farm near Broad Run, Virginia, and refuse to call Rules into session. On one occasion, Smith said he could not come to Washington because his barn had just burned down. That prompted Rayburn to quip, "I knew Howard Smith would do almost anything to stop a civil rights bill, but I never suspected he would resort to arson."

The Rules Committee had been a problem for Democratic leaders long before Smith became its chairman. It had been the strait through which all bills of consequence had to pass, and, by dominating its ranks from the late 1930s, Republicans and conservative Southern Democrats had held a kind of veto power over House action.

Rayburn had chafed at this. But he had also enjoyed a symbiotic relationship with most of Smith's predecessors over the years. Some were among his personal friends, and he found many of them useful in dealing with other committee barons (or as a convenient excuse for keeping certain bills from the floor when he wished).

The Speaker had yet another reason to hesitate before taking on what he would call "the worst fight of my life," and that was the uncertainty of the outcome. Rayburn hated to lose and hated to risk losing. He worked hard to avoid dramatic and public tests of his power and prestige. He lasted longer in the Speakership than anyone else because he worked his will through others, facilitating things in private.

Now he was risking a great deal on the belief that the conservative coalition could be beaten by frontal assault. One House liberal, Rep. Richard Bolling, D-Mo., calculated that the nominal Democratic majority of 261 included 60 "strong conservatives, mostly from the South." Even with a handful of crossover votes from liberal Republicans, the Democratic leadership would be short of a 218-vote majority.

Just how many of those votes could be counted on to choose Rayburn over Judge Smith was another question. Once Rayburn had resolved to break the power of Rules, he had to choose a strategy. The most direct would have been to replace one of the eight Democrats on the twelve-member committee with a member more loyal to the leadership. The logical target was William M. Colmer of Mississippi, the second most senior Democrat after Smith and, again after Smith, the most conservative. This could have been handled in the House Democratic Caucus (where Rayburn would prevail).

Rayburn at first gave his colleagues to understand he would go after Colmer. But when this brought howls of protest, Rayburn offered his expansion plan instead. Aides thought later that Rayburn had intended this all along and had suggested the purge first so as to portray enlargement as a compromise.

The problem was that enlarging the committee would require a majority vote of the whole House. That meant risking that Republicans and Southern Democrats would humiliate the Speaker and the president. Minority Leader Charles A. Halleck, R-Ind., decided to make the issue a party-unity vote and discipline those

who deviated. At the same time, Smith's active campaign to save his prerogatives and power found willing ears among southerners fearful that Kennedy and his Ivy League aides would soon move the party so far left as to jeopardize their own reelection campaigns.

Still, when Smith saw the Speaker making headway, he made him an offer. If Rayburn would back off, leaving Smith in charge, the Rules Committee would guarantee safe conduct to the floor for five bills designated by the administration—a core program consisting of a minimum wage increase, federal aid to education, more public housing, aid to depressed areas, and a program for medical care for the elderly under Social Security (Medicare).

But from the standpoint of the Speaker, Smith's compromise was an outrage. Rayburn aide D. B. Hardeman wrote in his diary that Rayburn had dismissed the chairman angrily, saying, "Shit, Howard, the president may have 40 bills in his program before he's through."

Rayburn had set January 26 for a vote on the expansion of the committee. As the date approached, Bolling and others believed they had the votes. But when they could not produce a hard list of names totaling 218, both the Speaker's staff and the White House got cold feet and put the vote off for five days.

The delay put the vote just after Kennedy's first State of the Union speech. By then, according to Kennedy aide and biographer Theodore Sorenson, the White House would have used "all the influence a new administration could muster—patronage, sentiment, campaign commitments and federal actions of all kinds." One North Carolinian pronounced himself shocked when a Cabinet member hinted at the loss of federal spending projects in North Carolina.

Historical accounts differ as to the effect of these extra days. Some insist that votes were added by the blandishments emanating from the administration; others suggest that wavering

As president in the mid-1960s, Lyndon Johnson, left, would benefit from the taming of the Rules Committee achieved in 1961 by Sam Rayburn, right, in behalf of John Kennedy, center.

votes were lost when members were offended by the heavy-handed tactics. Rayburn, according to Hardeman's diary, summed it up later by saying Kennedy's calls "didn't change a vote."

Rayburn's not-so-secret weapon was his long-standing friendship with Joseph W. Martin, the veteran from Massachusetts who had been Speaker during the Republican majorities of 1947–1949 and 1953–1955. Martin had been deposed in a bitter interpersonal fight with Halleck after the elections of 1958. But he still had his seat, and he still had his friends. And he let it be known that Halleck's unity vote would not bind him.

The showdown came January 31, and the nation's capital watched carefully to see how the Kennedy "New Frontier" would fare in the first test of its power. But in the House itself, Kennedy was less the issue than the two men, both nearly eighty, who had been locked in combat for weeks. On that morning, Rayburn came through the swinging doors from the

Speaker's lobby to a spontaneous ovation that spread across the aisle and into the packed and overflowing galleries. He basked in the moment briefly before banging the gavel twice and calling the House to order.

When Smith's turn came to speak, he walked slowly, slightly stooped, to the well. He complained that he had been allotted only eight minutes to speak. He denied having any quarrel with Rayburn and said any quarrel that existed was "all on his side." There was laughter in the chamber, even from the Speaker.

Then Smith promised he would go with the leadership "just as long and just as far as my conscience will permit me to do." This brought even more laughter from the rows of Democrats immediately before him. "Some of these gentlemen who are laughing maybe do not understand what a conscience is," the chairman said with a sniff.

Halleck gave the last speech opposing the resolution. He raised the specter of Rules in league with a liberal leadership. There would be a torrent of bills that were "unwise . . . ill-timed . . . socialistic." The House, he said, "would be overwhelmed by bad legislation." As Halleck shouted his concluding sentences, Rayburn descended from the rostrum and took a floor seat. When Halleck had finished, Rayburn stepped forward to speak. Once again, the chamber honored him with an ovation.

Rayburn's remarks were brief and addressed to "my beloved colleagues." He said he resented the accusation that he was trying to pack the committee with friends. Slyly, he admitted having supported the packing of Rules a generation earlier—when he had backed the bids for membership of his old friends Smith and Colmer. This brought more laughter, and a nod of acknowledgment from Smith.

But Rayburn's earnest tone was reserved for his plea. We have a new president, he said, and he has a new program: "Let us move this program; let us be sure we can move it."

Then came the vote. The House of 1961 had no electronic recording device, and important votes required an interminable call of the roll. The lead changed hands repeatedly; members sat nervously with tally sheets spread on their laps. When the clerk reached the name of Jim Wright, D-Texas, Rayburn was ahead by a single vote. When the full roll had been called, the clerk whispered the count to Rayburn: 214–209. Eleven members had failed to answer when their names were called, and the clerk returned to those names again.

Time magazine's MacNeil noted that each additional vote was followed by an involuntary but audible intake of breath from the galleries surrounding the chamber. On this call, six responded; three for each side. The clerk handed a card to Rayburn, who announced: "On this vote, there being 217 ayes and 212 nos . . ." The rest of his statement—declaring the resolution to be adopted—was lost in the cheering.

Moments later Smith could be seen making his way out of the chamber with members, staff, and reporters crowding around him. Asked repeatedly why he had lost, Smith replied: "We didn't have enough votes." Then he slid an unlit cigar into his mouth and continued on his way. By some accounts, his parting words were: "It's all baloney."

The Speaker in his last year and the president in his first had carried the day. The Rayburn-dominated Committee on Committees would shortly appoint B. F. Sisk of California and Carl Elliott of Alabama to Rules. At last, the 87th Congress could exhale and begin its labors.

As it happened, however, the fifteen-member Rules Committee would not send much of Kennedy's agenda to the floor in that Congress. The administration, distracted by confrontations with the Soviets abroad, scaled back its legislative initiatives. Bolling wrote later that Kennedy had begun to think that in defiance of tradition he could accomplish more on the Hill in a second term.

Rayburn went home in the summer of 1961 before the session had even ended, and died there November 16. Kennedy was assassinated in Dallas two years later. It would be Lyndon B. Johnson who, as during the 88th and 89th Congresses, reaped the legislative harvest of their fight to subdue Smith. Writing years later on the signficance of the event, Rep. Richard B. Cheney, R-Wyo. (1979–1989), would note the delayed effect: "Although the New Frontier profited little from Rayburn's final battle in the House of Representatives, without it, the Great Society would have been impossible."

Smith held his gavel until 1967, stoically watching a procession of bills he detested march past him into law. But he did outlive the other principals of the 1961 drama, including Johnson, dying in 1976 at the age of ninety-three.

J ohn F. Kennedy was elected president in November 1960, inaugurating a White House era strikingly different in substance and tone from its predecessor. The Kennedy interlude, sometimes called Camelot by admirers and detractors alike, remains fascinating in retrospect—in part because it was so brief.

Kennedy had come to Congress in 1946, still not quite thirty and riding on his status as a war hero and a son of Joseph P. Kennedy, a wealthy Boston financier and former ambassador to Great Britain. The young Kennedy moved to the Senate in 1952, married a beautiful and cultured heiress, and almost immediately began positioning himself for the presidency—he was briefly considered for vice president at the Democratic convention of 1956. Just forty-two when he began campaigning in 1960, Kennedy also had to deal with religious prejudice: no Catholic had ever been elected president. But he blunted the religion issue by winning the West Virginia primary that spring and overcame the age handicap by projecting maturity in his debate with Vice President Richard M. Nixon that fall.

Once in office, Kennedy hoped not only to "get the country moving again" but also to turn its attention to the future. He proposed the Apollo moon project early in his presidency and lived long enough to see the first U.S. astronauts launched into space and orbiting the Earth. But the hopeful side of the Kennedy period would be overshadowed by a series of crises and challenges.

The fledgling regime of Fidel Castro in Cuba revealed itself to be communist, and a U.S.-backed effort to topple it failed miserably at the Bay of Pigs. Shortly thereafter, the Soviet premier, Nikita Khrushchev, provoked the new president by building a wall between East Berlin and West Berlin.

Meanwhile, at home, Kennedy confronted unrest in the South, where the aspirations of the civil rights movement continued to rise. Issues of race and civil rights had slowly supplanted jobs and wages as the central conflict of domestic politics during the later Eisenhower years.

In 1960, even as Kennedy was campaigning for president as a friend of the civil rights movement, the stakes were being raised. When four black college students tried to integrate a lunch counter in Greensboro, North Carolina, that February, they inaugurated the era of the sit-in. Over the next eighteen months, more than 70,000 college students took part in such demonstrations throughout the South.

In 1962, under federal court order, the University of Mississippi admitted its first black student, James Meredith. Days of student protests turned to rioting and left two dead. The demonstration ethos reached its zenith in August 1963, when more than 200,000 marchers stood on the Mall in Washington, D.C., and heard Rev. Martin Luther King Jr. say: "I have a dream that this nation will rise up and live out the true meaning of its creed . . . that all men are created equal."

= 1963 =

Crossing the Line in the Dust

Alan Greenblatt

At his inauguration as Alabama governor in 1963, George C. Wallace renewed a popular campaign pledge. "I draw the line in the dust and toss the gauntlet before the feet of tyranny, and I say: Segregation now! Segregation tomorrow! Segregation forever!" Less than six months later, on June 11, the feisty Democrat moved to make good his vow by standing in a schoolhouse door to block the entrance of two black students, Vivian Malone and James Hood, into the University of Alabama.

Wallace knew he was playing on a national stage, the latest southern authority to resist the Supreme Court's ruling in *Brown v. Board of Education* that desegregation should proceed "with all deliberate speed." The bantam governor had directed aides to paint a literal "line in the dust" in the doorway, along with two semicircles that marked where the governor should stand for the television cameras.

Squared up against Deputy Attorney General Nicholas Katzenbach, President John F. Kennedy's representative, Wallace read a proclamation denouncing "Central Government." By confronting a white bureaucrat in place of the black students, the governor was able to make government the issue rather than race. "Standing in the doorway made Wallace a star," Richard Reeves notes in his biography *President Kennedy.* "On television he was the same size as the president."

Meanwhile, away from the cameras, Malone and Hood quietly reported to their dorms. Bowing to pressure off-camera, Wallace kept his campus from exploding as the University of Mississippi had the year before (when antiintegration rioters killed two men).

Kennedy also appeared on television June 11, prompted by events in Alabama to make a primetime address on civil rights. In 1960 Kennedy had run on a civil rights platform, but as president he had sought to avoid the issue. He was mindful that his other legislation was in the hands of the southerners who chaired two dozen of the thirty-eight congressional committees. "If we go into a long fight in Congress," Kennedy warned the Rev. Dr. Martin Luther King Jr., "it will bottleneck everything else and still get no bill."

But by 1963, the television images could no longer be ignored. "For the horrors of the American Negro's life," novelist James Baldwin wrote, "there has been almost no language." Television lent blacks its powerful voice and access to America's homes. Pictures of white lawmen turning dogs and fire hoses on nonviolent protest marchers in Birmingham, Alabama, won sympathy for blacks worldwide.

During a presidential visit to Rome in 1963, Pope Paul VI embarrassed Kennedy by telling reporters he prayed for the success of American blacks in their struggle.

On May 2, 1963, during the long campaign for civil rights in Birmingham, King choreographed a visual appeal to conscience. Although jailed for his role in the protests, King still organized a march of more than 1,000 schoolchildren

Gov. George Wallace, flanked by state police, guards University of Alabama door.

through streets lined with police. The pictures of snarling police dogs biting into children as young as five touched off riots in dozens of cities, as well as peaceful demonstrations in hundreds more. "Legislation was not possible until the dogs lunged at the peaceful marchers in Birmingham in 1963," historian Arthur Schlesinger Jr. would later recall.

Attorney General Robert F. Kennedy hoped to persuade his brother to act, warning that the nation might soon be engulfed in violence. The younger Kennedy acknowledged that before the election "we didn't lie awake nights worrying" about civil rights. But the issue had risen on the administration's agenda with the unfolding of events in Alabama (including the May 1962 beating of Justice Department official John Seigenthaler, who was left unconscious by a white mob in Montgomery).

Robert Kennedy finally won his brother over on the night of the Wallace showdown. "There comes a time when a man has to take a stand," the president said, and the White House staff rushed the unexpected speech to him minutes before airtime. Casting racial justice as a moral issue and a top priority, Kennedy announced he would send comprehensive civil rights legislation to Congress.

"The events in Birmingham and elsewhere have so increased the cries for equality that no city or state or legislative body can prudently choose to ignore them," the president told the nation. "It is a time to act in Congress."

Kennedy formally submitted his brother's draft legislation June 19, 1963, but its prognosis was not good. The young president, who had spent his fourteen years in the House and Senate in near-constant pursuit of higher office, was not popular on Capitol Hill. In his first two years in office, he had shown little leverage with the conservative coalition of Republicans and southern Democrats, and a weak Kennedy bill to ban literacy tests, used to bar blacks at some polling places, had been killed by a southern filibuster in 1962. "I can't get a Mother's Day resolution through that goddamn Congress," the president complained.

Six years before, Kennedy's vice president, Lyndon B. Johnson, had earned credit as Senate majority leader by pushing through the first civil rights legislation since 1875. Earlier in his twenty-year congressional career, Johnson had opposed antidiscrimination bills. But by 1957 Johnson had hopes of winning over a national constituency, and he refused to sign the Southern Manifesto, with its call for massive resistance to the *Brown* decision.

Johnson twisted arms and cut deals to ensure the votes for cloture in 1957. But by the time he was through amending the House bill, it was said to resemble the soup that Abraham Lincoln described as made from the shadow of a pigeon that had starved to death. Johnson aide Harry McPherson might have felt the 1957 debate "persuaded many southern Negroes that at last Congress intended to do them justice," but Sen. Richard B. Russell, D-Ga., who was the leader of the southern bloc (as well as Johnson's mentor), looked on passage of the weakened bill as "the sweetest victory of my 25 years as a senator."

With this history in mind, civil rights activists in 1963 pushed for as strong a bill as possible, so that something substantial would be left after all the congressional deal-making. "When we ask for one-half of a loaf, we get one-quarter of a loaf. We ought to ask for what we want and fight for it," argued James Farmer, leader of the Congress of Racial Equality. But the Kennedys realized that the activists could not deliver the Republican votes necessary for passage, so they immediately sought a compromise with the GOP.

Robert Kennedy nearly managed to drive away the Republicans before the game started. Testifying June 26 at the first subcommittee hearing on the 1963 bill, which aimed to ban discrimination in public accommodations and employment, the attorney general insulted House Judiciary Republicans by telling them he had not read or taken seriously their own civil rights bills, which were in some cases stronger than the administration's.

"Why should the GOP bail out the administration?" asked exasperated House Minority Leader Charles A. Halleck of Indiana. Yet Halleck knew that many Republicans supported the bill on principle. Civil rights supporters in the GOP feared that the administration would let the Senate gut the bill again. The chastened Kennedys let Judiciary's ranking Republican, William McCulloch of Ohio, rewrite the bill to his party's satisfaction over the last weekend of October 1963 and promised him veto power over any prospective Senate amendments. The deep moral conviction of this fiscal conservative swayed fence-sitting Republicans as no liberal argument could have. But as the rank and file grew aware of Halleck's and McCulloch's cooperation, someone put an umbrella, symbolizing British Prime Minister Neville Chamberlain and appeasement, on the Republican leadership desk on the House floor.

The major remaining obstacle in the House was Democrat Howard W. Smith of Virginia, chairman of the Rules Committee and long the chief undertaker for progressive legislation. Although enough Rules Committee members were in open revolt to force Smith's hand eventually, the old chairman succeeded in delaying the bill's progress long enough to open fissures in the fragile Kennedy-Halleck alliance.

After being criticized by the president and the press for the slow pace at which Congress was

Young black demonstrators file toward jail in Birmingham, Alabama, on May 4, 1963.

handling the bill, Halleck complained at a November 21 news conference that the president, "who had promised major civil rights legislation in 1961," had been dragging his feet and planning to blame Congress. Liberal Democrats such as Don Edwards of California began to worry that "it was kind of running out of gas again."

But as Halleck spoke in Washington, Kennedy was in Texas on a political mission that would end abruptly and tragically with his death from an assassin's bullet on November 22, 1963.

After assuming the presidency, Johnson looked first to passing the martyred president's priority legislation. Addressing a joint session of Congress on November 27, Johnson solemnly told the nation, "No memorial oration or eulogy could more eloquently honor President Kennedy's memory than the earliest passage of the civil rights bill for which he fought so long."

The public responded with mounting support. The House acted fairly quickly, passing the bill with strong bipartisan support, 290-130,

after nine days of debate in February 1964 notable for discipline and restraint. *Newsweek* reported that "what emerged was a stronger bill than Kennedy administration officials had thought feasible." The real challenge was still the Senate, where Russell and the other southerners were waiting.

"I had to produce a civil rights bill that was even stronger than the one they'd have gotten if Kennedy had lived," Johnson later said. Johnson told the Senate that no other legislation should be considered, even in committee, until civil rights was voted on. Putting his own ambitious agenda on hold essentially undercut the deadly delaying effect of any filibuster before it could begin.

The Senate began its deliberations February 17. The protests and riots that had roiled and embarrassed the South for a decade had spread north by 1964, increasing the calls for action, and for the first time civil rights supporters, including labor unions, launched an organized lobbying campaign in Congress.

Perhaps most important, the Leadership Conference on Civil Rights persuaded religious groups to lobby senators from western states where blacks and organized labor were not a presence, helping to frame the issue in starkly moral terms. "There has never been as effective a lobby maintained in the city of Washington as there is today," groused Senator Russell.

Catholic, Jewish, and Protestant seminarians began a round-the-clock vigil at the Lincoln Memorial in behalf of the bill April 19, 1964, when the filibuster was already two months old. Roger Mudd of CBS began a vigil of his own the day after Easter, broadcasting nine reports daily from the Capitol steps while the Senate lurched on.

Appearing on "Face the Nation," Russell conceded that "any possible compromise" had been made more difficult by Kennedy's "tragic fate." In contrast to 1957, when Russell had said, "My intention is to amend this bill if possible, but to defeat it in any event," his strategy in 1964 was not to compromise at all. He dared supporters to find the sixty-seven votes necessary to break the filibuster—something that had never been achieved on a civil rights bill.

The key, once again, was winning GOP support. Minority Leader Everett M. Dirksen of Illinois had reservations about the bill's strong fair-employment provisions, but he knew the time for horse-trading on civil rights was past.

Dirksen aimed to amend the bill just enough to answer conservative GOP concerns. Steve Horn, an aide to liberal Republican Thomas H. Kuchel of California, said, "Dirksen will go through his public acting process, take a licking, and then be with us." Dirksen quietly negotiated with the Justice Department for weeks, settling on a handful of amendments that softened some of the bill's language and allowed states and localities to comply voluntarily with public accommodations requirements before the power of the federal government was brought into play, undermining the South's appeal to states' rights.

The former actor withheld his public support until May 19, during the filibuster's twelveth week, when it would have maximum impact among Republicans who were eager to recess in time for the national GOP convention. "No army is stronger than an idea whose time has come," Dirksen said, quoting French novelist Victor Hugo.

Russell allowed privately that "the jig is up." The last gasp of the filibuster was heard June 9, when Robert C. Byrd, D-W.Va., began to read an 800-page speech arguing against cloture. His fourteen-hour marathon address was the longest speech of the longest filibuster in Senate history. But cloture was invoked, finally, June 10 by a vote of 71-29, with twenty-seven Republicans joining forty-four Democrats. The Senate passed the bill June 19, 1964, one year to the day after Kennedy had introduced it.

Civil rights supporters had been worn out. During his floor speech June 10, Dirksen twice swallowed ulcer pills handed to him by a page. Clair Engle, D-Calif., fatally ill and unable to speak, was wheeled onto the Senate floor to cast the last votes of his career in favor of civil rights, pointing to his eye to signify "aye."

The celebration was cut short for several of the principals, including the Kennedys. Sen. Edward M. Kennedy, D-Mass., was nearly killed June 19 in a plane crash. Senate Majority Whip Hubert H. Humphrey, who had been the floor manager for the bill, had to rush back to Minnesota where a son was about to undergo surgery for cancer.

The Republicans, too, were soon robbed of their sense of achievement because the man who would lead them in the next presidential election voted against the bill. "If my vote is misconstrued," said Sen. Barry M. Goldwater, R-Ariz., "let me suffer its consequences."

As a watershed in history, the assassination of President Kennedy in November 1963 has often been compared to Pearl Harbor. Those who were alive invariably remember where they were when they heard the news of either event. Pearl Harbor ended America's illusion of security in the world, but Kennedy's assassination seemed to destroy an even dearer sense of national innocence.

Historians argue over what might have happened had Kennedy lived to complete his term. Would he have been able to push the Civil Rights Act through? Would he have been reelected? And most haunting of all, what would he have done in Vietnam?

Some Kennedy admirers who opposed the Vietnam war have insisted that he would have throttled back the Vietnam commitment in a second term, if not sooner. The president's brother, Robert F. Kennedy, propounded a version of this view when he ran an antiwar campaign for president in 1968. Conspiracy theorists, such as filmmaker Oliver Stone, have extended this analysis to suggest that Kennedy was assassinated by extreme anticommunists (including elements of the armed forces) precisely because he was beginning to sour on the war.

The facts are more complex. Kennedy was a war veteran whose hawkish campaign for president in 1960 accused President Eisenhower of allowing the Soviets to achieve nuclear superiority—the supposed "missile gap." In the 1960 debates between Kennedy and Richard M. Nixon, it was Kennedy who took the more aggressive stand toward the Chinese islands of Quemoy and Matsu. Moreover, Kennedy's performance in the October 1962 missile crisis strongly indicates that he was willing to risk war—even nuclear war—where he thought it necessary to call the Soviets' bluff.

Toward the end of 1961, having spent his first year as president in almost continual confrontation with the Soviets, Kennedy ordered combat advisers to shore up the sagging army of South Vietnam. He knew that the battlefield situation was not especially encouraging and that the political situation in Saigon was tenuous at best. But he was loath to let any prize fall into the Soviets' laps in the year of the Bay of Pigs and the Berlin Wall.

Secretary of State Dean Rusk viewed Vietnam as a test case for responding to communist insurgency in the Third World. Rusk counseled Kennedy to meet that test sternly, and his advice was buttressed by the optimistic projections of the can-do Secretary of Defense Robert S. McNamara. Even more critical may have been Kennedy's own political experience. He had served in the Senate with Joe McCarthy in the 1950s and in the House of the Un-American Activities Committee in the 1940s. He knew what price could be exacted from those who let communism spread on their watch.

In February 1962, with questions already arising about the mission of the Americans he had sent to Vietnam, Kennedy had issued a public statement that U.S. advisers would return fire if fired upon.

The Gulf of Tonkin Incident

Phil Duncan

When President Lyndon B. Johnson took office in November 1963, the U.S. military had been involved in the fighting in South Vietnam for nearly two years. Johnson's predecessor, President John F. Kennedy, committed combat support advisers in December 1961 to train the South Vietnamese military in its fight against Vietcong guerrillas, who were supported by communist North Vietnam and equipped with Chinese and Soviet weaponry.

The fight was not going well. While the Vietcong were a focused and disciplined force, South Vietnam was having trouble establishing a stable government. A coup in November 1963 was followed by another in January 1964, and political uncertainty persisted through the year, hampering efforts to plot a war strategy.

But walking out on Vietnam was not an option for Johnson, who saw the conflict through the prism of the cold war. He felt America was obligated to resist communism in Vietnam, lest the ideology and might of a rival superpower spread throughout Southeast Asia. "Communists, using force and intrigue, seek a communist-dominated world," he said in an April 1964 speech.

In May, Defense Secretary Robert S. McNamara presented a plan to Johnson for stepping up U.S. involvement in the country. In response, Johnson asked Congress for an additional $125 million in aid to South Vietnam. Congress already had been asked to provide $500 million for South Vietnam that year, but the Vietcong were still gaining strength and even threatening Saigon.

McNamara, in his 1995 memoir, *In Retrospect*, recalls that "some of the Joint Chiefs of Staff" had wanted to send combat troops to Vietnam beginning in January 1964. McNamara said Johnson had wanted any such action to be "preceded by some form of congressional endorsement." In response, McNamara wrote, "the State Department had drafted a resolution in late May."

The leading GOP presidential candidate in the spring of 1964, Arizona senator Barry M. Goldwater, had gained widespread attention by criticizing Johnson's strategy in Vietnam as meek and muddled. In May Goldwater suggested that the United States use low-yield nuclear bombs in the jungle to interrupt supply lines connecting the Vietcong to their North Vietnamese sponsors.

Goldwater had two campaign themes, one domestic and one foreign, each rooted in the public's fear of menace from the left. He pledged to end "the abuse of law and order in this country," a veiled reference to the rioting that had occurred in several cities early that summer. In world affairs, Goldwater vowed that America would not "cringe before the bully of communism." The GOP platform noted that the Berlin Wall had been erected and an invasion of Communist Cuba botched since Democrats moved into the White House in 1961. The document also scored Democrats for presiding over "the slow death of freedom" in Laos and Vietnam.

South Vietnamese train to repel waterborne communist forces in August 1964, before the massive U.S. military buildup began in earnest.

The GOP nominated Goldwater in San Francisco in mid-July. As his running mate, he picked the Republican national chairman, Rep. William E. Miller of New York, who had opened the convention with a speech faulting the Democratic administration for not understanding the "perpetual threat of communism in this world."

Soon thereafter, on July 27, the Johnson administration announced that the United States would send 5,000 more advisers to its 16,000-person military mission in South Vietnam. Three days later, on the afternoon of July 30, sailors of the South Vietnamese navy, piloting four patrol boats they had just received from the United States, left their base at Da Nang to attack a reported enemy patrol-boat base in North Vietnam.

Reaching their destination about midnight, the boats shelled the North Vietnamese islands of Hon Me and Hon Ngu, which lie in the Gulf of Tonkin about three and four miles, respectively, from the mainland. It was the first naval shelling of North Vietnam, according to John Galloway, whose 1970 book, *The Gulf of Tonkin Resolution*, is an exhaustive account of the events of the time.

The day after the shelling, July 31, the U.S. destroyer *Maddox* entered the Gulf of Tonkin and patrolled in the vicinity of the two islands with orders to "stimulate" and measure North Vietnamese and Chinese radar. On the night of August 1 the *Maddox* sailed toward Hon Me, approaching from the same direction the South Vietnamese raiders had. The *Maddox* came within four miles of the island, then turned away to the south. On August 2 the *Maddox* reported picking up radio transmissions indicating "possible hostile action." The ship advised naval headquarters in Hawaii that continuing to patrol close to shore "presents an unacceptable risk." The *Maddox* received orders to resume its itinerary when "considered prudent."

Soon the *Maddox* was steaming back toward Hon Me. At about 11 a.m. August 2, the *Maddox* was eleven miles from the island when the ship detected three North Vietnamese patrol craft. It turned to head for open waters. At 2:40 p.m., the *Maddox* reported: "Being approached by high-speed craft with apparent intent to conduct torpedo attack. Intend to open fire in self-defense if necessary." According to the *Maddox*'s log, when the enemy boats were 9,800 yards distant, the *Maddox* fired twice, paused, then fired four more times. The American vessel then came under fire from the approaching boats.

Three boats closed to within three miles of the *Maddox*. Two launched one torpedo each. Both missed the *Maddox* by more than 100 yards. The third patrol boat, struck by a shell, stopped dead. Fighter planes from the aircraft carrier USS *Ticonderoga* swarmed in and damaged the other two patrol boats. The whole encounter took less than twenty-five minutes. The *Maddox* was undamaged.

After news of the incident reached Washington, Johnson called in reporters on August 3 and said he had ordered a second destroyer, the *C. Turner Joy*, to join the *Maddox* on patrol in the Gulf of Tonkin. Later that day, McNamara and Secretary of State Dean Rusk briefed members of the Senate Foreign Relations and Armed Services committees. The administration sent a note of protest to North Vietnam warning of "grave consequences" if there was "any further unprovoked offensive military action against the United States."

During the evening of August 3, South Vietnamese patrol boats staged another attack on the North, this time shelling military facilities on the mainland. At the time of this attack, the *Maddox* and the *C. Turner Joy* were about seventy nautical miles to the northeast.

The next night, August 4, the two American destroyers were again in the middle of the gulf, about sixty-five miles from land. At 9:30 p.m., the *Maddox* reported radar contact with unidentified vessels that were closing rapidly. When the approaching vessels were judged to be 8,000 yards distant, the *Maddox* fired star shells, but it was a moonless night with rough seas and the radar contact was never visually confirmed.

At 6,000 yards, the *C. Turner Joy* commenced firing, and in the next hour, according to McNamara's account two days later, "the destroyers relayed messages stating that they had avoided a number of torpedoes, that they had been under repeated attack, and that they had sunk two of the attacking craft."

However, differing reports from the two destroyers raised questions. The *Maddox* reported picking up twenty-two enemy torpedoes on sonar, but the *C. Turner Joy* detected none. During the most intense part of the encounter, the *C. Turner Joy* radar picked up unidentified vessels, but at that same time, the *Maddox*

radar did not. The *C. Turner Joy* claimed to have sunk one boat and damaged another, but no debris was ever found.

North Vietnam claimed that there was no attack at all, just a "sheer fabrication" of events by the United States so it would have an excuse to attack the North.

In Washington, it was about 11 a.m. August 4 when word arrived that the destroyers had been engaged. Even before a scheduled noon meeting of the National Security Council, Johnson told aides he would retaliate by ordering U.S. air strikes against North Vietnam.

That evening, Johnson called sixteen congressional leaders into the Cabinet Room at the White House to inform them that gunboat-support facilities in North Vietnam would be bombed. He told them he wanted a congressional resolution on Southeast Asia. The wording was discussed, and before leaving the White House, all the members present said they would vote for an expression of American resolve.

Johnson then prepared for an address to the nation. At 11:36 p.m. EDT, he spoke on television and radio. "Aggression by terror against the peaceful villagers of South Vietnam has now been joined by open aggression on the high seas against the United States of America," Johnson said. After explaining that air strikes were under way against North Vietnam, Johnson said he had met with congressional leaders and "informed them that I shall immediately request the Congress to pass a resolution making it clear that our government is united in its determination to take all necessary measures in support of freedom and in defense of peace in Southeast Asia."

That night, and again in a message to Congress the next day, Johnson noted that the U.S. political calendar had partly influenced his actions. "At a time when we are entering upon three months of campaigning," he said, "hostile nations must understand that . . . the United States will continue to protect its national interests and that in these matters there is no division among us." In his TV address, Johnson said, "Just a few minutes ago I was able to reach Senator Goldwater, and I am glad to say he has expressed his support of the address I am making to you tonight."

The bombing Johnson ordered was carried out by aircraft of the 7th Fleet. The United States claimed that about two dozen patrol craft were destroyed or damaged and said two American planes were lost and two damaged.

Congress quickly took up the Southeast Asia Resolution. The text had fewer than 450 words, and the core was this: "The United States regards as vital to its national interest and to world peace the maintenance of international peace and security in Southeast Asia. . . . [T]he United States is, therefore, prepared, as the President determines, to take all necessary steps, including the use of armed force, to assist any member or protocol state of the Southeast Asia Collective Defense Treaty requesting assistance in defense of its freedom."

To expedite passage, Senate Minority Leader Everett McKinley Dirksen, R-Ill., suggested skipping committee consideration. But the Senate's Democratic majority made time August 6 for a joint, closed-door session of Armed Services and Foreign Relations. There was perfunctory testimony from Secretaries McNamara and Rusk and Chairman of the Joint Chiefs of Staff Gen. Earle G. Wheeler. The resolution passed 31–1.

The lone dissenter was Oregon Democrat Wayne Morse, who had already denounced the resolution as a "predated declaration of war." Calling the United States a "provocateur, every bit as much as North Vietnam has been a provocateur," Morse suggested that U.S. ships had asked for trouble by patrolling close to the North Vietnamese coast at almost the same time North Vietnam was being shelled by South Vietnamese boats.

In his book, Galloway recounts that Democratic senator J. William Fulbright, the chairman of the Foreign Relations Committee, later regretted how the committee had acquiesced with so little scrutiny. "Imagine," Fulbright said three years later, "we spent all of an hour and 40 minutes on that resolution. A disaster. A tragic mistake. We should have held hearings. The resolution would have passed anyway, but not in its present form. At the time, I was not in a suspicious frame of mind. I was afraid of Goldwater."

After the Senate committee vote, McNamara, Rusk, and Wheeler testified before the House Foreign Affairs Committee, which promptly approved the resolution 29–0.

Fulbright was responsible for shepherding the resolution on the Senate floor. It was clear that most senators would support him. But during the nine hours that the issue was considered over August 6 and 7, some skepticism was expressed.

Democratic senators George S. McGovern of South Dakota, Allen J. Ellender of Louisiana, and Gaylord Nelson of Wisconsin wondered whether the U.S. ships might have invited attack, perhaps by escorting South Vietnamese boats that later fired on North Vietnam or by approaching the North Vietnamese shore.

Sen. Daniel B. Brewster, a Maryland Democrat, asked whether the wording of the resolution would authorize or approve the introduction of American fighting men to Vietnam or China. Fulbright said the resolution was not designed with that in mind, but it "would not prevent it."

Sen. John Sherman Cooper, R-Ky., made this query: If, "looking ahead, the president decided that it was necessary to use such force as could lead into war, will we give that authority by this resolution?" Fulbright responded in the affirmative and then argued that conditions of modern warfare made it difficult for the president to consult with Congress before taking military action. "Things move so rapidly that this is the way we must respond to the new developments," Fulbright said.

Nelson sought to amend the resolution to restrict its scope. He proposed to add this language: "Our continuing policy is to limit our role to the provision of aid, training assistance and military advice, and it is the sense of Congress, that except when provoked to greater response, we should continue to avoid a direct military involvement in the Southeastern Asian conflict." But Nelson ran afoul of a prearranged three-hour time limit for debate August 7; his amendment never came to a vote.

On the roll call for final Senate passage, one "nay" came from Morse, who argued strenuously that "our American officialdom in Saigon and our American officialdom in the Pentagon and the State Department" had colluded to provoke an incident with North Vietnam. By approving the resolution, Morse warned, "we are, in effect, giving the president of the United States war-making powers in the absence of a declaration of war."

A second "nay" came from Ernest Gruening, D-Alaska, who said the resolution gave the president a "blank check" for a war "not merely in South Vietnam, but in all Southeast Asia." Gruening feared "escalation unlimited" if the resolution passed. But their admonitions were overwhelmed by senators sharing the hope expressed by Fulbright, who said, "I sincerely believe that this action . . . will result in deterring any ambitions or reckless adventuresome spirit on the part of the North Vietnamese or the Communist Chinese."

The final vote in the Senate was 88-2. In the House, the debate took under an hour, and the vote for passage was 416-0.

Johnson signed the Tonkin resolution into law August 10. Two weeks later in Atlantic City, New Jersey, delegates at the Democratic National Convention approved a party platform that, in a section headlined "Peace," praised the president's handling of the Tonkin incident for having "repulsed Communist aggression."

In the fall campaign, Goldwater periodically pushed the theme that Democrats were soft on communism, but Johnson's actions in the highly publicized Tonkin incident had insulated him from that criticism. In November, the president took 61 percent of the popular vote, carrying every state except Goldwater's Arizona and five in the Deep South.

In February 1965, Johnson, relying on the Tonkin resolution for authority, initiated intensive U.S. bombing of North Vietnam and committed the first American combat troops to South Vietnam.

1965

In 1964 Lyndon B. Johnson, who had become president on John F. Kennedy's death, won a full presidential term in his own right. He did it in convincing fashion, with a phenomenal 61 percent share of the popular vote that eclipsed the landslides of Roosevelt and Eisenhower and which would not be equaled by those of Nixon and Reagan. He carried every state except the five of the Deep South and Arizona, the home state of the Republican nominee.

Johnson's achievement had several origins. Not least among them was the nation's grief over Kennedy's untimely death. The slain president's shaky standing in office was forgotten in the rush to mythologize him in death. Johnson handled the martyrdom masterfully, using it to unify the country, to drive the Civil Rights Act through Congress, and to establish an irrefutable claim to the nomination in 1964.

Johnson was also abetted by the Republicans, whose nomination contest featured two candidates with serious political liabilities. One was Nelson A. Rockefeller, the governor of New York, a favorite of the Eastern establishment, and the bearer of a name synonymous with vast wealth. The other was Barry M. Goldwater, the Arizona senator who had emerged as the spokesman of the party's ascendant right. Goldwater had long argued that the party needed to distinguish itself more from the Democrats—an argument summed up in one of his slogans: "A Choice, Not An Echo."

Goldwater won the nomination easily, showing far greater appeal in the Sunbelt states where the party (and the nation) was growing fastest. He was renowned not only as a fiscal conservative but as a voice for social tradition. Although he personally opposed segregation, he had voted against the Civil Rights Act in deference to states' rights and a limited central government.

The Republican convention of 1964 was a victory celebration for the party's core conservatives, many of whom had not been so satisfied with a nominee since Alf Landon in 1936. Offended by the tone of the platform and the podium speeches, Rockefeller and others walked out. On the final night, Goldwater gave a triumphal address that included the famous aphorism: "Moderation in defense of liberty is no virtue, extremism in pursuit of freedom is no vice."

Polls showed many voters put off by the Goldwater on display that July, and he lagged well behind Johnson throughout the fall. But if Republicans were disappointed not to win the White House, the real disaster befell them in races down the ballot. The tide of Johnson's election carried the Democrats to nearly 300 seats in the House and almost 70 in the Senate—exceeding even the heights they had scaled following the 1958 midterm elections.

The 1964 election gave Johnson more than a presidency he could call his own. It gave him a Congress willing to work his will. It gave him a power opportunity unmatched in postwar American history, and Johnson was never one to waste an opportunity.

Fulfilling the Great Society

Stephen Gettinger

Never before had a president given his State of the Union address on the day a new Congress convened. But nine hours after the 89th Congress took the oath of office January 4, 1965—and more than two weeks before his own inauguration—Lyndon Baines Johnson stood before a joint session in the House chamber, hailing "the excitement of great expectations."

The audience was unprecedented in its breadth: it was the first speech of its kind delivered for national prime-time television. But the audience was no grander than the sweep of Johnson's ambition: his agenda was the most far-reaching since the dawn of the New Deal.

Johnson demanded the first national health insurance for the aged, the first expansive federal assistance for education, the first stiff controls on polluters, the first federal patronage of the arts. He called for aid to cities, to the poor, to the police, to small farmers, to Appalachia.

Alongside these creations, Johnson sought an end to discriminatory immigration laws, an end to most federal excise taxes, and an end to voter-registration laws that kept southern blacks from the polls.

Near the conclusion of his historic speech, Johnson added a grace note of humility: "A president's hardest task is not to do what is right, but to know what is right." For the rest of that exceptional year of legislative performance, Johnson evinced no doubt about what he thought was right. In the speech, Johnson fleshed out the Great Society he had introduced in May 1964, describing it as "a place where the city of man serves not only the needs of the body and the demands of commerce but the desire for beauty and the hunger for community." It was a program to dispel the shadow of an assassinated president, John F. Kennedy, and to show the world the great heart and vision of this outsized Texan whose nomination for vice president had outraged Democratic liberals.

The election of 1964 had vaulted Johnson onto a plateau with his hero, former President Franklin D. Roosevelt. His 61 percent of the popular vote exceeded even FDR's 1936 triumph over Alfred Landon; indeed, it was the greatest landslide since the popular vote was first counted nationally, in 1832. On his coattails came huge Democratic congressional majorities: 68 of the 100 Senate seats, 295 of the 435 House seats.

Senate Minority Leader Everett McKinley Dirksen, R-Ill., dismissed Johnson's speech as "a perfect dream in a very imperfect world." Johnson's biggest obstacles, however, were Democrats.

The House Rules Committee had lost its iron grip in 1961, but Chairman Howard W. Smith of Virginia was a still-powerful enemy not only of civil rights bills, but also of federal aid to education (inspiring the in-house slogan "no rules for schools").

On the Ways and Means Committee, the folksy, Harvard-trained Wilbur Mills of Arkansas

President Johnson shakes hands with Health, Education and Welfare Secretary Anthony Celebrezze after signing the Medicare bill into law. Mrs. Johnson, Vice President Hubert H. Humphrey, center, and former president Harry S. Truman, seated at right, look on.

was at the peak of his powers. His committee was known as "the graveyard for Medicare." Worried about the "actuarial soundness" of Social Security, in 1964 he had bottled up a Medicare bill on a 12-12 vote.

In the first days of the new Congress, liberal House Democrats—watched by 1,400 senior citizens bused in from across the country—set out to tether the committee barons. They gave the Speaker power to circumvent the Rules Committee if it stalled legislation for more than twenty-one days. Ways and Means, which traditionally had allotted fifteen of its twenty-five seats to the majority, saw its ratio altered to 18-7 (with all the new Democratic seats going to pro-Medicare members). To warn southerners, the majority stripped of their seniority two Democrats who had openly supported GOP presidential candidate Barry M. Goldwater in 1964.

Later in January, Johnson summoned his congressional lobbying team, headed by Kennedy holdover Lawrence F. O'Brien, for an hourlong exhortation. He might have won by 16 million votes, he said, but the total was inflated by Goldwater's extremism, and his popular support was sure to subside. "So I want you guys to get off your asses and do everything possible to get everything in my program passed as soon as possible," he barked.

Few presidents have understood Congress as thoroughly as Johnson, who had been elected to the House in 1937 and to the Senate in 1949, serving as Senate majority leader from 1955 to 1961. Johnson began his day in the White House reading the *Congressional Record* (left by his bed at 7:15 a.m.) and ended it reading summaries of staff contacts with members. "There is but one way for a president to deal with the Congress, and that is continuously, incessantly and without interruption," he said.

Johnson laid out his marching orders to the 89th Congress in a relentless parade of sixty-three formal messages. Health care was the topic of the first missive, sent January 7, followed by education January 12, immigration the next day, foreign aid the following day, and defense January 18.

At his inauguration January 20, Johnson sanctified his program by lifting almost verbatim from a prose poem written for the occasion (but not delivered) by novelist John Steinbeck: "I do not believe that the Great Society is the ordered, changeless, and sterile battalion of the ants. It is the excitement of becoming—always becoming, trying, probing, falling, resting, and trying again—but always trying and always gaining."

Medicare did not merit even a complete sentence in the State of the Union speech more than two weeks before, but then the election had made its enactment a foregone conclusion. President Harry S. Truman had called for universal medical insurance in 1945, but the American Medical Association (AMA) had been able to fight off "socialized medicine."

Johnson had found Medicare to be a big applause line in stump speeches, and practically all the seventy-one new House Democrats supported it. Even Mills on Ways and Means announced after the election that he would move a bill.

To mute the AMA, Johnson left doctors' bills, out of his proposal, suggesting coverage through Social Security only for hospitalization. The AMA protested that coverage would be inadequate. Republicans united behind an alternative that would cover both hospitalization and doctor bills, but would remain voluntary.

On March 2, Mills dropped a bombshell. He suggested to Johnson aide Wilbur J. Cohen, a "three-layer cake" of compulsory hospitalization coverage, voluntary insurance for doctor bills, and a combination of existing programs that would guarantee medical care for the poor. "It was the most brilliant legislative move I'd seen in 30 years," said Cohen. "In effect, Mills had taken the AMA's ammunition, put it in the Republicans' gun, and blown both of them off the map."

Johnson leaped into the high-stakes game, telling Cohen: "Call them and raise them if necessary, but get this bill now." Drafted overnight, the new plan was approved, 17–8, by Ways and Means on March 23. Two weeks later, the bill was passed by a 313–115 vote as Rep. John D. Dingell, D-Mich., presided over the House (in memory of his father, who had offered the first nationalized medical plan in 1943).

On education, Johnson cut another legislative Gordian knot. For decades, federal aid to education had been blocked by ancient fears about integration, federal control, and a breach in the wall between church and state. (Kennedy, the first Catholic president, had been frustrated on education aid in part because he would not help parochial schools.)

The Civil Rights Act of 1964 ended the integration argument. Then Johnson brought together the antagonists and offered a new idea to resolve the latter two anxieties. Aid would go not to schools but to school districts, based largely on the number of resident children who were impoverished, regardless of whether those children went to public or parochial schools. The proposal "represents a fantastically skillful break in the stalemate occasioned by the church-state dilemma," testified a spokesman for the United Presbyterian Church.

The House passed the education bill in three days with only one minor change. Fearing mischief in a conference committee, the administration browbeat the Senate into killing all amendments and passing an identical bill. It did so at 7:43 p.m. on Friday, April 9. By 8 p.m., Johnson had ordered that a formal copy be prepared

Five days after Johnson signed the Voting Rights Act, the Watts section of Los Angeles exploded in rioting.

within twenty-four hours, rather than the usual ten days. On Sunday, he flew to Texas and signed it in the one-room schoolhouse he had attended and in front of his first teacher, "Miss Katie."

Johnson wanted to downplay civil rights, seeking a break from the effort it had taken to break the Senate filibuster against the Civil Rights Act of 1964. But the Rev. Dr. Martin Luther King Jr., fresh from receiving the Nobel Peace Prize, seized the initiative January 2, announcing a campaign against voter registration barriers, such as literacy tests and poll taxes. It began in Selma, Alabama, where blacks made up 58 percent of the population but only 3 percent of voters.

King's crusade generated a crisis March 7, when a local sheriff named Jim Clark led a gang of deputies in an assault to stop the marchers at the Edmund Pettis Bridge outside Selma. Johnson held back on sending federal troops to wrest control from Gov. George C. Wallace and let televised images of brutality do the preaching.

But pressure escalated several days later when a Boston minister died after a beating by a white gang in Selma. To prepare for a special joint session of Congress on March 15—scheduled, again, for prime time—Johnson's staff

worked all night on a speech that never made it to the teleprompter because he was adding personal touches up to the last minute.

"I speak tonight for the dignity of man and the destiny of democracy," Johnson began. "Outside this chamber is the outraged conscience of a nation." In the emotional climax, he declared, "It is not just Negroes, but really it is all of us, who must overcome the crippling legacy of bigotry and injustice." Here he paused, raised his arms, and then spoke slowly the words of the anthem sung by the marchers: "And . . . we . . . shall . . . overcome." The chamber rose to its feet in a clamor; Senate Majority Leader Mike Mansfield, D-Mont., was close to tears.

The voting rights bill marched through Congress with dispatch, the only question being how much stronger to make it. Democratic senator Allen J. Ellender of Louisiana vowed to debate "as long as God gives me strength," but southern strategist Richard B. Russell, D-Ga., was ill, and a full-blown filibuster never developed. After a desultory debate over five weeks, the Senate passed the bill May 26 by a vote of 77-19.

Johnson revived an old tradition by going to the Capitol to sign the measure August 6, doing so in the ornate President's Room off the Senate floor—where, 104 years earlier, Abraham Lincoln had signed a bill freeing slaves who had been pressed into Confederate service. "Today we strike away the last major shackle of those fierce and ancient bonds," Johnson said.

But the limits of legislative power were highlighted five days later when the Watts section of Los Angeles exploded in the worst racial riots of the nation's history, leaving thirty-four people dead and the neighborhood in smoldering ruins. Riots followed in Chicago and Springfield, Massachusetts, and for many white voters, the moral crusade became tinged with fear.

Bill-signing ceremonies, designed by Johnson himself, were the president's favorite recreation. He flew to his alma mater, Southwest Texas State College, to sign a bill creating the first general college scholarships. He drove to the National Institutes of Health outside Washington to sign a bill setting up health research centers. He went to the Statue of Liberty to sign a bill loosening nationality quotas for immigration.

But it was his signing of the Medicare bill July 30 in Independence, Missouri, that cemented his place in history. Despite a record-setting barrage of advertisements by the AMA and a doctors' threat to boycott elderly patients, the bill coasted through both chambers in final form by 3 to 1 margins. Senate floor manager Russell B. Long, D-La., boasted that the bill "does more to meet more human problems than any other measure ever passed." Johnson took an entourage to the hometown of the eighty-one-year-old Truman. "He's old and he's tired and he's been left all alone down there," Johnson told Cohen. "I want him to know that his country has not forgotten him." In a characteristic musing, he added, "I wonder if anyone will do the same for me."

There were plenty of other signings to keep him occupied. Congress took no recesses that year, not even in the August heat, instead muscling bill after bill to the White House. House Republican Conference chairman Melvin R. Laird of Wisconsin complained: "Unless the legislative branch stands for something more than a rubber stamp, it is not Republicans who will be a minority; it will be the entire Congress, dwarfed and dragooned by a great and overbearing executive branch." Sometimes, Congress went the rubber stamp one better, giving the president more than he asked for on Medicare, voting rights, education aid, and an expansion of the War on Poverty.

By the fall, new laws eliminated excise taxes, created the National Endowments for the Arts and the Humanities, offered the first rent subsidies, imposed the first standards for automobile exhaust and water quality, and required the first warning labels for cigarettes. Johnson's only significant defeats came on his push for home rule for the District of Columbia and for the repeal of the section of the Taft-Hartley labor law that protected state right-to-work laws.

In remarks prepared for a Salute to Congress dinner October 7, Johnson stated unequivocally, "Tonight, the president of the United States is going on record as naming this session of Congress the greatest in American history." He did not deliver that speech because the House was working late, trying to clear the Highway Beautification Act as a present to the first lady, Lady Bird Johnson.

Congress kept at it for two more weeks, churning out a farm bill, aid for medical education, authorization of 200 public works projects, and a federal pay raise. Goldwater called it "the Xerox Congress," and Dirksen complained that the legislative output was an "echo, not a choice." But on the last full day of the session, October 22, Speaker John W. McCormack of Massachusetts labeled the 89th "the Congress of fulfillment. It is the Congress of accomplished hopes. It is the Congress of realized dreams."

Vietnam did not intrude on the average American's consciousness until the mid-1960s, but it had been part of the American foreign policy puzzle since World War II. During that war, the Japanese seized the Southeast Asian territory the West called French Indochina, taking France's colonies as their own. After 1941 the United States began supplying weapons and other matériel to guerrillas resisting the Japanese in the region. One such cadre was led by a Paris-educated Vietnamese named Ho Chi Minh.

Ho and his followers hoped the United States would support their national aspirations when the war was over. But after Japan's defeat, the French sent their armed forces to reclaim their colonies. The Truman administration, focused on unifying and defending Europe, sided with the colonial powers against the various insurgent nationals of the Third World—many of whom were communist revolutionaries. Subsequently, when Ho and his Vietminh guerrillas turned their fire on the French, they used weapons provided by the Soviet Union and, later, by China.

By the early 1950s France was unable to support its army in Southeast Asia. The Eisenhower administration, still trying to negotiate an end to the war in Korea, dispatched $60 million to the French cause in Indochina in May 1953. More money followed that September, and by the following year it was estimated that American dollars were financing three-fourths of the French war effort.

In April and May 1954 the chairman of the Joint Chiefs of Staff urged President Dwight Eisenhower to intervene in relief of the besieged French stronghold at Dien Bien Phu. The Vietnamese had hauled artillery into place over mountain footpaths, and they were pounding the French into submission. Eisenhower refused to commit U.S. forces, in part because it was already too late. In July 1954 the French sat down with the Vietminh in Geneva and cut the country in half.

In South Vietnam the French tried to protect their interests by installing a Catholic, European-educated elite in the capital city of Saigon. Ho and his cohort held sway in the northern capital of Hanoi but continued to infiltrate the South through the Vietcong, a guerrilla force of peasant soldiers. By the time John F. Kennedy arrived in the White House, the Vietcong were bidding for control of the countryside and regularly roughing up the South Vietnamese army.

The efforts of U.S. advisers in 1962 and 1963 did little to change the battlefield situation, while in Saigon the political picture worsened. Less than three weeks before Kennedy's death, an American-inspired coup d'état in Saigon resulted in the death of President Ngo Dinh Diem.

Within months of taking office, Lyndon B. Johnson had occasion to assert his commitment to Vietnam via the Gulf of Tonkin resolution. Later, Johnson the presidential candidate shifted gears and played the peacemaker. "We seek no wider war," he said.

= 1966 =

Vietnam and the Voices of Dissent

Ronald D. Elving

When the 89th Congress returned from holiday recess in January 1966, the number of Americans killed in Vietnam had not reached 2,000. But the previous year's escalation of the war was continuing, and the U.S. troop commitment had exceeded 180,000. The casualty rate was accelerating, and uneasiness in Washington was growing.

Some of the dissent came from the same few senators who had questioned the 1964 Gulf of Tonkin resolution, the authority President Lyndon B. Johnson relied on to expand the U.S. effort. But in the winter of 1965-1966, the nascent congressional opposition to the war would acquire a new leader and symbol in Arkansas Democrat J. William Fulbright.

As chairman of the Senate Foreign Relations Committee, Fulbright occupied a position of traditional importance in policy making. Johnson had bowed to this position in 1964, when he asked Fulbright to carry the Gulf of Tonkin resolution in the Senate. Fulbright had reluctantly agreed, hurrying the resolution through without a hearing.

But as the war worsened, Fulbright came to regret Tonkin and to doubt the wisdom of U.S. behavior abroad. Johnson had dispatched troops to the Dominican Republic in April 1965 to quiet civil unrest, prompting Fulbright to give a floor speech in September denouncing reckless use of American military might. By the winter, he would be ready to apply the same objections to Vietnam. "He had evolved that swiftly

from friendly critic to dissenter," wrote Haynes Johnson and Bernard Gwertzman in their 1968 biography of the senator.

Fulbright's transformation from servant of the White House to savant of the opposition led to the first real clash over Vietnam in Congress. For six dramatic days early in 1966, the Foreign Relations chairman publicly dissected the administration policy under hot television lights and worldwide media scrutiny. It was the first debate about Vietnam to be witnessed by the nation as a whole.

For the first time, the nation heard Secretary of State Dean Rusk and other administration officials being asked direct questions about timetables and the prospects for success. For many, it was the first time those answers had sounded so evasive and discouraging.

Fulbright's public show did little to slow the war itself, but it served to open a second front. The hearings brought antiwar sentiments out from the back benches, academic salons, and scattered street demonstrations to the forefront of public debate.

Fulbright was in some ways an unlikely choice to be Johnson's chief antagonist. The two shared a regional background as well as party affiliation. As Senate majority leader, Johnson had helped arrange Fulbright's rise to the Foreign Relations chairmanship in 1959, and their longstanding friendship had stayed warm well into 1965.

But Fulbright stood apart from most politicians, largely because he inclined toward the

The intellectual, contemplative J. William Fulbright was an unlikely choice to be Johnson's chief antagonist. But his change of opinion would lead to the first real clash over Vietnam in Congress.

intellectual, contemplative life. He was the favorite son of a leading, self-made businessman in Fayetteville. His father's mansion stood on a hill overlooking the campus of the University of Arkansas, where the future senator began taking courses in 1920 at the age of fifteen. The young Fulbright was not merely bookish: he became captain of the university tennis team and the hero halfback of the football team. His professors urged him to apply for a Rhodes scholarship.

At Oxford, Fulbright discovered an interest in what he called "reading just to learn." Compared with the products of English boarding schools, he felt himself dreadfully unprepared

academically. The effects of this experience would be visible long after in his scholarly manner and style of dress (one reporter referred to him as "well-waistcoated").

After Oxford, Fulbright enrolled in law school at George Washington University, graduating second in a class of 135. He taught briefly at George Washington before returning to Arkansas to teach at the law school and run a 110-acre farm. In 1939 the University of Arkansas board of trustees made the well-liked young law professor president of the university when he was just thirty-four.

Motivated largely by an interest in foreign policy, Fulbright ran for Congress in the wartime election of 1942. As a freshman on Foreign Affairs he offered a resolution committing the United States to join an international organization for the purpose of keeping the peace in the postwar world. The resolution was passed and two years later fulfilled in the signing of the United Nations charter.

Moving to the Senate in 1945, Fulbright showed himself willing to beard a president of his own party. After the GOP captured both Houses of Congress in 1946, the freshman senator suggested President Harry S. Truman resign in favor of a Republican so that one party could have full control of foreign policy. Later, Fulbright would chair hearings into administration corruption, prompting Truman to label him "an overeducated SOB."

In the 1950s, Fulbright was noted as the one senator who refused to appropriate money for the subcommittee investigations of Sen. Joseph R. McCarthy, the anticommunist Republican crusader from Wisconsin. But he was also remembered for defending segregation when federal marshals came to enforce the integration of schools in Little Rock. Fulbright believed in a gradual pace of change in racial matters and clearly regarded anything more radical as political suicide.

But if this stand kept him in the Senate, it kept him out of the Cabinet. When John F. Kennedy became president in 1960, he reportedly wanted to make Fulbright his secretary of state. The influential columnist Walter Lippmann privately urged Kennedy to do it. But objections from civil rights leaders and liberals in Congress prevented him, and the job went instead to Rusk, a career State Department man renowned for professional loyalty and steadfast anticommunism.

When Kennedy was killed and Johnson sworn in in November 1963, Fulbright had every expectation of continued harmony with the White House. But Johnson was soon pulled in a new direction, dictated both by the global politics of the cold war and by domestic political dynamics. Republicans had shed their historic isolation and urged worldwide resistance to communism, often outflanking Democrats on the issue. Fulbright would later explain his haste on the Tonkin resolution by saying he feared that the GOP presidential candidate in 1964, Sen. Barry M. Goldwater of Arizona, would treat any delay as evidence the ruling party was "soft on communism."

Thereafter, however, Fulbright found himself disturbed by the mounting military effort in Southeast Asia. When he gave his speech on the Dominican incursion, Vietnam was the real source of his objections and of Johnson's annoyed response.

Fulbright tried to patch things up, sending the president a long, flattering letter. But late in the year he was dispatched to Australia on official business and denied use of a military jet. It took him four days to reach his destination by prop plane. Along the way, Fulbright pored over a book about China's mistreatment by the West. His staff noted that he seemed profoundly affected by it.

As 1966 began, the administration asked Congress for two supplemental appropriations bills, one for $12 billion in extra military spending associated with Vietnam and another for $415 million in additional foreign aid—$275 million of which was to go to Vietnam. To have comparable impact in 1995 dollars, each of these figures would have to be quadrupled.

Fulbright had no jurisdiction over the military appropriation, but Foreign Relations had authorizing control over foreign aid. On this authority he scheduled hearings on the bill to begin January 28.

The first witness was Rusk, the prim and practiced secretary of state. Rusk, too, had been raised in the rural South (Cherokee County, Georgia) and gone to Oxford: on the front page of the *New York Times*, diplomatic correspondent Max Frankel referred to Rusk as "the Georgia hillbilly who became a Rhodes scholar."

Rusk did not want to testify in public, imploring the committee to close the hearing. But the senators refused, and Rusk had to bear the television lights (Fulbright himself sometimes donned dark glasses against the glare) as well as the weight of the interrogation.

Rusk was questioned exhaustively, partly because he said so little. He mostly repeated the straightforward view that North Vietnam had invaded its neighbor country and the United States had a formal treaty obligation to help— along with a moral duty and a political interest in doing so. "What we face in Vietnam is what we faced on many occasions before," Rusk said, "the need to check the extension of communist power in order to maintain a reasonable stability in a precarious world."

Each senator in turn sought to pry something more from him. Republicans such as ranking member Bourke Hickenlooper of Iowa went after allegations of administration mismanagement. The Democratic doves, such as Wayne Morse of Oregon, tried to trap Rusk on the origins of the Vietcong and the unpopulari-

Secretary of State Dean Rusk poses at a map of Southeast Asia with Sens. Bourke Hickenlooper, background, and J. William Fulbright, who presided over Rusk's Senate grilling in 1966.

ty of the Saigon government. The Democratic hawks, such as Russell B. Long of Louisiana, asked Rusk to take some credit for military successes in the field. Rusk refused to take any of the bait.

"We wish only that people of South Vietnam should have the right and opportunity to determine their future in freedom," he said, "without coercion or threat from the outside."

Fulbright presided over the grilling of Rusk with what he considered dispassionate detachment—a demeanor admirers found appealing and detractors regarded as arrogant. When he did speak up, he tried to be low key. After Rusk compared Vietnam to the appeasement of Hitler, Fulbright replied: "There is some feeling that, perhaps, we have intervened in a family quarrel here."

Fulbright regarded the first day of hearings as a success and looked forward to the next session, scheduled for a week later, with Secretary of Defense Robert S. McNamara as the wit-

ness. But once again he had underestimated the reaction from the Oval Office.

Johnson summoned congressional leaders to the White House two days later on Sunday, January 30. There he pointedly ignored Fulbright and announced that the bombing of North Vietnam—suspended since before Christmas—would resume. He also made it clear that McNamara would not testify in open session. He called a news conference the same day and said that such testimony might cost "the lives of a good many of our men."

Johnson then flew to Hawaii to meet with the South Vietnamese military leaders who had recently seized control of the Saigon government. Journalist Tristram Coffin later recalled how Johnson took with him four Cabinet officers, the chairman of the Joint Chiefs of Staff, and the national security adviser. But if the idea was to deprive Fulbright of witnesses, it backfired. For in place of the administration heavyweights, Fulbright called an array of other witnesses with strong credentials, some of whom were prepared to question not only the strategy and tactics of the war but also its basic necessity.

Among these was James M. Gavin, the nation's youngest division commander in World War II and later ambassador to France. Gavin had been to Southeast Asia to make an assessment, and his view was that it would take overwhelming numerical superiority to secure the countryside.

Also called was George F. Kennan, a former ambassador to the Soviet Union and an originator of the cold war "containment doctrine." Kennan, too, cast a cold eye on Rusk's premises. "Vietnam is not a region of major military and industrial importance," Kennan said, and nothing that happened there would be crucial to global affairs.

As the first Senate Foreign Relations chairman to stage such an intraparty rebellion since William E. Borah who resisted Calvin Coolidge's incursion into Nicaragua in the 1920, Fulbright was a sudden celebrity and intensely controversial. To the burgeoning antiwar movement, he became an overnight saint. To supporters of the war he was little more than a traitor. Goldwater came close to saying so when he said Fulbright "lends support and aid and comfort to our enemies." *National Review* magazine called the chairman a "Judas goat." Former vice president Richard M. Nixon announced that GOP candidates for Congress that year would make an issue of Democrats taking "the appeasement line" on Vietnam.

Fulbright was stunned by the volume of mail and telephone calls. He believed he was conducting the hearings impersonally, hoping to minimize the element of confrontation between him and Johnson. But just as the White House could not deny the newsworthy nature of the proceedings, neither could Fulbright escape the personal dimension of the story.

CBS carried a special report called "Fulbright: Advice and Dissent," in which correspondent Eric Sevareid asked Fulbright if he accepted the basic Rusk analogy between Hitler's aggression and that of Ho Chi Minh, the president of North Vietnam. "I'm afraid I do not," Fulbright said. "This is a very complicated situation."

The final session of the hearings was held February 18, a Friday. Rusk returned for another session and remained under questioning for seven hours. Fulbright biographer Eugene Brown noted a particularly "bristling colloquy" between chairman and cabinet secretary when Rusk said Fulbright seemed to think "we should abandon the effort in South Vietnam." This brought what Brown called a "pained denial" from Fulbright, who said "I am not questioning our motives, I think our motives are very good." A month later, Fulbright returned to the point in saying, on the Senate floor, "I do not question the motives, all I question is the wisdom."

In the end, all that Fulbright and his committee could do was question. They changed few minds, at least in the short term. The supplemental aid package was approved by overwhelming margins in the Senate as well as the House.

But Fulbright had forced much of the nation to confront the difficult questions at the center of the debate. Beyond that, the hearings renewed a longstanding struggle between the president and the Congress over the conduct of foreign policy.

Vietnam would remain an active issue for nearly a decade and cost more than 58,000 American lives. Communism would remain the focus of foreign policy for another quarter century. But the issue of policy control between the branches is as old as the republic and is likely to last as long.

The American political season of 1968 was perhaps the ugliest of the twentieth century. For the first time in the United States, the field of presidential primary candidates was narrowed by assassination when Robert F. Kennedy was gunned down on the June night he won the Democratic primary in California. But Kennedy's was not even the first historically significant assassination of the year. In April Rev. Martin Luther King Jr. had been murdered by a sniper in Memphis, touching off days of devastating riots in the nation's big cities. In Washington, D.C., protracted civil unrest reduced some of the capital city's oldest commercial corridors to smoking ruins.

But even before King's murder, President Lyndon Johnson had announced the end of his political career by saying he would not accept his party's nomination for another term. Johnson had seen his dream of a Great Society foiled by rioting in Los Angeles in 1965 and in Detroit and a dozen other cities two years later. His hopes for a decisive victory in Vietnam likewise had been dashed.

Johnson hoped that, if he sacrificed the presidency, his administration could negotiate a peace with the Vietcong and the North Vietnamese. He also hoped that the same gesture would free his party to campaign on his achievements in civil and political rights, Medicare, and antipoverty programs. But his chosen successor, Hubert H. Humphrey Jr. of Minnesota, accepted the nomination at the convention in Chicago amid disturbances on the floor and in the street outside. The world saw televised images of the Chicago police fighting pitched battles with demonstrators.

While some were obsessed with Vietnam that summer, others were fixed on "law and order," the phrase that had replaced "states' rights" in the political argot of the South and received frequent mention elsewhere as well. Gov. George C. Wallace of Alabama, the man in the doorway, also ran for president in 1968 and carried five states along with 13.5 percent of the national popular vote.

The Republican nominee in 1968 once again was Richard M. Nixon, the former vice president, who promised he had a secret plan to end the war in Vietnam. More subliminally, Nixon pledged to restore the America of the 1950s, skillfully manipulating the issues on which Goldwater had been so ham-handed in 1964. While never defending the Jim Crow South, Nixon recruited the active support of Sen. Strom Thurmond of South Carolina, who had converted to the GOP in 1964.

Over the preceding months and years, the far-sighted Nixon had spent time with many southern conservatives—urging them to support a Republican alternative in the White House. He had told them the South would be the basis for his nomination and election in 1968. He also let it be known that he understood the southern attitude toward the Supreme Court. Nixon promised Thurmond and others that, if elected, he would appoint at least one true southern conservative to the Court.

Collision Over the Supreme Court

Rhodes Cook

Richard M. Nixon became president in 1969, after one of the most traumatic political years in the nation's history. The assassinations of the Rev. Dr. Martin Luther King Jr. and Sen. Robert F. Kennedy had cast a pall over the 1968 presidential campaign. The wound on the body politic inflicted by the continuing Vietnam War remained raw.

Against this backdrop, the Republican Nixon and the Congress, still in Democratic control, struggled to make their way. While they found agreement on some issues—a military draft lottery, a nuclear nonproliferation treaty, and an extension of the income tax surtax—they were often at loggerheads. And no conflict would be more bitter than the battle to define the Supreme Court and its role in an increasingly volatile society.

Twice, Nixon tried to put southerners on the Court who shared his conservative view of the Constitution. Twice, the Senate denied his nominees confirmation. Not since 1930 had a president seen even one of his Supreme Court nominees rejected by the Senate. And not since the nineteenth century had a president suffered the rejection of two.

The two nominees, Clement F. Haynsworth Jr. and G. Harrold Carswell, were both considered "strict constructionists" who would interpret the Constitution with what was called "judicial restraint."

Just as important, Haynsworth was from South Carolina and Carswell from Florida; their selection was part of Nixon's vaunted southern strategy, an effort to draw Dixie conservatives into the GOP and make it the nation's majority party.

Campaigning in 1968, Nixon had criticized the Supreme Court under Chief Justice Earl Warren for "coddling criminals." He had promised to appoint justices more receptive to the viewpoint of police and prosecutors. It was a strategic issue for Nixon, as he sought to woo voters away from the independent candidacy of Alabama governor George C. Wallace and build a new base for the Republican Party in the South and in socially conservative, blue-collar precincts of the North. By blocking Haynsworth and Carswell, the Senate stymied Nixon's efforts to reconfigure both the Court and the political landscape.

The double defeat has been remembered as an affront to the South and, conversely, as a confirmation of political support for the Court's civil rights decisions of the 1950s and 1960s. Others regard it as a classic reassertion of the Senate's constitutional power to advise and consent.

Nixon's first opportunity to fill a Court vacancy went smoothly. Early in 1969 he appointed Warren E. Burger, a judge for the U.S. Court of Appeals in the District of Columbia, to replace the retiring Warren as chief justice. Burger, a Minnesotan, won quick confirmation.

Then, in May, Nixon got a new and surprising opportunity to fill a second seat when Justice Abe Fortas resigned. When Nixon first an-

Sen. Strom Thurmond, R-S.C., left, introduced Supreme Court nominee Clement F. Haynsworth Jr., center, a fellow South Carolinian, to the Judiciary Committee in September 1969.

nounced, in August, his choice of Haynsworth to replace Fortas, few thought the nomination would have much trouble.

Haynsworth, fifty-six, offered impressive credentials. A graduate of Harvard Law School and a veteran of the federal bench, he was chief justice of the 4th U.S. Circuit Court of Appeals, which is based in Richmond and covers the mid-Atlantic states.

Civil rights activists argued that the 4th Circuit had been guilty of foot-dragging in school desegregation, but Haynsworth said such criticism was based on views expressed in the past, "when none of us was thinking or writing as we are today."

Opposition to Haynsworth, though, gradually developed around the issue of judicial ethics. Fortas had put this concern on the radar screen in a new way, resigning because of charges that he had accepted an outside fee from the family foundation of a convicted stock manipulator. Haynsworth's problem was not nearly so glaring, but conflict-of-interest questions arose

from his stock holdings. Haynsworth had ruled for a corporation in a labor case in 1963 while he owned stock in a company that did business with the corporation. He also had bought stock in 1967 in a corporation involved in a case before his court. Haynsworth had voted in the corporation's favor in that case before buying the stock, but before the decision was announced.

Haynsworth defended his actions in hearings before the Senate Judiciary Committee in late September, maintaining that he had never personally profited from a decision made by his court. But he urged the Senate to resolve any substantial doubts about the propriety of his actions. Democratic senator Sam J. Ervin Jr. of North Carolina came to Haynsworth's defense, saying that as a former lawyer in the 4th Circuit, he had read all of Haynsworth's opinions. Ervin said they had been written with the "cold neutrality of the impartial judge."

Leading officials in the Nixon administration dismissed criticism as routine. "If we'd put up one of the twelve apostles it would have been

Two days after Nixon nominated G. Harrold Carswell, left, in January 1970 a reporter turned up a 1948 speech in which Carswell embraced white supremacy.

the same," said Attorney General John N. Mitchell.

But a string of witnesses from civil rights groups and organized labor heartily disagreed. George Meany, president of the AFL-CIO, labeled Haynsworth antilabor and indifferent to the "legitimate aspirations of Negroes." Meany also said the nominee lacked a strong sense of ethics.

When the hearings had ended but the committee had yet to vote, fissures became evident within Republican ranks. The Senate's lone black member, Edward W. Brooke, R-Mass., wrote Nixon on October 1 to request the withdrawal of Haynsworth's nomination.

A week later, two members of the GOP Senate leadership announced their opposition to the nomination. Assistant Minority Leader Robert P. Griffin of Michigan, who had been a leading critic of Fortas, said that "legitimate and substantial doubt" had been raised about Haynsworth's sensitivity on questions of ethics.

On the same grounds, Margaret Chase Smith of Maine, chairman of the Senate Republican Conference, said she could not apply one standard to Fortas and another to Haynsworth. On October 9 a divided Judiciary Committee voted ten to seven to report Haynsworth's nomination. Among the ten voting for Haynsworth were five Democrats (including Ervin, Robert C. Byrd of West Virginia, and Thomas J. Dodd of Connecticut). Two Republicans, Griffin and Charles McC. Mathias Jr. of Maryland, joined the committee's other five Democrats in opposing the nominee.

Senate Minority Leader Hugh Scott of Pennsylvania, a member of Judiciary, voted to report the nomination despite his lack of enthusiasm for it. He said anyone nominated by the president deserved to have his qualifications judged by the full Senate.

Haynsworth's lagging prospects brought words of defiance from the White House. Terming the allegations against his nominee "a vicious character assassination," Nixon told reporters October 20 that he would not withdraw the nomination even at Haynsworth's request.

Both sides increased their lobbying as the nomination headed to the floor in mid-November. The administration argued that organized labor was driving the opposition. One White House loyalist, first-year GOP Senator Bob Dole of Kansas, said the vote on Haynsworth "is going to demonstrate how much power labor has in America."

The White House enlisted various elements of the Republican Party to put pressure on GOP senators. Sen. Charles S. Percy, R-Ill., reported that ten of the eleven House Republicans from his home state descended on his office to urge him to vote for Haynsworth. The office of Ohio GOP senator William B. Saxbe reported receiving "hundreds of threatening letters" from state residents. "It's as strong as anything we've seen," said one Saxbe aide.

When the vote was taken November 21, Vice President Spiro T. Agnew was dispatched to preside, in case he was needed to break a tie. But after a tense, ten-minute call of the roll, Haynsworth had only forty-five votes, with fifty-five cast against him. The vote was more regional than partisan. Nineteen Democratic senators, sixteen of them from the South, supported the nomination.

Seventeen Republican senators opposed it, including the party's top Senate leaders: Scott, Griffin, Smith, and John J. Williams of Delaware, the chairman of the GOP Committee on Committees and a zealous advocate of high Senate ethical standards. Of a dozen senators publicly uncommitted before the vote, only one—J. William Fulbright of Arkansas—broke for Haynsworth.

Democratic senator Ernest F. Hollings of South Carolina, Haynsworth's chief sponsor, blamed the White House for failing to line up Senate GOP leaders. "We weren't in the ballpark the last six weeks," Hollings complained.

"You can't win if you can't get your leadership."

Nixon reacted angrily to the defeat, promising that in selecting a new nominee, he would employ the same criteria that he had used in picking Haynsworth. On January 19, 1970, he announced his choice of Carswell, a fifty-year-old Duke University graduate who was in his first year on the 5th U.S. Circuit Court of Appeals, the New Orleans-based circuit for most of the Deep South.

Few senators were eager for another fight with the White House, but problems were quickly apparent. Two days after the announcement, a television reporter uncovered a speech that Carswell had made in 1948 while running for a seat in the Georgia legislature. "I yield to no man as a fellow candidate or as a fellow citizen," Carswell had said, "in the firm, vigorous belief in the principles of White Supremacy, and I shall always be so governed." Then came the story of how Carswell had participated in converting a public golf course in Tallahassee into an all-white private club in order to keep it segregated.

When hearings before the Senate Judiciary Committee began in late January, Carswell appeared before the panel to defend himself. "I am not a racist," he said. But witnesses told of Carswell's hostility from the bench to black civil rights attorneys. The dean of the Yale Law School ventured that Carswell had "the most slender credentials of any man put forward in this century for the Supreme Court."

The issue of qualification became the mantra of Carswell's critics. Judiciary reported out the nomination February 16 by a vote of 13 to 4, but supporters were generally tepid in their approval, while detractors were scathing. "He is a mediocre man," said Sen. Joseph D. Tydings, D-Md.

When Carswell's nomination reached the Senate floor in mid-March, his supporters tried to respond to the criticism directly. The Judiciary Committee's ranking Republican, Roman

L. Hruska of Nebraska, denied that Carswell was a mediocre judge, but added: "Even if he was mediocre, there are a lot of mediocre judges and people and lawyers. They are entitled to a little representation, aren't they, and a little chance? We can't have all Brandeises and Cardozos and Frankfurters and stuff like that there." Aides to Hruska said later that the remark was made in jest, but Carswell's critics seized on it to buttress their arguments that the nominee was unfit to serve on the Court.

In a letter to Saxbe on April 1, an exasperated Nixon charged the Senate with trying to usurp his constitutional powers. "The question arises," he wrote, "whether I, as President of the United States, shall be accorded the same right of choice in naming Supreme Court Justices which has been freely accorded to to my predecessors of both parties."

Senate Majority Leader Mike Mansfield of Montana fired back that the Senate, in advising and consenting, shared the appointive power with the president.

As the reckoning neared, the White House focused on three undecided Republicans—Marlow W. Cook of Kentucky, Winston L. Prouty of Vermont, and Smith of Maine. Nixon met face-to-face with Cook and Smith, who remained uncommitted. Prouty finally told the administration that he would vote for Carswell if it was the deciding vote.

But when the vote was taken April 8, it was soon evident that Prouty's vote would not make the difference. Early in the roll call, Cook voted no and a gasp came from the packed Senate gallery. The nomination was going down.

Prouty and Smith also followed with "no" votes, as did Democrats Fulbright and William B. Spong Jr. of Virginia, both of whom had voted for Haynsworth.

Carswell lost, 51-45. Thirteen Republicans had voted against the president's nominee, even though this time all the GOP leaders except Smith voted to confirm. Among the seventeen Democrats who voted for Carswell, fourteen were from the South.

Dole suggested that the president wait until after the November elections to submit another nomination. "It may be easier," said Dole, "to change the Senate than the U.S. Supreme Court—in fact, it may be a prerequisite."

Nixon agreed to a point, saying that the Senate as "presently constituted" would not confirm anyone "from the South who believes as I do in the strict construction of the Constitution."

But Nixon was not willing to wait until after the 1970 elections to try again. Within a week of Carswell's defeat, he nominated Harry A. Blackmun, a friend of Warren Burger's since their boyhood in Minnesota. In 1973, Blackmun would write the abortion rights opinion, *Roe v. Wade*, that shocked and galvanized abortion rights opponents for decades thereafter.

As for Carswell, he quit the appeals court to mount an unsuccessful bid for the GOP Senate nomination in Florida, campaigning against the "ultraliberal" Senate that had rejected him.

But many members of the upper chamber applauded what they had done. Said Fulbright: "The Senate has reasserted itself."

Although the Senate twice refused to confirm his appointments to the Supreme Court, President Richard M. Nixon had a reasonable working relationship with Congress during his first term. Democrats were in control of both chambers, and many were embittered by the loss of the White House. But the leaders of the 91st Congress (1969-1971) were highly pragmatic politicians. Speaker John W. McCormack of Massachusetts and Senate Majority Leader Mike Mansfield of Montana had known Nixon since serving in the House with him in the 1940s.

There was still a bipartisan consensus in favor of a continuing commitment in Vietnam. At the same time, Nixon knew he needed to reduce that commitment or risk losing his consensus. He pursued an expanded version of the peace talks that had been underway in Paris since the previous year, and, within six months of taking office, he began a steady reduction of the number of U.S. troops in Vietnam.

Nixon also recognized the importance, or at least the usefulness, of cooperating on popular items on the Democratic agenda. In his first year in office he did not veto a single bill. During his first term he signed legislation allowing eighteen-year-olds to vote and creating both the Environmental Protection Agency and the Occupational Safety and Health Administration.

Nixon was also fortunate in his first term, basking in the glory of the Apollo moon landings, which began in July 1969, and exploiting the split between the Soviets and the Chinese. He also benefited from the misfortunes of potential Democratic rivals. Sen. Edward M. Kennedy of Massachusetts, the brother of John and Robert and a presidential prospect for 1972, drove off a bridge at Chappaquiddick and caused the death of a young woman who worked for him. The next Democratic front-runner, Sen. Edmund S. Muskie of Maine, stumbled in the first primary and sank from sight.

Nevertheless, Nixon mounted his reelection effort as if preparing for Armageddon. The campaign raised unprecedented amounts of money, kept substantial portions of it in cash, and used some of it to silence a gang of burglars caught inside the Democratic Party's headquarters in the Watergate office complex in June 1972. The story of Watergate, and of the campaign's involvement, would emerge piecemeal over a period of months in the *Washington Post*.

The Democrats, meanwhile, battled their way through another contentious primary season and another fractious convention. They spurned Sen. Hubert H. Humphrey, the former vice president, and nominated their most idealistic peace candidate, Sen. George S. McGovern of South Dakota. In November, Nixon carried every state but Massachusetts and came within a hair of equaling Johnson's 1964 vote share.

Watergate played almost no part in the voting decisions of 1972. But within a few months, the trickle of revelations about the scandal would swell into a torrent.

= 1973 =

"Senator Sam" and the President's Men

Alan Greenblatt

Early in 1973, Sen. Sam J. Ervin, D-N.C., was chosen to preside over the Senate Watergate Committee, a special investigating panel handpicked by the chamber's two party leaders and charged with investigating breaches of the law and abuses of power in President Richard M. Nixon's 1972 reelection campaign. The choice would prove fateful for both chairman and president.

"Senator Sam" was seventy-six years old and an unlikely candidate for liberal icon status. Through nearly two decades in the Senate he had played Hollywood's concept of a Solon from the Old South, rumpled and jowly but possessed of a silver tongue. He had given his party's northern liberals fits, filibustering their bills with lengthy passages memorized from the King James Bible. He opposed civil rights bills and Medicare and supported the Vietnam War from start to finish. He was a major reason why Nixon, in the words of biographer Stephen E. Ambrose, "liked Southern Democrats more than he did most Republicans."

But Ervin's pro-Nixon reputation made him all the more attractive to Senate Majority Leader Mike Mansfield, D-Mont., who picked him to chair what was formally called the Senate Select Committee to Investigate Presidential Campaign Practices. Mansfield's hunch was that Ervin, who was also chairman of the Government Operations Committee, would appear less partisan than some younger buck with presidential ambitions. "Sam is the only man we could have picked on either side who would have the respect of the Senate as a whole," Mansfield said.

Yet even Mansfield could not have foreseen how momentous his choice would prove. As the Watergate hearings stretched out across the summer weeks of 1973, Ervin's role evolved from master of ceremonies to central figure and beyond that to something more. Much of the nation sat riveted to the live television coverage, engrossed by Ervin's lengthy recitations from the Constitution. When the chairman admonished witnesses about founding principles that the Nixon White House had abused, it was apparent that his loyalty to those principles exceeded his sympathy for the president. And in that shift the senator reflected the mood of the nation.

Most of the country got its first look at the self-styled "old country lawyer" when he opened the committee's first hearing on May 17, 1973, calling for order with a colorful gavel provided him by friends among the Cherokee. Ervin was joined on the dais that day by the committee's vice chairman, Howard H. Baker Jr., R-Tenn., along with three other Democrats (Daniel K. Inouye of Hawaii, Herman A. Talmadge of Georgia, and Joseph M. Montoya of New Mexico) and two other Republicans (Edward J. Gurney of Florida and Lowell P. Weicker Jr. of Connecticut).

In that leadoff session, Ervin intoned that the men who had been caught breaking into the of-

In summer of 1973, Sens. Sam Ervin, center, and Howard Baker, left, quizzed a procession of Nixon aides in an effort to answer the question: "What did the president know and when did he know it?"

fices of the Democratic National Committee (DNC) in Washington's Watergate complex the previous June 17 "were seeking to steal . . . not the jewels, money, or other property of American citizens, but something much more valuable—their most precious heritage: the right to vote in a free election."

Ervin also rejected suggestions that the break-in was no more than "a third-rate burglary," as White House spokesman Ron Ziegler had put it, and emphasized that the perpetrators had ties to the administration and to the reelection campaign.

This connection had been revealed within hours of the initial arrest, as two of those involved were officials of the Committee to Re-elect the President. But the initial assumption among most people, including journalists and Justice Department prosecutors, was that the burglars were engaged in an unauthorized prank of their own.

"My only reaction to the case had been a vague feeling that every political campaign had a few crackpots who cause embarrassment," wrote Fred Thompson, the top staff lawyer for Baker on the committee, in his 1975 book, *At That Point in Time.* (Thompson would be elected to his former boss's seat in the Senate in 1994.) The dismissive view of Watergate had prevailed through the campaign year of 1972, which saw Nixon reelected in a landslide that carried forty-nine states. But soon thereafter, the White House plan to contain the damage rapidly came apart.

In the first months following the burglary, the cover-up had been managed by a young lawyer named John W. Dean III, the presidential counsel. Dean's job was to conceal the complicity of Nixon's staff not only in the Watergate burglary but in myriad other campaign "dirty tricks" and illegal acts that would later be called the "White House horrors" by Nixon's former law partner, attorney general, and campaign director, John N. Mitchell.

Early in 1973, Dean became overwhelmed with the difficulty of his task and began looking for ways to avoid becoming the fall guy for the cover-up. By spring, with questions multiplying in the media and the law enforcement community, Nixon was compelled to clean house. Dean was fired April 30. The same day, Nixon accepted the resignations of White House Chief of Staff H. R. (Bob) Haldeman, domestic policy czar John Ehrlichman, and Attorney General Richard G. Kleindienst, who had been involved in the Justice investigation.

Dean turned to the Senate committee, hoping to be granted limited immunity from prosecution for crimes he might testify to committing in the course of open hearings. By carefully leaking information to the press about what he knew, Dean made himself irresistible as a potential star witness who had been close to the core of the case.

Dean opened his week of testimony June 25 by reading a damning 245-page statement. The reading consumed about six hours, with Dean pausing only for sips of water and a lunch break. The nation watched with a mix of amazement, admiration, and aversion. Everything about Dean appeared neutral, from his brown suit to his flat voice. Pale and precise and wearing a newly bought pair of owlish glasses, Dean radiated a lawyerly authority as he accused the president and others of high crimes and misdemeanors.

Dean described a "do-it-yourself White House staff, regardless of the law." He revealed that the White House kept an "enemies list" of entertainers, businessmen, journalists, and others thought hostile to the administration. Dean

entered the list for the record along with the recommendations he had made on "how we can use the available federal machinery to screw our political enemies" with tax audits and other forms of harassment.

But the most damaging item on Dean's long list was his allegation that Nixon was informed about the Watergate cover-up no later than September 15, 1972, six months earlier than Nixon had admitted to knowing. Moreover, Dean asserted, he and Nixon had discussed Nixon pardoning the burglars on March 21, 1973, and Nixon had assured his counsel that raising a million dollars to continue making "hush money" payments to prevent the implicating of higher-ups would not be a problem.

As Nixon recounted in his 1978 memoirs, "It no longer made any difference that not all of Dean's testimony was accurate. It only mattered if *any* of his testimony was accurate." It was Dean's word against the president's, and if many dismissed Dean as a stool pigeon out to save his own skin, a source for verification would soon be revealed.

Deep in Dean's testimony was the suggestion that one of his meetings with Nixon might have been tape-recorded. Moreover, memos submitted to the committee by one of Nixon's attorneys struck Thompson's deputy counsel, Donald G. Sanders, as having the appearance of an audiotape transcript (Sanders was a former FBI agent). Sanders managed to confirm his surmise by interviewing Alexander P. Butterfield, who had coordinated the day-to-day operations of the White House as Haldeman's deputy and who knew an extensive taping system had been in place since February 1971.

Sanders's interview with Butterfield took place on Friday, July 13. On the following Monday, Butterfield was getting his hair cut at the Sheraton Carlton Hotel when Assistant Chief Counsel James Hamilton contacted him by phone to testify publicly that day. Butterfield

John Ehrlichman, left, Nixon's domestic policy chief, oversaw the White House "Plumbers," who burglarized the office of an antiwar activist's psychiatrist in September 1971.

refused, then watched on the barber's TV as Hamilton entered the ornate Senate Caucus Room, scene of the hearings in progress, and whispered in Ervin's ear. Hamilton was soon back on the telephone, warning Butterfield that he should be in Ervin's office by half past noon or the Senate's sergeant-at-arms would arrest him on the street. Still in the barber shop, Butterfield called Leonard Garment, the attorney then coordinating the White House response to Watergate. "Get a good haircut," Garment advised. "You'll have a national audience today."

Shortly after 2 p.m., Butterfield was in the Senate Caucus Room. Fred Thompson asked: "Mr. Butterfield, are you aware of the installation of any listening devices in the Oval Office of the president?"

"I was aware of listening devices, yes, sir," Butterfield answered, and suddenly the possibility arose that a definitive answer might be found to the crucial question of the hearings: "What did the president know and when did he know it?"

That question had been asked persistently by Senator Baker, who appeared to some as if he felt he had something to prove. Some had questioned whether Baker could be nonpartisan. Dean had directly assailed Baker's credibility, noting that the Tennessean had met secretly with the president to discuss the Senate investigation well before the hearings began. But Baker could show that he had refused Nixon's suggestions for staffing the GOP side of the committee, and his balanced questioning had contrasted strongly with that of Senator Gurney, the committee's one avowedly pro-Nixon member.

With Butterfield's statement in hand, the committee the next day sent Nixon a formal request for the tapes. Nixon declined, saying that to provide such confidential material would violate the separation of powers.

On July 18, with national sentiment in the balance, John Ehrlichman began his testimony. Ervin got the better of him in an exchange about an earlier break-in perpetrated by some of the same burglars who had entered the DNC's Watergate offices. Ehrlichman oversaw a group called the Plumbers (meant to plug leaks) who broke into the offices of Dr. Lewis Fielding in September 1971, hoping to find material that could discredit his patient Daniel Ellsberg.

Ellsberg had leaked a vast store of documents on the U.S. military's role in Vietnam that had been circulated within the Pentagon. The documents, known as the Pentagon Papers, were published in several newspapers and deeply embarrassed the administration. Ehrlichman argued that concern for national security justified the Fielding break-in. Ervin would have none of it.

"Foreign intelligence activities had nothing to do with the opinion of Ellsberg's psychiatrist about his intellectual or emotional or psychological state," Ervin said. Ehrlichman asked, "How do you know that, Mr. Chairman?"

"Because I can understand the English language," Ervin replied. "It's my mother tongue." The largely anti-Nixon audience in the hearing room applauded, and even the stern-faced Ehrlichman could not suppress a grin.

The committee followed up its request for the tapes with a subpoena that Nixon "respectfully" rejected July 26. By a show of hands in open session the committee voted to fight in court for custody of the evidence. Ervin's dismay at being stiffed by the White House was exacerbated when former chief of staff Haldeman came to testify and said he had taken twenty-two of the tapes in question home to review them. Haldeman's summary of what he heard would later lead to a conviction on perjury charges, but at the time the committee was mostly angry that an ordinary citizen in disgrace could take home the tapes overnight when a committee created by a unanimous vote of the Senate could not hear them at all. This was a "strange thing," drawled Ervin in mordant tones.

The fight for the tapes moved into the courts, where the Ervin committee's claim had to compete with that of Special Prosecutor Archibald Cox, who had been appointed to pursue the Watergate matter for the Justice Department. John J. Sirica, chief judge of the U.S. District Court in Washington, ruled in favor of Cox's subpoena, but not the Senate's.

At this point in mid-October, Nixon floated a compromise. He proposed allowing a conservative Southern Democrat, Sen. John C. Stennis of Mississippi, to hear the tapes in order to verify a White House summary of them. Having lost their court bid for the tapes, Ervin and Baker seemed to have little to lose by agreeing to the Stennis gambit, and the White House announced it had their agreement on October 19.

Thus emboldened, Nixon took on Cox's subpoena by ordering Attorney General Elliot Richardson to fire Cox. Richardson refused and promptly resigned. His deputy, William Ruckelshaus, did the same. Nixon finally found someone willing to carry out his order: Solicitor General Robert H. Bork.

As news of the October 20 Saturday Night Massacre spread, cars passing the White House created a cacophony of blaring horns in response to a "Honk for Impeachment" sign held up by a protester. Inside the West Wing, Ron Ziegler announced that Cox had been fired and that the special prosecutor's office was being abolished. The new White House chief of staff, Alexander M. Haig, ordered the FBI to seal Cox's office, an operation captured by network television with the look and air of a coup d'état.

The next day, House GOP Conference Chairman John B. Anderson of Illinois predicted that "impeachment resolutions are going to be raining down like hailstones." In the coming months, the Watergate limelight would indeed shift to the House, where the impeachment process must begin. At the same time, the Supreme Court would consider whether the tapes could be subpoenaed for use in criminal trials, and its decision in July 1974 would strip Nixon of his last defense.

But while the Senate Watergate Committee faded, the newfound fame of its leaders lingered. Baker emerged with high respect and was elected his party's leader in the Senate in late 1976. Ervin retired at the end of 1974 but remained a media favorite with "Uncle Sam" fan clubs distributing his fleshy profile and chaotic eyebrows on sweatshirts, posters, and watches. So popular was Ervin's sonorous bass voice that record companies released albums of him singing "If I Had a Hammer" and reciting "The Night Before Christmas."

Article I of the Constitution specifies that Congress will have the power to raise and spend money—the "power of the purse." Tax bills in particular were to originate in the House of Representatives, giving rise in modern times to the legendary power of the House Ways and Means Committee.

Beginning in the 1830s, both chambers split the money decisions into two stages—one that authorized expenditures and one that actually appropriated the money to pay for them. The idea of this bifurcated process was to insulate pure spending decisions from the distraction of policy decisions. But over the years, the distinction has rarely been either clearly drawn or fully enforced.

Eventually, each chamber developed a powerful committee devoted to appropriations, and the members of these committees evolved their own special culture. Often more bipartisan than Congress as a whole, this culture also has been more conservative in some respects than Congress as a whole. It has been undeniably stable. From 1947 until 1994, for example, only four men served as chairman of the House Appropriations Committee. One, a Republican from New York, held the job for just four years. The rest of the era was shared among three Democrats: Clarence Cannon of Missouri, George Mahon of Texas, and Jamie L. Whitten of Mississippi.

Through most of its history, Congress had no budget process and no budget. Authorizing committees set out dollar figures and Appropriations either honored them or not. The tax-writing panels tried to do their best to keep up, mindful of the changing fashions regarding voters' tolerance for taxes versus public debt. In the 1920s, for example, the government was eager to retire the debts accumulated in World War I. In the 1980s the pressure for a tax cut was felt more acutely than the pressure to decrease the annual budget shortfall.

During the Nixon administration, the costs of the Vietnam War and the Great Society had necessitated both high taxes and unusually big deficits (by the standards of the time). Returned to office with a mandate in 1972, Nixon put Congress on notice immediately that he intended to spend billions less than authorized and appropriated—not just in future fiscal years but immediately. His budget director announced in February 1993 that some $8.7 billion in spending that the president had previously signed off on would now be impounded.

The impoundment mechanism of the executive branch had been used before, but not applied to such enormous figures or in such dramatic circumstances. Nixon was reaching for the purse strings not just as a means of enforcing economy but as a means of altering priorities and redirecting policy. He was issuing the most direct challenge imaginable to the core of Congress's power. And it added impetus to the pleas of inside reformers and outside critics alike who had long urged Congress to adopt a congressional budget and live within its confines.

The Power of the Purse

John R. Cranford

As Richard M. Nixon began his second term as president, encouraged by a landslide election victory in November 1972 and not yet seriously weakened by the spreading infection of Watergate, he was determined to have his way on matters of federal spending, whether Congress granted its permission or not.

"This Congress has not been responsible on money," Nixon told a televised news conference January 31, 1973. "The difficulty, of course . . . is that the Congress represents special interests."

Nixon followed through on this slap by throwing down the gauntlet. "I will not spend money if the Congress overspends, and I will not be for programs that will raise the taxes and put a bigger burden on the already overburdened American taxpayer," he vowed.

Congress swiftly took up the challenge, and the duel began. The battle between the Republican president and the Democratic Congress would run for nearly eighteen months, and it would stimulate the reinvention of congressional spending procedures in the Congressional Budget and Impoundment Control Act of 1974. That law still orders federal fiscal policy more than two decades later.

The stage had been set in October 1972 for a fundamental confrontation between the branches over which holds the government's purse strings. Nixon's first steps toward the constitutional brink came when he proposed a mandatory ceiling of $250 billion on spending for fiscal 1973, $20 billion more than had been spent in fiscal 1972.

The House went along with the president's proposal, which would have granted him broad authority to reduce or eliminate spending on individual programs. But the Senate balked.

Nixon responded by vetoing bills he considered inflationary, among them the Water Pollution Control Act Amendments of 1972, allocating $11 billion for 1973 and 1974 for sewage treatment projects. Congress overrode this particular veto within a day. But Nixon was ready with another round of escalation.

Punctuating his view that Congress was unwilling to make the government live within its means, Nixon began impounding—flatly refusing to spend—billions of dollars Congress had appropriated. This included $6 billion for sewage treatment grants to states and cities, $2.5 billion from the Highway Trust Fund, and billions more for other programs.

Impoundment was a well-established practice of presidents almost since the founding of the Republic, but none before had employed it on such a scale or for the purpose of killing programs outright.

In 1803 Thomas Jefferson deferred for a time spending $50,000 on gunboats to patrol the Mississippi River—an action he justified by citing the just-completed Louisiana Purchase, which had relocated the country's western border and enhanced the prospects for peace. Harry S. Truman impounded $735 million appropriated in

FILE PHOTO

"The constitutional right of the president of the United States to impound funds," Nixon said, "is absolutely clear." But no president before him had employed impoundment on such a scale or for the purpose of killing programs outright.

1949 for the Air Force, an amount that he judged an unwarranted imposition on the peacetime economy.

Invoking Jefferson and Truman, Nixon justified his impoundments at the January 31 news conference. "The constitutional right for the president of the United States to impound funds . . . is absolutely clear," he said.

But it was not absolutely clear to everyone. William H. Rehnquist, Nixon's most recent appointee to the Supreme Court, had reached exactly the opposite conclusion four years earlier, while serving as an assistant attorney general.

In a memorandum, Rehnquist wrote, "It is in our view extremely difficult to formulate a constitutional theory to justify a refusal by the president to comply with a congressional directive to spend."

Nixon's claim was also disputed by Sen. Sam Ervin, a North Carolina Democrat whose "country lawyer" demeanor belied his status as the accepted constitutional expert in Congress. On January 2, 1973, Ervin led a group of seventeen Senate leaders who intervened as "friends of the court" in a case brought by the state of Missouri to release the money Nixon had impounded from the Highway Trust Fund in 1972.

"This practice of impoundment is contemptuous of Congress," Ervin said. "The power of the purse belongs exclusively to Congress under the Constitution."

Two weeks later, he introduced a bill to require the president to gain permission from Congress to withhold money Congress had directed to be spent. On January 30, he convened five days of joint hearings of the Government Operations Committee and the Judiciary Subcommittee on Separation of Powers—both of which he chaired—to challenge the administration on its impoundment policy.

When Agriculture Secretary Earl L. Butz at first failed to attend the hearing, Ervin was enraged. "I don't recognize the power of the president to determine what witnesses a congressional committee should have," Ervin said.

Often supportive of the president's first-term policies, Ervin was now becoming riled by Nixon's behavior and that of his administration (as the senator's role in the unfolding of the Watergate affair would demonstrate later that year).

Five days later, Ervin's hearings took on an even angrier tone when Joseph T. Sneed, newly appointed as deputy attorney general, offered a sweeping legal defense of Nixon's impoundments. Sneed said Ervin's bill would "reverse

170 years of presidential practice [and] undercut the president's existing authority to combat inflation, unemployment and a wide range of economic ills."

The president, Sneed said, had "an implied constitutional right" to impound appropriated money. Presidential impoundment "to promote fiscal stability is not usurpation; rather it is in the great tradition of checks and balances upon which our Constitution is based."

His comments drew expressions of outrage and disbelief. Edmund S. Muskie, D-Maine, said he was reminded of "a speech made by the president of the Philippines as a justification for eliminating the national assembly." Lawton Chiles, D-Fla., said Sneed was granting the president "a divine right" to eliminate any program he chose.

Sneed until 1972 had been dean of the Duke University Law School—Nixon's alma mater, where the president's oil portrait hung in the moot courtroom (until it was snatched by pranksters in 1974). A month after Sneed's Capitol Hill appearance, Ervin amused an appreciative crowd in that same room at Duke, recounting his reply to Sneed's contention that Nixon's impoundment authority was rooted in the president's constitutional responsibility "to take care that the laws be faithfully executed."

"The state has the power to execute a man for a capital crime," Ervin joked. "Does that mean the president has the authority to execute the laws under that definition?"

Impoundment had few advocates on Capitol Hill, other than Senate Minority Leader Hugh Scott, R-Pa., who said in a January 26 radio broadcast: "Scott's law is that, if the Congress can't add, the president must subtract, so the taxes don't multiply."

But if public support for Nixon's actions was weak, the sense that Congress had to get its fiscal house in order was nonetheless widespread. The federal budget was growing rapidly and with it the deficit. The budget had been in the red an average of $3.7 billion a year for the two prior decades, and occasionally had shown a surplus, the last time in 1969. But the deficit had swelled to $23 billion in fiscal 1971 and again in fiscal 1972, a trend that showed no sign of abating.

"The answer to impoundment can't be merely political—a lot of rhetoric on both sides," argued Al Ullman of Oregon, the second-ranking Democrat on the House Ways and Means Committee. "It's got to be structural in the Congress."

Before 1974 there was no congressional budget process, much less a congressional budget. Laws such as the Water Pollution Control Act Amendments of 1972 did not merely authorize the spending of billions of dollars, they required it. As the Supreme Court would rule in 1975, such laws obligated the government, even though the money had not been separately appropriated in the traditional fashion.

So, during debate over a must-pass bill raising the federal debt ceiling in 1972, Congress voted to create a Joint Study Committee on Budget Control. Ullman was named co-chairman. Six months later, on April 16, 1973, the thirty-two House and Senate members of the panel, all drawn from the Appropriations, Finance, and Ways and Means committees, gave unanimous approval to the idea of creating budget committees in both chambers, with the power to set an overall budget and firm limits on subcategories of spending. Seeking an end to deficits altogether, the joint committee proposed that Congress would have to offset any expected deficit for the coming year with a tax surcharge on individual and corporate incomes.

The time seemed ripe for Congress to act. On April 2, the 8th U.S. Circuit Court of Appeals agreed with Ervin and his colleagues, and ruled that Nixon's Highway Trust Fund impoundment was illegal.

Rep. Richard Bolling of Missouri, both an insider and a reformer, said the law's prospects depended "almost entirely on the will of the members of this House and of the other body."

The next day, Ervin's Government Operations Committee approved his anti-impoundment bill, 13-3. Believing that Congress would not accept limits on the president without some gesture toward controlling spending, the committee first adopted an amendment sponsored by Muskie to impose a budget ceiling for fiscal 1974, and give Nixon authority to meet it by reducing spending evenly across the board.

The Senate passed Ervin's bill May 10 by voice vote. In separate roll calls, the Senate agreed to the impoundment language, 66-24, and the spending ceiling, 86-4.

The House was more conservative than the Senate, and more concerned that the deficit was a problem to be reckoned with. But on June 22 the Rules Committee weighed in with its version of an anti-impoundment bill. Where the Senate would have required the president

to spend any impounded money unless Congress voted to concur in the president's action, the House put the burden on Congress to vote to reject the president's action. Adoption of a simple resolution to reject an impoundment would have been sufficient, however.

On a nearly party-line vote of 254-164, the House passed the bill July 25. But it was plain the House would not give its approval to a conference report on impoundment control without action on Congress's own budget process.

Delicate negotiations in both chambers got under way in an effort to rewrite the budget control recommendations of the Joint Study Committee, and to balance liberal and conservative distrust of the proposal.

In the House, Richard Bolling of Missouri, third-ranking Democrat on the Rules Committee and a longtime student of the budget, took charge of navigating among the appropriators, authorizers, and revenue-raisers to craft procedures that would protect institutional prerogatives and still permit some measure of control.

By late fall, bills had been drafted in both chambers. Bolling's work produced a bill to create House and Senate budget committees, with a new joint staff to match the expertise of the president's Office of Management and Budget. It called for adoption of budget resolutions setting broad spending and revenue targets for the government, and established a timetable for action. It proposed moving the start of the fiscal year from July 1 to October 1 to give Congress more time to do its work.

The House passed Bolling's version December 5 by a 386-23 vote. Ervin's Government Operations Committee approved its similar version November 28. Staff negotiations involving both chambers produced a revised Senate bill in March 1974 that retained much of the Bolling structure, but continued to fine-tune the budget resolutions and "reconciliation" bills that would be used to bring spending in line with budgets.

The Senate passed the Rules Committee bill, 80-0, on March 21, and over the next ten weeks House and Senate conferees agreed to further compromises, most of which had the effect of giving congressional committees more, not less, leeway in the process. Spending ceilings became less restrictive, and caps on spending subcategories were set by broad functional divisions that did not correspond with the jurisdictions of appropriations subcommittees.

Final congressional action was swift. The House adopted the conference report June 18 by a 401-6 vote. Three days later the Senate cleared the bill, 75-0.

By the time the bill was presented to Nixon for his signature on July 12, he was an enthusiastic supporter of what he called "the most significant reform of budget procedures since the Congress and this country began." Whatever objections he previously voiced about the restraints it placed on impoundments had dissipated. But by this time, Watergate had reduced the president to near irrelevance in Washington; his resignation would come in less than a month.

There were skeptics, however. Rep. H. R. Gross, R-Iowa, a legendary critic of congressional profligacy, called the new budget law "another resort to gimmickry." Gross, who was retiring, predicted that Congress would "quickly find ways to warp and bend the reform rules laid down here today."

Bolling may have been most prophetic: "Whether it does succeed will depend almost entirely on the will of the members of this House and of the other body of this Congress."

For people who record the news or follow it closely, 1973 was among the most exciting and exhausting of the century. President Richard M. Nixon celebrated his second inauguration on January 20, beginning a week that brought three other events of milestone significance.

The event with perhaps the most far-reaching implications was the announcement January 22 that the Supreme Court had ruled in the case of *Roe v. Wade*. By a 7-2 vote the justices invalidated all laws restricting a woman's right to an abortion in the first six months of pregnancy.

On January 27 a four-party agreement was signed in Paris regarding Vietnam. Not coincidentally, on the same day, the Pentagon announced that the military draft in place since shortly before World War II would no longer be needed, completing the transition to an all-volunteer army begun earlier in the Nixon presidency.

In February the United States and China agreed to set up permanent liaison offices in each other's capital city. In March the last U.S. combat troops left Vietnam. In April the last of 590 prisoners of war returned home from Vietnam. At the end of that month, Nixon accepted the resignations of his chief of staff, his top domestic adviser, and his attorney general—all of them crippled by Watergate.

Beginning in June, the nation was transfixed by the Senate Watergate hearings. Then the scandal moved offstage for a period of lawyerly investigation and negotiation. But the descent of Nixon continued. His approval rating in the Gallup Poll, which began the year near 70 percent, spiraled down to around 25 percent by October.

Also in October, Congress and the nation were distracted by an assault on Israel by Egypt and Syria on Yom Kippur, the highest of Jewish holy days. Israel needed substantial U.S. aid to recover its battlefield footing, but it survived. The Arab states lashed out in frustration, stopping oil exports to the United States for five months.

Even as the fighting raged, Vice President Spiro T. Agnew resigned after pleading "no contest" to tax evasion charges. He had failed to declare the payments he had taken from contractors when he was governor of Maryland in the 1960s. Two days later, Nixon named a new vice president, as he was empowered to do by the Twenty-fifth Amendment. The successor was Gerald R. Ford of Michigan, the Republican leader in the House. In contrast to Agnew, Ford was a genial Hill veteran, respected, and even liked by members in both parties. Before the end of October, the president lost his attorney general, fired another, and fired the special prosecutor who had been handling the Watergate case.

In November the House and Senate mustered the two-thirds vote to override Nixon's veto of the War Powers Act—imposing new limits on the president's military prerogatives. Nixon's continued tenure in office was no longer just a threat to his party but a threat to the long-term standing of the presidency itself.

= 1974 =

The High Drama of Impeachment

Alan Greenblatt

The televised Senate Watergate Committee hearings that were a constant black eye for President Richard M. Nixon throughout the summer of 1973 were winding down. But the panel's discovery that Nixon had bugged the Oval Office began a fight for the tape recordings that could answer the committee's famous question, "What did the president know, and when did he know it?"

After Special Prosecutor Archibald Cox subpoenaed the tapes, Nixon ordered him fired, and on October 20, 1973, the president decapitated the Justice Department of its top officials for refusing to carry out this order. Even some members of Congress who were sympathetic to Nixon declared, after the Saturday Night Massacre, that the president was no mere bystander to crimes committed by his out-of-control staff.

A lone impeachment resolution had been introduced that summer by Rep. Robert F. Drinan, D-Mass., but within days of the massacre there were dozens. The time had come, as Nixon loyalist, Sen. George D. Aiken, R-Vt., put it with the hint of a dare, to "either impeach him or get off his back." With members clamoring, on October 23 House Speaker Carl Albert, D-Okla., handed responsibility for an investigation over to the House Judiciary Committee and its new chairman, an obscure New Jersey Democrat named Peter W. Rodino Jr.

It would have been difficult to imagine Rodino's longtime predecessor in the chair, Brooklyn Democrat Emmanuel Celler, presiding over the impeachment proceedings. Although Celler was a stalwart liberal, he also was an old Nixon pal. But Celler had unexpectedly lost his seat in the 1972 primaries, and the gavel fell to Rodino.

An opera fan and something of a dandy in dress, Rodino was the sort of man who listed his civic awards in the *Congressional Directory* and proudly pointed to the creation of a national holiday honoring Christopher Columbus as his signal legislative achievement.

Rodino's anonymity was a plus in Albert's accounting. "I didn't want to go to one of the more spectacular members of the House or someone who wanted to be a movie star," the Speaker said. Innately cautious, Rodino pursued a strategy of quiet accretion of evidence, patiently building an overwhelming case to win over some of the GOP committee members and protect the politically charged process from accusations of partisanship.

Rodino let two months pass before he even selected his special counsel, John M. Doar, a lifelong Republican who had headed the Justice Department's Civil Rights Division under Attorney General Robert F. Kennedy.

"My task was to make the process of impeachment work, whether to a trial or vindication didn't matter," Doar said. He holed up his staff of 100, half of them lawyers (including Bernard W. Nussbaum, a future White House counsel, and a freshly minted Yale Law School graduate named Hillary Rodham), under police protection on three floors of the old Congres-

House Judiciary Committee Chairman Peter W. Rodino Jr., holds aloft his gavel waiting for a signal to begin the panel's proceedings July 24, 1974. Rep. Harold D. Donahue, D-Mass., is at left.

sional Hotel, behind the Longworth House Office Building. Sifting first through grand jury and Senate Watergate Committee material, they eventually gathered forty volumes of evidence totaling 2 million words.

Some GOP leaders pressed the committee to finish its work by the spring of 1974 to clear up the matter before the height of the election season. But Rodino allowed Doar months to work on the case while the committee met only sporadically in closed session to protect members from locking themselves into a public position.

Nixon thought his impeachment would turn not on precedent or law but on public opinion, and the president was definitely slipping in that court throughout the winter and spring of 1974. Still, Nixon took cold comfort in the fact that Congress enjoyed less regard than he did. ("Even lower than mine!" Nixon wrote of the institution's poll ratings in his 1978 memoirs.)

Nixon mounted a campaign to restore his public image, which the media lampooned as Operation Candor and a good deal of which backfired. On November 17, he made a much-hyped appearance before newspaper editors at Walt Disney World, the new amusement park in Florida. Embroiled in a tax evasion controversy, Nixon sputtered: "People have got to know whether or not their president is a crook. Well, I am not a crook."

Nixon had improperly claimed a half-million-dollar tax deduction for donating his vice-presidential papers to the National Archives, backdating the gift. On April 2, the IRS presented Nixon with a bill for $432,787 in back taxes, news that the *New York Times* trumpeted with a triple-deck headline worthy of Pearl Harbor. Nixon's approval rating dropped to 26 percent.

Doar and his staff had been consumed with the thorny question of what exactly constituted an impeachable offense. The Constitution stipulates "treason, bribery, or other high crimes and misdemeanors," but the latter phrase was ambiguous, and there was precious little precedent for the committee to build on. Republicans took up the argument that a specific criminal charge was necessary to impeach; Andrew Johnson, the only president yet impeached, was charged with violating an act of Congress.

But on February 21, Doar released a forty-nine-page report to the committee concluding that focusing only on criminal activity "would frustrate the purpose that the framers intended for impeachment." Although ranking Republican Edward Hutchinson of Michigan distanced himself from this finding, the special Republican counsel signed off on it, and Rodino gave it his blessing.

"It has been my view all along that grounds for impeachment need not arise out of criminal conduct," the chairman said. The staff would look for a pattern of abuse, not necessarily a specific crime.

Nixon was still fighting on another front, seeking to withhold additional tapes from the new special prosecutor, Leon Jaworski.

Nixon's lawyers admitted in November that a crucial tape, recorded three days after the break-in at Democratic National Committee headquarters at the Watergate complex, contained a gap of eighteen and a half minutes. (Two other tapes under subpoena were missing entirely.) White House Chief of Staff Alexander M. Haig suggested that perhaps "some sinister force" had caused the erasure, but a team of scientists chosen jointly by the White House and its prosecutors quickly determined that the tape had been recorded over at least five times.

This apparent destruction of evidence was a public relations disaster, lowering the president's credibility rating in a Harris Poll to 21 percent. The media had a field day when Nixon's secretary Rose Mary Woods posed for pictures, contorting herself to demonstrate how she might have erased the tape accidentally by answering the phone while her foot depressed the wrong button of the tape recorder.

In April the House Judiciary Committee joined the fight for the tapes, issuing a subpoena of its own. On April 29 the president went on national television to announce that he would give transcripts of forty-three conversations to the committee.

The committee did not accept the transcripts in lieu of the tapes, but their release nevertheless caused a firestorm. Despite heavy editing, in many cases by Nixon himself, their informal and conspiratorial tone offended a public unused to gutter speech from national leaders. For instance, Nixon told his top aides, "I don't give a shit. I want you all to stonewall it. Let them plead the Fifth Amendment, cover up or anything else that will save the plan. That's the whole point." In the White House version, "expletive deleted" marked the spots where the president had indulged in profanity, and a new phrase entered the national lexicon.

"I realize that these transcripts will provide grist for many sensational stories in the press," Nixon said, and he had never been so right. Even loyal Republican newspapers in the Midwest began calling for Nixon's resignation. Even if it were true, as columnist Joseph Alsop pointed out, that crudeness was not an impeachable offense, the burden of proof shifted to the president, who was fighting to keep the case's hard evidence, the tapes, to himself.

On Saturday, July 24, the Supreme Court blocked Nixon's last avenue of legal defense, releasing a unanimous decision to require the president to hand over all the relevant tapes to Jaworski, tapes that everyone expected would provide the "smoking gun" skeptical members had demanded.

That same evening, before those tapes were made available, the committee took up the

WHITE HOUSE PHOTO/CONSOLIDATED NEWS PICTURES

Nixon hugs daughter Julie Eisenhower on August 7 after telling his family of his decision to resign the presidency.

question of impeachment in televised sessions, then a rare phenomenon requiring a special vote of the House. With each member allotted fifteen minutes to make a statement, all the cards would be on the table.

In an uncharacteristically forthcoming moment a month before, Rodino had told reporters he expected all twenty-one Democrats would vote for impeachment. Charles E. Wiggins, R-

Calif., the president's most adamant defender on the committee, could count on far fewer votes. Both sides were struggling for the hearts and minds of the publicly undecided moderates. Their votes were not necessary to the outcome, but they would determine whether the committee's verdict was perceived as fair.

Rodino had patiently wooed the committee's three Southern Democrats and several of the Republicans. "I'm staying up until 2 a.m. reading, trying to reflect, to place in context eight or nine thousand pages of evidence . . . and see if it stacks up against the meager phrases of the Constitution," said first-term Republican William S. Cohen of Maine.

The bipartisan rump group, led by Tom Railsback, R-Ill., was known, to its chagrin, as the fragile coalition; its members preferred to call themselves "the magnificent seven." With Rodino's blessing, they met for several hours before the hearing to see if they could come up with language for articles of impeachment that could achieve consensus. Their districts had all gone heavily for Nixon in the last election, and they were bound by policy to him; but they felt bound by conscience and the law to leave the reservation.

Rodino held the gavel halfway aloft, waiting for a cue from a TV prompter to bang it down at 7:45. "I, as the chairman, have been guided by a simple principle," he announced, "that the law must deal fairly with every man."

Barbara Jordan, D-Texas, captured the gravity of the proceedings. Leaning forward intently, she said in her deep, powerful, voice that lent her words a Churchillian heft: "My faith in the Constitution is whole, it is complete, it is total, and I am not going to sit here and be an idle spectator to the diminution, the subversion, the destruction of the Constitution."

The Democrats' point that no man is above the law was turned, judo-like, against them by

Wiggins, who represented part of the president's former congressional district. Wiggins had said he thought Doar had "a goddamned weak circumstantial case" and challenged the Democrats "to act like lawyers."

Although conceding "wrongful acts" on the part of the White House staff, Wiggins said July 24 that in all of Doar's multiple volumes, "there is not a word, not a word, ladies and gentlemen, of presidential knowledge of awareness or involvement in that wrongful act." Lacking evidence of specific wrongdoing on Nixon's part, Wiggins argued, there could be no impeachable offense.

One by one, the "undecided" Republicans voiced deep doubts about the president. Railsback recited, step by step, the allegations of Nixon's involvement in Watergate to devastating effect. Rep. M. Caldwell Butler, R-Va., said, "The pattern of misrepresentation and half-truth that emerges from our investigation reveals a presidential policy cynically based on the premise that truth itself is negotiable." It became clear that they would vote against the president.

When it came time on July 26 to vote on the first article, charging Nixon with obstruction of justice, Paul S. Sarbanes, D-Md., a junior but widely respected member, was allowed to introduce the final language. The TV camera panned to each member as the vote was taken. Butler had said July 24 he would vote for impeachment, "but there will be no joy in it for me," and that set the tone. Members mainly kept their heads down or arms folded as they quietly spoke their "ayes." Democrats voted first, sealing the outcome, but then came six "ayes" from the Republicans, including Railsback, Butler, and Cohen.

Butler described the mood in his diary: "Just a total feeling of sadness for our country. With all due respect to those who think that there were those of our colleagues who were happy with it—I don't think so."

Rodino voted last, his voice cracking into a weary gasp as he agreed to impeach the president. The vote was 27-11. Soon the room had to be cleared in response to a false rumor of a kamikaze plane headed its way.

On subsequent days the panel approved two additional articles, charging abuse of power and contempt of Congress for refusing to honor its subpoenas. An article on the secret bombing of Cambodia, introduced by John Conyers Jr., D-Mich., was voted down, as was one regarding tax evasion.

The next week, the "smoking gun" turned up in a tape made six days after the Watergate break-in that showed Nixon had conspired to cripple the investigation. After the committee had been briefed August 5, Wiggins, teary-eyed, announced, "I have reached the painful conclusion that the president of the United States should resign." If not, "I am prepared to conclude that the magnificent career of public service of Richard Nixon must be terminated involuntarily."

Nixon's resignation speech August 8, the first ever by a president, garnered the largest TV audience to that time, but it was his televised farewell speech to his staff the next day that would be remembered. After joking about having to find a way to pay his taxes, Nixon told emotional, rambling stories about his parents' struggles before uttering his own epitaph: "Always remember, others may hate you, but those who hate you don't win unless you hate them, and then you destroy yourself."

The new president, Gerald R. Ford, who had been House minority leader just nine months earlier, announced, after being sworn in at noon August 9, "Our long national nightmare is over." On August 20, with an exquisite sense of anticlimax, the House voted, 412-3, to accept the Judiciary Committee's impeachment report.

As all-consuming as the Watergate story was for the political community, average Americans were often more exercised about something else in the winter of 1973-1974. For many, the real outrage of that season was the energy crisis generated by the Arab oil embargo. Not only were motorists waiting in endless lines to buy gas, but they were also paying unimaginable prices for it.

Beginning in October, as the Yom Kippur war ended, and lasting until mid-March 1974, the embargo shut off the flow of oil from the Middle East. It also caused the price of a barrel of oil to leap from less than $5 to more than $20 almost overnight.

In the 1960s, filling up the family car cost about twenty-five cents a gallon; and gas wars would sometimes drive that price still lower. Midway into the 1970s, gasoline sold for nearly a dollar more per gallon, and there was talk of $1.50 or even $2. Respected economists and scientists reminded Americans that the price of fuel had long been far higher in Europe and elsewhere in the world. The Constitution had no article guaranteeing cheap energy in perpetuity. Yet Americans had come to regard cheap energy as the next thing to a birthright.

For the first time, millions became aware that nearly half the oil used in the United States was coming not from Texas or Oklahoma but from faraway countries—most of them clustered around the Persian Gulf and implacably hostile to Israel, a U.S. ally of enormous political significance.

While domestic fields in the United States still held considerable supplies of oil (and truly vast supplies of natural gas), it had long been cheaper for the big oil companies to pump the crude of the Middle East, which was so abundant and so easily recoverable that production costs were comparatively minuscule. No one had factored in the cost of an interruption in the supply.

The result of the embargo and price increase was a deepening of the postelection recession already underway in 1973. This recession was not typical because prices did not decline along with wages and employment levels. Instead, prices were driven higher by the cost of energy. Products made with petroleum cost more, and so did everything made or transported by machines that burned fossil fuels.

This combination of economic slowdown and inflation came to be called stagflation, and it had serious economic and political consequences in the short term and the long. It further soured swing voters on the Nixon-Ford administration, contributing to the election of a freshman class with seventy-five Democrats in 1974.

In the longer term, the first oil shock (and its companion in 1979) depressed wages and sapped the sense of job security. Real incomes began to show recovery by the late 1980s, but the popular conviction that the American economy was no longer taking care of its own persisted into the 1990s.

= 1974 =

"Watergate Babies" Take Power

Ronald D. Elving

Our long national nightmare is over," said Gerald R. Ford as he took the oath as president August 9, 1974, replacing the disgraced Richard M. Nixon. But for Republicans, the storm stirred by the Watergate scandal was still gathering. Within weeks, it would strike Capitol Hill with gale force and lasting consequences.

For the GOP, warning flags had flown over the 1974 election season from the outset. Congressional elections midway through a president's second term invariably bruise the incumbent's party. Moreover, in 1974 the decade's first oil shock was still fresh, and unemployment and inflation were on the rise.

Disenchanted with the president they had reelected two years earlier, many voters were distressed by the blanket pardon Ford granted him in September. Neither Nixon nor Ford was on the ballot that November, but voters found plenty of other Republicans on whom to visit their vengeance.

Election Day drove the number of Republican governors down from eighteen to thirteen and the number of Republican senators down from forty-two to thirty-eight. But the heaviest blow fell on the GOP's long-suffering minority in the House, which dropped to just 144 seats after having struggled up to 192 in the 1972 election.

The result was the emergence of a new generation of Democrats, many of whom wanted to change their own party and reform Congress as much as they wanted to punish the party of Nixon. In the House, these newcomers would reverse the recent trend toward Republicans in congressional voting that had threatened the Democrats' twenty-year dominance. By their sheer number, and by the savvy reelection politics they would practice and perfect, these "Watergate babies" would help the Democrats maintain their grip on the chamber for twenty more years.

Democrats had plenty of statewide winners that November. Among their new governors were Edmund G. "Jerry" Brown Jr. in California, Michael S. Dukakis in Massachusetts, Richard D. "Dick" Lamm in Colorado, and Ella Grasso in Connecticut. Among their new members of the Senate were Dale Bumpers of Arkansas, John Glenn of Ohio, Patrick J. Leahy of Vermont, Wendell Ford of Kentucky, and Gary W. Hart of Colorado.

But the new class in the House received an unusual share of the postelection attention for their youthfulness, their cohesion, and their common debt to Watergate. The class numbered 92 in all, the largest new crop of representatives since the 118-member Class of 1948.

But even more important was the lopsided party split: seventy-five Democrats to just seventeen Republicans. The GOP members included several who would make their mark, including Reps. Henry J. Hyde of Illinois and Bill Goodling of Pennsylvania (both of whom survived to become committee chairmen in the 104th Congress), as well as Bill Gradison of Ohio and the

Les AuCoin is sworn in by Speaker Carl Albert in January 1975, becoming the first Democratic House member from the northwest corner of Oregon since the 1890s.

incomparable Millicent H. Fenwick of New Jersey (the model for Lacey Davenport in the "Doonesbury" comic strip). Several of the Republicans first elected that fall would later move to the Senate (Larry Pressler of Ohio, Bob Kasten of Wisconsin, Charles E. Grassley of Iowa, and James M. Jeffords of Vermont).

But when people talked about the Watergate babies, they meant the Democrats. They were young—half of them not yet forty years old. Many were self-starter candidates who had sought their nominations without the aid—or even against the will—of local party and labor organizations. One newcomer, Protestant minister Robert W. Edgar from suburban Philadelphia, had begun his campaign by looking up the Democratic Party's number in the phone book.

They were also intensely ambitious. The class included future governors James J. Blanchard of Michigan and James J. Florio of New Jersey. It also included five Democrats who would later be elected to the Senate: Tim Wirth of Colorado, Max Baucus of Montana, Christo-

pher J. Dodd of Connecticut, Tom Harkin of Iowa, and Paul Simon of Illinois. Many more would end their careers trying for the Senate or for governorships.

Typically, the Watergate babies received their first campaign training as volunteers for presidential "peace candidates" in 1968 and 1972. (One such young Democrat, Bill Clinton, was nominated for a House seat from Arkansas but lost.)

As Wirth would sum it up a decade later: "We were the children of Vietnam, not World War II. We were products of television, not of print. We were products of computer politics, not courthouse politics. And we were reflections of JFK as president, not FDR."

Most of these new Democrats had not simply inherited traditional party districts but had wrested their jobs away from the GOP. The two most senior members of the House minority were defeated by upstart Democrats in long-held GOP territory. The massacre reached all levels of seniority and spread to all regions. Recent Republican gains in the South were rolled back, as ten of the party's seats in the region reverted to the Democrats.

New York elected eleven freshmen in 1974, one-fourth of its delegation, and every one was a Democrat. Among the least probable were Long Island's Thomas J. Downey, who at twenty-five would be the youngest member of Congress since the early 1800s, and Ithaca's Matthew J. McHugh, whose base had last gone Democratic for the House in 1912.

Paul E. Tsongas became the first Democrat elected to the House from Lowell, Massachusetts, in the twentieth century. Les AuCoin became the first Democrat elected from Oregon's northwest corner since the 1890s. And in rural Indiana, a college professor named Philip R. Sharp became the first Democrat to represent his part of the state since it was admitted to the Union.

Within days of the election, early birds among the House freshmen were landing on Capitol Hill to prepare for the December party meetings that would organize the chamber for the new session. Wirth even set about interviewing staff for a freshman caucus. Senior House Democrats would grudgingly assign the group "office space" in a closet in the basement of the Longworth building, where exposed pipes gurgled to announce every toilet flush from the floors above.

There were those, however, who took the new kids seriously. Urban liberals such as Richard Bolling of Kansas City, Missouri, Phillip Burton of San Francisco, and James G. O'Hara of Detroit had been battling the seniority-based power system that long had favored rural conservatives. They had pushed through a new rule subjecting all committee chairmen to an approval vote by all Democratic members of the House at the start of each Congress. The next vote would include the seventy-five members of the Class of 1974.

"We actually had the audacity to hold meetings at which we interviewed the committee chairmen," recalled Sharp. "It was extraordinary. I'm not sure we were totally aware how different that was."

One chairman who ignored the class's invitation to chat was F. Edward Hebert, a seventeen-termer from Louisiana and chairman of the Armed Services Committee. Hebert saw no reason to kowtow to any freshmen—until his staff explained the veiled threat of a bloc vote against him in caucus. Hebert acceded to a Saturday session with the freshmen, but could not quite bring himself to bend the knee. At one point in his interview, he even referred to the assembled members-elect as "boys and girls," prompting stares of disbelief. When the caucus met to vote on committee chairmanships in early January 1975, Hebert lost by nineteen votes, with all but a few of the freshmen voting against him.

Another high-profile victim that January was W. R. "Wild Bill" Poage of Waco, Texas, who had been running the Agriculture Committee for more than a decade. Poage thought he had little to fear from the new class, in part because Thomas S. Foley of Washington, the chairman of the left-leaning Democratic Study Group and a popular figure among the younger members, was in his corner. Foley made a memorable speech to the caucus urging Poage's reelection. But when the votes were in, Poage had done poorly with the freshmen and lost. Foley was elected in his place.

Also riding the tumbrel that day was Wright Patman, the legendary populist chairman of the House Banking and Currency Committee and another Texan. Patman in his eighties still made a show of bearding governors of the Federal Reserve Board who testified before him. But he had been born in 1893 and was simply too old-school for the new generation.

The dismissal of these three senior barons not only established the rule of the caucus over the committee structure but elevated the status of junior members within the caucus. No chair-

Ways and Means Chairman Wilbur Mills met his downfall after an embarrassing public incident with an exotic dancer.

man could now afford to ignore any Democratic member, regardless of committee assignment or longevity.

But the feudal system of the House suffered more that winter from the downfall of Wilbur Mills of Arkansas, the longtime chairman of Ways and Means. And while Mills's story was principally one of self-destruction, the votes of the Watergate babies pushed him off the ledge.

Mills had first been elected in 1938 at the age of twenty-nine and had been chairman of Ways and Means since 1958. Committee Democrats, in addition to handling all legislation on taxes, trade, welfare, and Social Security, also made all the majority party's assignments to all the other standing committees of the House (as they had since 1911).

Mills had peopled his panel with allies over the years, building his power over other members' careers. A master of both the substance and the politics of his legislative realm, Mills at sixty-five had accumulated as much power as one man could in Congress and easily eclipsed his party's lackluster Speaker, Carl Albert of Oklahoma.

But in October 1974, police in Washington stopped a speeding car in the wee hours near the Tidal Basin. A woman burst from the vehicle, ran to the water's edge, and flung herself in. Rescued from the chilly water, she turned out to be an exotic dancer named Annabella Battistella, performing in Washington under the nom de plume "Fanne Foxe, the Argentine Firecracker." Back in the car, police found the portly Mills slumped in the back seat, his face scratched and bleeding, apparently too drunk to attempt an escape.

Although his Arkansas district reelected him that fall, Mills was weakened on the Hill. Reformers were able to round up the votes for a rules change enlarging Ways and Means from twenty-five seats to thirty-seven and diluting Mills's influence. They got the votes they needed from the Class of 1974. Mills offered Representative Burton a compromise plan in the week of Thanksgiving but was told it was too late. The chairman was, by some reports, despondent.

That weekend, the wire services carried a photo of him shuffling onto a Boston burlesque stage during a performance by Fanne Foxe. Mills was admitted to a hospital for observation. Within days, the caucus decided that all committee assignments would henceforth be made by the Steering and Policy Committee. In January, Mills offered no resistance when the caucus leaders moved to replace him as chairman of Ways and Means.

In retrospect, the significance of the Class of 1974 seems beyond dispute. The election of that fall stalled a general Republican advance in Congress, postponing the equilibrium correction between the two parties that would otherwise have been expected in the mid-1970s by historical precedents. It took the GOP two full decades to recover.

Legislatively, the class helped prevent the Ford administration from building a record prior to the presidential election of 1976. Beyond that, the class made major contributions to the energy and environmental legislation of the decade and lent the votes that powered the postwar Democratic reform efforts in the House to their apogee.

Yet the memory of the Watergate class has been tinged with rue and even bitterness. In part because much of the reform agenda was accomplished within scant weeks of the new class's arrival, the remainder of their first term had a feeling of anticlimax. Divisions emerged: energy issues split the class by region; abortion split it by religion. "Anyone who thought the freshmen would be doing anything together beyond the first month was mistaken," said class member David W. Evans of Indiana.

Soon, the frustration of congressional routine set in and recriminations began. Bob Carr of Michigan, a former campus radical who remained a firebrand as a House freshman, provided a symbolic example in June 1975 when he gave an angry floor speech calling on Albert to resign as Speaker. Not a single voice was raised in support of Carr, and more than a few of his classmates were embarrassed at the outburst.

"We had a manic-depressive six months," said Tsongas. "The system has swallowed us up," said Norman Y. Mineta, a California class member who would serve more than two decades. "Maybe we were a little oversold from the beginning," said class member Mark W. Hannaford of California.

Over the years, the Class of 1974 would account for few leaders in the caucus: Butler Der-

rick of South Carolina became a chief deputy whip before retiring in 1994. In contrast, the "Watergate echo" class elected two years later could boast a majority leader and a majority whip (Richard A. Gephardt of Missouri and David E. Bonior of Michigan, respectively).

In fact, the most meaningful posts to be occupied by the Watergate babies over the years have been in the committee system they once voted to subordinate to the caucus. (In the last two years of Democratic majority control in the 103d Congress, class members Mineta, George Miller of California, and John J. LaFalce of New York were chairmen of standing committees, while classmates Carr, Sharp, Henry A. Waxman of California, Harold E. Ford of Tennessee, and Andrew Jacobs Jr. of Indiana chaired major subcommittees.)

In retrospect, the most permanent accomplishment of the class seemed to be its survival. "They decided the most important thing in the world was to get reelected, no matter what," said senior Iowa Democrat Neal Smith. "The day they hit here they started campaigning for the next election."

Bringing in computers, aggressively pursuing media attention, and raising the art of constituent service to new heights, the class helped bring the phrase "entrenched incumbent" into vogue. Although most big classes pay a high price in the next election, only two Watergate babies who sought a second House term in 1976 were denied.

Richard M. Nixon's fall from power reverberated long enough to dominate not only the midterm election cycle of 1974 but also the presidential cycle of 1976. Jimmy Carter emerged in the early Democratic primaries largely by projecting an image of directness and simplicity in contrast to Nixon's devious worldliness. Carter spoke of America needing a government "as it good as its people."

As a former one-term governor, Carter had the least government experience of the major candidates in 1976. Apart from his Navy years, he had spent his life in Georgia. But in the climate of the mid-1970s, these facts were seen more as assets than liabilities. He appealed to farmers as a former peanut grower. He appealed to religious conservatives as an unabashed Baptist—"a born-again Christian." And he even did well with African Americans, who respected his record of opposition to racism.

In the fall campaign, Carter was able to hang Nixon around the neck of President Gerald R. Ford. It was not just that Ford had been chosen by Nixon, but that Ford had granted his disgraced predecessor a blanket pardon for any crimes committed. While others went to jail for their roles in Watergate, the former president could not even be charged. For all who sensed something wrong in this, Ford would always be tainted.

Once in office, Carter pursued an agenda of extraordinary ambition. He papered Capitol Hill with proposals to revamp welfare and the tax code and congressional budgeting. He wanted the country to treat his energy program as "the moral equivalent of war." Carter and his Georgia coterie were brimming with ideas on the domestic front, but most met with cool receptions, at best, in Congress.

Frustrated at many turns on domestic policy, Carter had remarkable success in his first ventures into foreign policy. He will always be remembered for the peace accords signed by Israel and Egypt at Camp David in 1978, five years after the Yom Kippur war. In 1979, however, Carter suffered terrible reversals in foreign affairs—the unforeseen revolution in Iran, the taking of American hostages in Tehran, and the Soviet invasion of Afghanistan.

In each of these episodes, Carter was seen as a good-hearted idealist brought up short by the hard realities of the world. One reason he was cast in this Wilsonian caricature was his insistence on discussing politics in terms of good and evil, right and wrong. But American conservatives also had come to view Carter as dangerously naive because he had "given away" the Panama Canal, which had been a U.S. asset since the earliest years of the century.

Carter saw the canal as an asset best preserved by a transfer of responsibility to the host country. Many others in academia and politics saw it the same way, including many Republicans and even some conservatives as unassailable as William F. Buckley. But by securing Senate consent in the Panama treaty in 1978, Carter may have guaranteed bad reviews of his performance in the crises of 1979 and 1980.

= 1977 =

War of Words Over the Canal

Phil Duncan

On the first Saturday in November 1977, as a big crowd assembled at Neyland Stadium in Knoxville for the University of Tennessee football game, there was trouble in the air. Not for the home-team Volunteers, who won, but for one of the spectators: Tennessee senator Howard H. Baker Jr.

Circling above the stadium was a light plane towing a banner with the message, "Save Our Canal." The airborne exhortation reminded Baker that conservative GOP activists were intent on thwarting President Jimmy Carter's plans to shift the Panama Canal to the jurisdiction of Panama. Baker, leader of the Republican minority in the Senate, had yet to take a position.

Baker's coolness had irked many on the GOP right, who did not see the issue as a close call: ceding control of the canal diminished U.S. prestige, they felt. The waterway had been a symbol that projected America's power abroad ever since construction began in the administration of Republican president Theodore Roosevelt in the early 1900s.

A leading spokesman for the "Save Our Canal" movement was former California governor Ronald Reagan. He had made the waterway an issue in his 1976 bid for the GOP presidential nomination, often proclaiming, "We bought it, we paid for it, we built it and we intend to keep it."

During eight months of intense dispute beginning in September 1977, the canal debate would reveal deep fissures between and within the parties over the proper course of American foreign policy. It also renewed the historic struggle between the executive and legislative powers for control over that policy. And it foreshadowed much of the ideological clash that would dominate the pivotal presidential election of 1980.

Soon after nudging Gerald R. Ford from the White House in the 1976 election, Carter served notice that shifting control of the canal to Panama would be a centerpiece of his efforts to change the image of American foreign policy. It would symbolize a "new partnership" with the peoples of Latin America, "vivid proof . . . that a new era of friendship and cooperation is beginning, and that what they regard as a last remnant of American colonialism is being removed."

In the previous three administrations, there were discussions with Panama over changing the canal's status. Carter put the talks on a fast track, entrusting them to veteran foreign policy hands Sol M. Linowitz and Ellsworth Bunker. In March 1977, they announced substantial agreement with Panama on the language of a new treaty.

From the outset, however, the new treaty language sparked controversy not only in the United States but also in Panama, where it was attacked by both the left and the nationalist right. Both sides argued that Panama's leader, Brig. Gen. Omar Torrijos, owed his position to the United States and therefore could not hold out for Panama's best interests in negotiations.

The Panama Canal Zone, shown during a 1906 visit by President Theodore Roosevelt, had been under U.S. control for more than seventy years when Jimmy Carter sought a change in its status.

In June 1977 Carter administration officials acknowledged that domestic resistance to ceding the canal was significant enough that the Senate could not muster the two-thirds vote needed for approval. Carter, getting personally involved in wooing skeptics, said America would keep "partial sovereignty" over the Canal Zone until 2000 and subsequently retain the right to defend the canal, ensuring U.S. ships priority passage in emergencies.

In August, treaty negotiators announced an agreement "in principle," and a September 7 signing ceremony was scheduled for Washington. Carter and Torrijos initialed two treaties, one setting out the terms of transferring the canal to full Panamanian control by December 31, 1999, and a second giving the United States an indefinite right to assure the neutrality of the canal from any threat.

Determined to secure an aura of bipartisan respectability for the treaties, Carter dispatched teams to brief Ford and former secretary of state Henry Kissinger on them. Ford and Kissinger both subsequently declared that ratification was "in the national interest of the United States." Those two endorsements and one later from actor John Wayne were public relations coups, but scarcely guaranteed Senate approval.

Less than a week after the signing ceremony, the leader of the president's party in the Senate, Robert C. Byrd of West Virginia, declared that the treaties would not come to the Senate floor until 1978, insisting that earlier consideration would result in their defeat. An August Gallup Poll survey reported 47 percent opposing ratification and 37 percent in favor.

For the rest of the year, conservative opponents of turning over the canal vigorously attacked. They aimed to convince voters that the treaties were a unilateral U.S. surrender of prestige. Sen. Strom Thurmond of South Carolina said that with Panama in charge of the canal, it would soon come under the control of the Soviet Union and Cuba.

Republican senator Bob Dole of Kansas and other critics proposed numerous amendments aimed at correcting alleged flaws and omissions in the documents. But Carter's State Department called these "killer" amendments, requiring a reopening of formal negotiations with Panama.

In late September, Byrd began talking about structuring consideration of the treaties so as to allow senators to propose "reservations or understandings" in lieu of formal amendments. He said such legislative vehicles would influence the future interpretation and administration of the treaties without necessitating any renegotiation. Over the next six months, the "reservations and understandings" avenue was heavily traveled by senators on both sides of the issue and even by the administration itself.

In October, Dole called attention to a confidential State Department cablegram sent from the American Embassy in Panama that he said showed "vast differences of interpretation" between the two countries on major provisions in the treaties, especially regarding the American right to defend the canal after 1999. State Department spokesman Hodding Carter III criticized Dole for publicizing the cable, but before the month was out, Carter and Torrijos had issued a statement clarifying the neutrality treaty.

Both the United States and Panama, the statement said, "shall have the right to act against any aggression or threat directed against the canal." Further, both countries' ships would be allowed "to go to the head of the line of vessels in order to transit the canal rapidly" in emergencies.

With an eye on Panamanian sensibilities, the statement also stipulated that the neutrality treaty granted America no "right of intervention . . . in the internal affairs of Panama," and that any U.S. military action to protect the canal "shall never be directed against the territorial integrity or political independence of Panama." Far from being mollified, many critics of the treaties saw Carter's and Torrijos's effort at clarification as proof that the treaty needed to be amended or rejected outright.

In the U.S. news media, there was growing criticism that the Carter administration was so mired in Panama that American diplomacy in other areas was suffering. Clearly, the campaign for the treaties needed a boost.

On October 23 the Torrijos government trumpeted the outcome of a plebiscite on the treaties that endorsed them by better than 2 to 1. The following month, in a dramatic gesture that energized the process, Torrijos pledged he would resign if the U.S. Senate felt he was an obstacle to passage of the treaties.

Torrijos made the promise to a group of seven senators he had invited to his summer home. One of them was Byrd, who returned to Washington sounding more upbeat. By December, he had scheduled the start of floor debate for February, and he was predicting the president would prevail.

Treaty advocates also were encouraged in late 1977 that Minority Leader Baker continued to study the pacts and keep his counsel in the face of intense pressure from the GOP right. In addition to efforts such as the aerial lobbying at the Tennessee football game, Baker reported receiving about 22,000 letters on the treaties, fewer than 500 favoring ratification.

Among those working to mobilize grassroots opposition to the treaties, the ardor was akin to the final weeks of a close election campaign. Two of the most active groups, the American Conservative Union and the Conservative Caucus, reported raising and spending nearly $1.5 million by early 1978. Many who fought the treaties later became the leaders and soldiers of the "Reagan Revolution" that in 1980 propelled the Californian into the White House.

On January 16, Howard Phillips, national director of the Conservative Caucus, was asked

Carter and Torrijos initial the Panama Canal treaties on September 7, 1977. In the ratification fight, crucial support came from Senate GOP leader Howard H. Baker Jr., who conditioned his vote on inclusion of language guaranteeing both countries' right to defend the canal.

by Congressional Quarterly how treaty opponents were faring in their fight. "Right now," he said, "I think we are losing." That day, Baker's long-awaited decision had come: he would support ratification, provided the Senate could add a "package of guarantees" on major defense provisions, along the lines of the Carter-Torrijos statement of understanding.

Three days earlier, Byrd had removed any lingering doubts about his position by declaring that he would vote for the treaties "and work for their approval." Like Baker, Byrd advised adding "some form" of language to the pacts clarifying America's right to defend the canal and to assure that U.S. ships could get priority passage in any emergency. Another boost for ratification came January 30, when the Senate Foreign Relations Committee voted with only

one dissent to send the treaties (including the October statement of understanding) to the floor.

Carter laid out his case for the treaties in two addresses to the nation, first in his State of the Union speech January 19 and then in a February 1 "fireside chat" from the White House.

The first day of the ratification debate by the full Senate, February 8, was carried live on National Public Radio (the first time Senate proceedings had been so broadcast). Senators faced a two-step process: first under consideration was the neutrality pact, which spelled out U.S. rights and responsibilities in defending the canal after 2000 and in sending its warships through the waterway in emergencies. Second, senators would vote on the basic treaty turning the canal over to Panama by the end of 1999.

Supporters were said to have sixty-two votes. They were five shy of two-thirds, but they easily mustered the simple majority needed to defeat a series of "killer amendments" in the course of several weeks.

Still, even after agreeing to include the October statement of understanding with the treaty, proponents were short of sixty-seven votes until two more concessions by Senate leaders broke the logjam.

First, Georgia Democrats Herman E. Talmadge and Sam Nunn announced for the treaty March 14 after the leadership agreed to support a reservation they proposed. It stated that the pact did not prevent the United States and Panama from working out an agreement in the future for basing U.S. troops there after 1999.

Second, treaty proponents won over freshman Democrat Dennis DeConcini of Arizona after he talked with Carter in mid-March and won support for his reservation. It allowed the United States "to use military force in Panama" after 2000 to keep the canal open if it were closed for any reason.

Shortly before the vote, a few other senators moved into the "yea" column, partly out of concern that Carter's authority to conduct foreign policy would be undermined by defeat of the treaty. Democrat Russell B. Long of Louisiana said March 15 that the "moral leadership" of the United States overseas would be compromised if the treaty was rejected.

On March 16, with all 100 senators answering the roll call from their desks, the neutrality pact was ratified, 68-32. Byrd said that had proponents been short of sixty-seven votes, he could have relied on a switch by "three or four" of the senators who voted against the treaty.

With that victory secured, the leadership felt fairly confident about prospects for the basic treaty. But that confidence soon was shaken by

an outpouring of anger from Panama over the DeConcini reservation. Many in that country felt it gave the United States a free pass to exercise "gunboat diplomacy" in Panama. Torrijos fired off letters of complaint to Carter and to 115 heads of state through their representatives at the United Nations.

The Senate put off a final vote on the basic treaty until after the Easter recess. Conservative groups mobilized a last-ditch effort to influence senators at home for the break.

Meanwhile, administration officials talked with DeConcini to try to find a way out of the dilemma. But they made no headway, and the Senate leadership asked the White House and the State Department to back off and leave the negotiations to the Senate alone. The Senate's next scheduled floor session on ratification was canceled, reportedly for fear that senators' arguments might further inflame the Panamanians.

On Sunday, April 16, Byrd and the treaties' floor managers, Frank Church, D-Idaho, and Paul S. Sarbanes, D-Md., met with the Panamanian ambassador and Deputy Secretary of State Warren Christopher with a compromise in hand that DeConcini could accept. A reservation would be added to the basic treaty stating that the United States would not intervene in the "internal affairs of Panama" or interfere with "its political independence or sovereign integrity" in the course of keeping the canal open, neutral, and secure. Torrijos's government accepted the compromise.

Still, treaty proponents remained anxious. Three other senators who had voted for the neutrality pact were, for various reasons, wavering on the basic treaty. In the end, they stiffened. The April 18 tally for ratification was 68-32, as all senators voted just as they had on the neutrality pact.

T he political phenomenon of Ronald Wilson Reagan began with Barry M. Goldwater's ill-fated presidential campaign of 1964. Late in that lopsided contest, the Republican Party bought an expensive block of time on national television and entrusted it to Reagan. Although years past his prime as a movie actor and television personality, Reagan delivered a personal pitch for Goldwater that sang.

Two years later, he was nominated for governor of California and defeated the supposedly unbeatable Edmund G. "Pat" Brown. Two years after that, his star was rising so fast in the party that he launched a brief bid for the presidential nomination, bowing out just before the convention nominated Richard M. Nixon. Running for reelection in 1972, Nixon would call Reagan the "superstar" of his campaign.

By 1974 Reagan had completed two terms as governor and was ready for another challenge; he considered running for the Senate. But it looked like a Democratic year, so he waited for his next opportunity. It came quickly, with Nixon's resignation and Gerald R. Ford's elevation to the presidency. Reagan gave the new man a little more than a year before declaring him insufficiently conservative and entering the 1976 presidential primaries himself.

Ford ran a rather lackluster campaign, but eked out a close win in the New Hampshire primary. Reagan made a comeback in North Carolina in March and contested the nomination all the way to the convention in Kansas City. After that defeat, it appeared that Reagan, sixty-five years old, had seen his last race. But he stayed alive on radio during the later 1970s, and the Panama Canal debate seemed to revitalize him. He entered the Republican primaries in 1980 as the man to beat. He lost the Iowa caucuses to George Bush, but won New Hampshire in convincing fashion and swept the important events thereafter en route to smooth nomination in Detroit that July.

The Democratic convention was a comparatively ragged affair. Sen. Edward M. Kennedy had contested the nomination, and, while he did not come close to displacing President Jimmy Carter, his challenge divided the party and made a vulnerable incumbent more so. Americans were still being held hostage inside the U.S. embassy in Tehran. And the "misery index" Carter had spoken about as a candidate in 1976—the combination of the unemployment rate and the inflation rate—had doubled during his presidency. Reagan would find a simple theme in the fall campaign by asking voters: "Are you better off than you were four years ago?"

Launching the general election campaign in September, Reagan stood on the steps of the Capitol with a crowd of Republican congressional candidates and signed a pledge. It said that, if elected, they would work together to enact a tax cut worth 10 percent a year for three years—across the board, for all brackets. The bill was named for sponsors Jack F. Kemp in the House and William V. Roth Jr. in the Senate.

The Reagan Revolution

Robert W. Merry

The week of Ronald Reagan's inauguration as the fortieth president of the United States, in January 1981, *Time* magazine hit the newsstands with a cover that pictured a crumbling dollar sign and the headline: "Reagan's Biggest Challenge: Mending the Economy." *Newsweek* was more blunt: "The Economy in Crisis," blared its cover that week, "Why It's Out of Control."

Reagan assumed national stewardship on a balmy January Tuesday amid widespread feelings that the country was indeed in crisis. Unemployment was at 7.4 percent that month. The economy, as measured by the gross national product, had declined 1.9 percent the previous year. The prime interest rate stood at a commerce-crunching 21 percent. And inflation, that insidious thief that siphons off economic value wherever it can be found, was approaching an ominous 12 percent.

"What the Great Depression was to the 1930s," said economist Walter Heller, "the Great Inflation is to the 1980s." In a widely quoted postelection memorandum, Rep. David A. Stockman, R-Mich., soon to be Reagan's budget director, declared the nation to be on the brink of "an economic Dunkirk."

It was into this miasma of trouble and trauma that Reagan marched, first as an unlikely inheritor of national leadership, then as a bold innovator full of resolve and confidence. The country's economic ills had arisen over many decades, he told Americans that inaugural Tuesday, and they would not go away in mere weeks or months. "But they will go away," he said in the familiar and reassuring voice that was becoming his primary political weapon. "They will go away because we as Americans have the capacity now, as we have had in the past, to do whatever needs to be done to preserve this last and greatest bastion of freedom."

Reagan, approaching his seventieth birthday as his presidency began, brought to the economic wars a new weapon called supply-side economics. This beguilingly simple doctrine held that the economy was being stifled by high tax rates that suppressed economic initiative and verve. The concentration was on "marginal tax rates"— the rates imposed on the last dollar earned. Those were the rates, argued the supply-siders, that sapped Americans' zest for saving, working, and investing. Slash those rates, they maintained, and the economy would come roaring back.

Indeed, said the supply-siders in what was to become their most controversial argument, the resulting rush of economic activity would generate ever-greater tax revenues, filling up federal coffers, and attacking the government's persistent budget deficits in a most painless way.

But the new president wouldn't rely exclusively on this supply-side bonanza to subdue the deficit. He would attack the federal government and shrink the leviathan state. As *Newsweek* put it on a February cover featuring new budget director Stockman: "Cut, Slash, Chop."

David Stockman, who left Congress to be Reagan's program-slashing budget director, said at the dawn of the administration that the country faced "an economic Dunkirk."

The plan was, first, to slash or kill scores of federal programs, including food stamps, rural electrification, make-work jobs programs, urban development grants, synthetic fuels subsidies, and trade assistance for workers displaced by foreign competition. Second, the call was for a 33 percent cut in individual income tax rates over three years.

Capital gains taxes would be slashed to 20 percent from 28 percent, and for business there would be drastically streamlined depreciation schedules, allowing corporations to write off investments in plant and equipment much faster.

All this, said Reagan, would remove the deadening hand of government from the dynamos of commerce and return the nation to those heady years of the 1950s and 1960s when economic growth fueled the nation and ensured its destiny.

The country seemed ready for such a mix of revolution and conservatism. The election that had swept Reagan into power the previous November had also given the Republicans control of the Senate for the first time in twenty-six years. And, in the House, the Democrats' margin of control was narrower than it had been in recent memory. With only 243 members, the majority leadership would lose control of the floor if only twenty-six Democrats allied themselves with the GOP on a given vote.

Reagan turned to the television airwaves as the medium for his forceful yet folksy rhetoric to stir up support among the masses, who in turn would send waves of political pressure back to Washington. The aim was to unleash the political equivalent of a tank offensive, to roll over the congressional Democrats and their steadfast and wily national leader in Washington.

The Democrats' leader was Thomas P. "Tip" O'Neill of Massachusetts, the white-maned polar bear of a man who served as Speaker of the House and personified the Democratic philosophy of government that Reagan sought to obliterate. O'Neill had once boasted about getting a grant into the federal budget to fund research on how to increase the height of an average dwarf by a couple inches. In light of the Reagan election, he said, he knew that sort of thing had become unfashionable, but he added, "I'm proud of what I did."

Reagan and O'Neill were both likable Irishmen who shared an easy back-slapping manner. But they were not destined to get along. Reagan's men had bristled when the president-elect had traveled to Capitol Hill for a visit with the Speaker and O'Neill said with a certain condescension: "You're in the big leagues now." Later, during a postinauguration meeting, the Speaker chastised the president for not providing enough details in his economic plan. "It shocks me how he talks to a president," one Reagan aide told *Newsweek*.

Reagan set out with dramatic flair to show he was ready for the big leagues. In the weeks after his inauguration he dominated the airwaves and the national debate with his avuncular political rhetoric.

On February 5, he addressed the nation from the Oval Office and presented a stinging critique of recent economic policy and a ringing call for support. He held up a dollar bill, describing it as "a dollar such as you earned, spent or saved in 1960." Then he reached into his trouser pocket and pulled out a quarter, a dime, and a penny.

"Thirty-six cents," he said. "That's what this 1960 dollar is worth today."

He held up charts showing trend lines in federal spending and federal taxes. "As you can see," he said, "the spending line rises at a steeper slant than the revenue line."

Two weeks later he addressed a joint session of Congress. "The people are watching and waiting," he warned the members. "They don't demand miracles. They do expect us to act. Let us act together."

Then on March 30 an event occurred that at first threatened to halt Reagan's revolution—but in the end gave it new force. As the president left the Washington Hilton Hotel after a noon speech, a young gunman named John Hinckley unleashed a barrage of pistol fire. One hollow-nosed bullet struck the president's limousine, skidded along a rear panel, flattened out into the shape of a dime, and then sliced into the president's torso below the armpit. It glanced off the seventh rib and plunged into his lung.

Secret Service agents shoved Reagan into the rear of the limo and sped off to George Washington University Hospital, where the president underwent emergency surgery. "I forgot to duck," he said with a smile when his wife, Nancy, stricken with fear, arrived. That breezy line, recounted to the nation, conveyed an impression of a president facing mortal danger with heroic joviality. It wasn't until later that the nation learned just how close to death—and how shaken—the president was.

The convalescence was remarkably rapid for a man of Reagan's age, and by April 28 he was back in the thick of battle, addressing another joint session of Congress on the nation's need for his economic prescriptions. "The American people," he declared, " . . . demand, and they have earned, a full and comprehensive effort to clean up our economic mess." His words—and the nation's sympathy for the wounded president—provided powerful thrust to his program.

Only a few months after taking a would-be assassin's bullet outside the Washington Hilton, President Reagan celebrates passage of his tax cut package with congressional allies in the Oval Office.

Meanwhile, his program was making its way through the thickets of Congress. On the day of Reagan's April 28 speech, the Senate Budget Committee met, and Chairman Pete V. Domenici, R-N.M., was able to shepherd through a budget resolution that comported with the president's plan.

Already the House Budget Committee, under the leadership of the conservative James R. Jones, D-Okla., had approved a stringent fiscal blueprint that moved in Reagan's direction—calling for about $15 billion in spending cuts in fiscal 1982. Jones had hoped to create a bipartisan consensus in his committee, but he couldn't. At the urging of the White House, Republicans refused to sign on, offering a more stringent fiscal plan of their own. They were rebuffed.

But on the House floor May 7 the full force of Reaganism was felt. Despite desperate Democratic efforts to hold the party's conservative flank, it crumbled. Sixty-three Democrats joined with all the chamber's Republicans to adopt the GOP plan, which called for $36.6 billion in fiscal 1982 cuts. House Republican leader Robert H. Michel of Illinois predicted before the vote that it would redirect the nation.

"Let history show that we provided the margin of difference that changed the course of American government," he said.

Five days later the Senate followed suit, adopting its resolution by a 78-20 vote. The minor differences between the two versions were ironed out easily in conference, and both chambers quickly approved the conference report. That set the stage in the summer for a subsequent showdown over a budget-reconciliation bill needed to enforce the fiscal savings called for in the budget resolution.

Meanwhile, the tax issue was moving along a parallel track. The Senate Finance Committee, led by Chairman Bob Dole, R-Kan., easily approved a three-year tax plan that was almost identical to the president's proposal (although the individual tax-rate cut was scaled back to 25 percent over three years). That placed considerable pressure on the Democratic-controlled House Ways and Means Committee and its new chairman, Dan Rostenkowski of Illinois.

Rostenkowski sought a middle ground, opting for a scaled-back tax cut plan that he said had the spirit of Reaganism but avoided fiscal irresponsibility. Like Jones on the budget, Rostenkowski hoped his proposal would form the basis for an eventual compromise. But the Republicans were not buying.

Treasury Secretary Donald T. Regan declared the chairman's tax cuts "puny," and the White House signaled it would seek to roll the chairman on the House floor.

What followed would become famous as "the bidding war." Hoping to build support for their respective plans, the White House and Rostenkowski each threw in juicy tax provisions benefiting specific interest groups: tax breaks for the oil industry, big corporate preferences, quicker depreciation schedules.

In Ways and Means, Rostenkowski placed the Reagan plan aside and marked up his own proposal. It was approved by his committee on a party-line vote July 23. As the issue headed for the House floor, it appeared it could go either way—for Reagan or for Rostenkowski.

But by going to the airwaves once again in a July 27 appeal to the nation, Reagan turned the tide in his favor. He generated a barrage of support from across the country that proved irresistible to skittish Democratic lawmakers, forty-eight of whom crossed over to support the president's plan. It passed the House on July 29, 238-195.

It was a dramatic moment. The *Wall Street Journal* article on the bill called Congress's action on taxes "a giant stride in the direction of experimental economics." Senate Republican leader Howard H. Baker Jr. of Tennessee echoed that sentiment in stronger language. The Reagan tax plan that was soon to become law, he said, was "a riverboat gamble."

Two days later the conference report on the reconciliation-spending bill reached both House and Senate and cleared both by overwhelming margins. By now, it was abundantly clear that Reagan was in command of fiscal policy. Each time a vote was called for, greater numbers of Democrats defected to the president's banner.

But if the final votes on July 31 were a bit anticlimactic, nobody missed their significance. House Budget Committee Chairman Jones called the final actions "clearly the most monumental and historic turnaround in fiscal policy that has ever occurred." Said Reagan: "The simple truth is that Congress heard the voice of the people, and they acted to carry out the will of the people."

Ronald Reagan's first year in the Oval Office is remembered primarily for its successes. In addition to securing federal spending cuts and tax rate reductions, the new president in 1981 appointed the first woman justice of the Supreme Court, broke the air traffic controllers' strike, and survived a gunshot wound at close range. Even NASA's newest advance, the space shuttle *Columbia*, won plaudits in a test run.

But the nation's ailing economy was slow to respond to treatment, largely because interest rates remained high. In 1979 President Jimmy Carter had appointed Paul Volcker chairman of the Federal Reserve. Volker's task was to reduce the double-digit inflation spurred by the oil shock of the Iranian crisis, and he proved that a Fed chairman appointed by a Democrat could be as tight as any Republican appointee.

His money policy brought inflation down, but it also caused a recession in 1980 that contributed to Carter's defeat in November. Although the economy improved for a while in 1981, Volcker remained worried about the consumer price index and kept a firm grip on the money supply. The economy turned truly sour in 1982. By November unemployment reached 10.4 percent, the highest reported since 1940.

Republicans in Congress ran for reelection that fall insisting that the downturn was temporary. The GOP slogan was "Stay the Course"—give the new Reaganomics a chance to turn the economy around. But voters can be fickle, especially in hard times, and many feared that the extended period of postwar growth had finally sputtered out. This economic insecurity made people wonder about the adequacy of the "safety net" Reagan had promised to preserve.

All this, plus the pendulum swing back from the 1980 election, contributed to a solid comeback for the Democrats in 1982. Democrats won twenty of the thirty-three Senate seats on the ballot and took back three-fourths of the ground they had lost in 1980 in the House. The conservative coalition that had dominated Congress for two years was weakened. The first, intoxicating phase of the Reagan era had passed.

As if to prove the point, 1983 was a year of great difficulty for the administration. In October, 241 American troops, part of a peacekeeping force in Beirut, were killed by a suicide truck bomber. That same week, however, U.S. forces flexed their muscles in the Caribbean, overrunning a weak Marxist government on the island of Grenada. The justification was the protection of American students there, but Latin America took the invasion as a demonstration and a warning. The White House had become increasingly alarmed about the behavior of the Sandinista government in Nicaragua, and many believed military intervention there was imminent.

Indeed, many of the strategists of the State and Defense Departments in the early 1980s wanted to commit U.S. forces in Central America. But it was clear that Congress, including the reinforced Democratic majority in the House, would resist.

= 1985 =

Reagan and the Rebels

Anne Q. Hoy

Secretary of State George P. Shultz and national security adviser Robert C. McFarlane watched over the Senate from gallery seats reserved for distinguished guests. They were certain that the White House had mounted its best effort. Now the chips would have to fall where they may.

At stake was an administration request for a comparatively minuscule amount of money: $14 million. However, the money was for a controversial element of President Ronald Reagan's Central America policy, and the next two days would determine how fully the president was in command of U.S. foreign policy.

It was April 1985, nearly six months after Reagan had retained the White House by overwhelming Democrat Walter F. Mondale in every state save Minnesota, Mondale's home state. With that mandate, Reagan hoped to provide direct assistance to the Nicaraguan Democratic Force, about 15,000 insurgents opposed to the leftist Sandinista-led government in Nicaragua. A year earlier, the Democratic-controlled House had succeeded in blocking covert aid to the rebels.

Shultz and McFarlane, the president's point men, came to the gallery on April 23 to ensure that the Republican-controlled Senate, despite its own misgivings, would continue to support the administration's murky Nicaraguan policy. Riding on the outcome of this vote was any chance the administration might have to prevail in the House.

Congressional and public support for U.S. involvement in the war in Nicaragua had always been tentative, and some recent blunders had weakened it further. The CIA had directed the mining of Nicaraguan harbors a year earlier—using what it called "unilaterally controlled Latino assets"—and had failed to inform Congress adequately about the operation. The agency also had a hand in a number of seaport raids in Nicaragua in 1983 and in a manual that called for U.S.-backed rebels "to neutralize" Nicaraguan government officials. All this had hobbled the administration's effort to build consensus for its policy.

For years, Reagan's push to fund the rebels had been an irritant in his relations with Congress. But the president, his persistence legendary, responded to the uproar by throwing the full weight of his office behind the effort. Instead of backing off, he raised the stakes.

Resistance was especially fierce in the House. Members were responding to a public that was still uneasy about U.S. entanglement in an ill-defined guerrilla war. Simply put, Nicaragua too easily summoned to mind snapshots of Vietnam.

The administration's aid had begun in 1981 as a covert activity. So Reagan's team did not immediately make a public case for the aid or lay out its objectives. But by 1984, the program was an open secret—reported in the news media and hotly debated in the halls of Congress.

By 1985 what had initially been justified as a secret operation to stem the flow of Cuban

In April 1985 Reagan sought $14 million in aid for Nicaragua's contras, a 15,000-man rebel militia seeking to overthrow their country's leftist government.

arms from Nicaragua to guerrillas in El Salvador had become an effort to rid the Americas of a communist sanctuary in Nicaragua.

For Reagan, the rebels' cause was a challenge to the United States and its resolve to thwart communism. Reagan applauded them as the "moral equivalent of the Founding Fathers," and backing them became an overriding, even consuming, White House mission—the subject of stacks of presidential speeches and internal polls. None of the polls was encouraging, though, and the issue ignited a fierce debate within the administration over how Reagan should seek to bend public opinion his way.

But in mid-April, a week before the critical Senate vote, the call for $14 million in direct military aid was doomed by a defection. Sen. Sam Nunn, a highly influential Georgia Democrat who had previously supported contra aid, came out against the package.

In a Senate floor speech closely watched by the White House, Nunn urged the administration to shift course, emphasize diplomacy, press for economic sanctions, seek a cease-fire, and "put the military option on the back burner."

Nunn's shift moved the White House. Within days, hints of a willingness, to compromise emerged. Shultz and McFarlane were plunged into a round of lengthy negotiations with fourteen senators considered to be wavering in their support for the contra aid.

The talks had begun in the Cabinet Room in the White House on April 22, with McFarlane heading Reagan's team. On the day of the Senate vote, negotiations migrated to the Capitol. There was much back and forth, but not much give and take.

A complex parliamentary situation was working against the president. Congressional opponents of contra aid, led by Rep. Edward P.

Boland, a Massachusetts Democrat, had set the terms of the 1985 debate a year earlier, constraining Reagan's political options.

In an amendment to a massive spending bill, Boland had barred any covert aid to the contras for that fiscal year, but reserved $14 million for "military or paramilitary operations in Nicaragua." Reagan was free, under the law, to ask Congress for the money for military purposes in 1985. But, as designed, he faced certain defeat because political support for direct "military or paramilitary" aid did not exist.

This formulation demanded that any alternative be negotiated with Congress and guaranteed Congress a hand in an important part of Reagan's foreign policy. Procedurally, it gave one chamber veto power over the policy. Indeed, Sen. John C. Danforth, R-Mo., later complained that the negotiations constituted "a bizarre spectacle of senators going to the White House to negotiate the most minute nuances" of foreign policy.

The talks, however, displayed an extraordinary level of executive and legislative deal-making. From the start, both sides agreed that the money should be restricted to "humanitarian" aid, a term not easily defined. Other significant sticking points emerged. McFarlane and his team, for example, insisted on direct talks between the Sandinista government and the contras. Democrats balked.

Finally, both sides had gone as far as they could. By the morning of the Senate vote, the White House had abandoned the group negotiations and set a new course. Reagan would lay out his views in a letter, pledging to use the money only for food, clothes, medicine, and "other assistance for their survival and well-being—and not for arms, ammunition, and weapons of war."

With this new tactic, Reagan picked off senators one by one, and had particular success with Democrats. Sen. Lloyd Bentsen, D-Texas,

for example, won tougher language on potential economic sanctions against Nicaragua; the White House won Bentsen.

In the end, Shultz and McFarlane's confidence proved well founded. The Senate approved Reagan's request for humanitarian aid, 53-46, despite nine Republicans abandoning their president—one more than had opposed aid to the contras in 1984. But in the House, the two-day debate took on a far more partisan and bitter flavor, with the odds stacked significantly against the president.

As the debate began, Democrats boasted a majority against Reagan's request, with ten to thirty votes to spare. House Democratic leaders made the going even tougher by moving up their votes by a week, a move Reagan branded "immoral." The tactic forced the White House to split its lobbying effort between the Senate and House, and robbed Reagan of even an hour to absorb any political advantage from the narrow Senate victory.

Reps. Michael D. Barnes of Maryland, chairman of the Foreign Affairs Subcommittee on Inter-American Affairs, and Lee H. Hamilton of Indiana, chairman of the House Intelligence Committee, had fashioned the Democrats' "constructive alternative." The Democrats' plan drew sharp criticism. Reagan derided it as "a shameful surrender" in an April 20 radio address, and Rep. Henry J. Hyde, R-Ill., echoed: "It is disarmament; it is surrender."

Nevertheless, on April 23, the House rebuffed Reagan, voting 180-248 against the $14 million aid package the Senate had accepted. The next day, the House went even further by rejecting two alternative aid packages—one Democratic and one Republican, essentially leaving the policy in limbo.

The House first rejected a GOP alternative backed by the White House. Minority Leader Robert H. Michel, R-Ill., did the honors, offering an amendment calling for $14 million in hu-

Just as contra aid seemed decisively defeated, Nicaraguan President Daniel Ortega, in trenchcoat, damaged his own cause in the U.S. Congress by going to Moscow to seek $200 million from the Soviets.

manitarian aid to the contras. In a critical concession, the amendment directed that the money go through the Agency for International Development, not the CIA.

As often happens in high-stakes votes, the "yeas" and "nays" tracked each other throughout the fifteen minutes of voting on April 24. When the time expired, the count was even, and House Speaker Thomas P. O'Neill Jr., D-Mass., plucked a "nay" card from the table in the well, prepared to break the deadlock. But with the clock running in overtime, Edward R. Roybal, D-Calif., and Henry B. Gonzalez, D-Texas, entered the chamber and cast the deciding votes: The amendment was narrowly rejected, 213-215.

O'Neill then rushed the House into a final vote on the underlying Democratic resolution. For the first time that day, the tally was lopsided and the resolution went down: 123-303.

House Minority Whip Trent Lott, R-Miss., vowed to fight on, calling the House votes "only one small skirmish in a rolling battle." The stunning House votes rattled Shultz and left Michel visibly shaken, incredulous that the House had turned down every option.

The House had delivered Reagan one of the most serious setbacks of his presidency. Still, the GOP alternative had failed by only two votes. It would not take long for the White House and its allies to build on this narrow margin and regain the initiative.

Less than a week later, Washington awoke to news that Nicaraguan President Daniel Ortega had made a pilgrimage to Moscow, seeking some $200 million in aid. Ortega's stunningly ill-timed trip deeply offended many Democrats and Republicans. Reagan quickly saw an opening.

Speaker O'Neill asked Democrats to draft legislation to provide humanitarian aid to the contras; several moderate and conservative House Democrats followed suit, agitating to revive the aid issue. The 1986 congressional elections were now approaching and many members, particularly from the South, worried about appearing "soft on communism."

In a largely symbolic move, the president imposed a trade embargo on Nicaragua on May 1. Revving up the rhetorical engines, Reagan called Ortega "the little dictator who went to Moscow in his green fatigues." Southern members worried that an all-out war in Nicaragua would send refugees flooding over the border.

As early as May, the stage was set for more votes on Nicaragua. The Senate reaffirmed its support for contra aid on June 6 and 7, approving $38 million for food, clothing, and other non-military aid in fiscal years 1985 and 1986. In the House, the debate had shifted decisively. Even opponents of aid betrayed a sense of resignation.

Still, when the debate began there was plenty of finger-pointing. Republicans said that the Democrats stood for appeasement and isolationism—they were the Neville Chamberlains of the mid-1980s.

O'Neill countered that the president would be satisfied only with "complete victory" in Nicaragua. "He can see himself leading a contingent down Broadway, with a big smile on his face, kind of like a grade-B motion picture actor, coming home the conquering hero," O'Neill said.

But Reagan continued to win converts; many Democrats now embraced his view that Nicaragua needed to lift press censorship, ease repression of dissidents, and make other internal changes.

Two concessions made by the White House were pivotal: the aid would be used for humanitarian purposes, and agencies other than the CIA would be considered to be administering the aid. As he had done in April, Reagan also sent a letter, this time to Rep. Dave McCurdy, D-Okla., a recent supporter, laying out his views.

When it came to a vote, the procedure played out much as it had in April, but the outcome was reversed. The House on June 12 refused, 196-232, to extend indefinitely a legal ban on any U.S. aid for "military and nonmilitary operations in Nicaragua"—a ban proposed by Boland that the House had consistently supported since 1983.

The House then turned back, 172-259, a Democratic alternative by Richard A. Gephardt, D-Mo., calling for any action to be delayed six months to foster the peace process.

The fix was in. In a dramatic shift, the House then agreed to supply $27 million in nonmilitary aid to the contras, adopting, 248-184, an amendment Joseph M. McDade, R-Pa., offered in behalf of Michel. The amendment was backed by McCurdy, even though the Democrats blocked his name from appearing on the amendment lest it lend a bipartisan tone.

A downcast Majority Leader Jim Wright, D-Texas, left the Capitol saying, "I hope for the best, but fear the worst."

The Nicaraguan question played a relatively small part in the elections of 1984. The passage of the Boland amendment in the House in 1983 (named for House Intelligence Committee Chairman Edward P. Boland) had greatly constrained administration efforts to aid the anticommunist "contra" rebels, and polls showed little public support for more direct intervention. A dust-up in Congress followed the April revelation that the CIA had participated in mining Nicaraguan harbors, and the Sandinista threat to neighboring countries came up during the presidential primaries. But through most of the campaign, the issue remained just below the surface.

It could be said that many issues remained just below the surface in 1984, because President Reagan ran a classic incumbent reelection campaign. It asked the voters to choose only between personalities and general philosophies about the direction of government. Many conservatives were dissatisfied with the gauzy approach and wanted a more ideological clash. The economy had finally begun growing again in 1983 and 1984, as interest rates declined in response to lower inflation. Reagan's popularity was again on the upswing. So why not use the opportunity to build a mandate for more of Reagan's agenda? Surely this was the time to press for constitutional amendments on school prayer, abortion, and a balanced budget.

But the president's inner circle began the year uncertain about the course of events. They were especially wary of making the election a referendum on what some called the Reagan Doctrine: a pledge to aid anticommunist insurgencies anywhere in the world. While it was popular to cheer the mujahedeen fighting the Soviets in Afghanistan, the sight of U.S. troops shipping out for combat overseas still brought to mind the divisive images of Vietnam.

The president's campaign managers could not anticipate that the Democrats would have a protracted and debilitating nomination fight. Nor could they have known the eventual nominee, former vice president Walter F. Mondale, would promise to *raise* taxes. So they chose a cautious strategy that emphasized the recent economic improvements and Reagan's personal charm. Their signature thirty-second "spot ad" on television featured uplifting music and soft-focus scenes of idealized life while the narrator intoned: "It's morning in America." The closest Reagan's campaign came to mentioning the threat of global communism was an ad that likened the Soviet Union to a large bear foraging in the woods.

The result was a magnificent landslide reelection for the president, who carried forty-nine states (like Richard M. Nixon in 1972) and nearly matched Lyndon B. Johnson's vote share of 1964. The Senate remained in Republican hands. The only sour note for the GOP was that it won just 192 seats in the House, far below its hopes. The high reelection rates across the board suggested a degree of voter satisfaction.

= 1986 =

The Iran-Contra Eruption

Carroll J. Doherty

After about two hours of poring over files and documents in a cramped office in the Old Executive Office Building, the Justice Department officials were glad to be breaking for lunch.

The two men were to meet their boss, Attorney General Edwin Meese III, at the Old Ebbitt Grill on 15th Street, a recently renovated restaurant popular with Washington's political crowd. Meese had ordered the two men—his chief of staff, John Richardson, and Assistant Attorney General William Bradford Reynolds—to conduct what he thought would be a routine inquiry into a highly charged issue: the Reagan administration's secret arms sales to Iran, disclosed about three weeks earlier.

What the investigation uncovered was anything but routine. Over lunch, Reynolds told Meese that he had stumbled onto a scheme so astounding, so utterly audacious, that they could only hope it had not actually been implemented. Meese, President Ronald Reagan's aide-de-camp going all the way back to California's political wars in the 1960s, quickly sized up its import.

"The effect for the administration could have been the political equivalent of a nuclear bomb," he wrote later. It very nearly was. On that sunny Saturday afternoon in November 1986, Reynolds had unearthed the first evidence that a pair of White House aides had wrested control of U.S. policy toward Iran and Nicaragua away from the State Department,

Congress, and perhaps the president. The administration was still struggling to contain the fallout from disclosures that Reagan, whose tough-on-terrorism rhetoric helped propel him into the White House in 1980, had approved shipments of weapons to Iran, the equivalent of Murder Inc. in the world of state-sponsored terrorism.

Now came a bombshell memo discovered by Reynolds's file search that suggested that profits from those arms sales had been secretly diverted to assist Nicaragua's antigovernment rebels—called contras—during a time when Congress had prohibited military aid for them.

Meese's worst fears were realized the next day, when he confirmed that the "diversion" had indeed occurred. The Iran-contra affair was about to explode into the most damaging political scandal of the Reagan era.

The White House managed to keep the story under wraps for two more days. But the president and his inner circle knew it had to come out, and the following Tuesday, November 25, the administration went public.

At a tumultuous White House press conference, the president—looking shaken and older than his seventy-five-years—said he had not been "fully informed" of the arms dealings. Reagan announced that he had fired Lt. Col. Oliver L. North, a Marine who served as the National Security Council (NSC) staff aide. North had engineered the diversion. Reagan also accepted the resignation of Vice Adm. John M. Poindex-

The public learned of the diversion of Iran arms-sale profits to the contras on November 25, 1986, when President Reagan announced that he had not been "fully informed" and turned the microphone over to Meese, right.

ter, his national security adviser, who had known of the dealings.

Then Reagan departed, leaving his attorney general to try to explain how $10 million to $30 million in profits from the Iranian arms sales (the exact amount was not known at the time and ended up being far less) went to the contras without the president's or his Cabinet's knowledge.

Meese calmly fielded questions for about forty minutes, mixing speculation and erroneous information with the few hard facts he possessed. But there was one question that neither Meese nor anyone else could answer that Tuesday before Thanksgiving: Can this presidency be saved?

The revelations rocked Capitol Hill. Congress had been routinely, almost casually, circumvented in the entire affair, despite laws restricting aid to the contras and requiring timely notification of covert operations.

The president's political stock was already slipping, as evidenced by the GOP's loss of the Senate majority in midterm elections that had been held early that November. Reagan now faced the prospect of serving the final two years of his presidency under a cloud.

The shock from the Iran-contra eruption was felt well beyond the realm of electoral politics, however. Many lawmakers were deeply skeptical of Reagan's defense that he was ignorant of the scheme. Even if true, Reagan's assertions amounted to a tacit admission that he had been asleep at the switch while his aides were running unauthorized and possibly illegal covert actions. Staunch administration loyalists questioned whether the aging president had lost his grip on the nation's foreign policy. "It's in pretty bad disarray," said Rep. Dick Cheney, R-Wyo.

Democrats, their power ascendant after gaining control of both chambers for the first time in six years, raised similar concerns in harsher terms. "What this says is that nobody really seems to be in charge of the foreign policy of this country," said Robert C. Byrd, D-W.Va., who was to take over as Senate majority leader when the 100th Congress convened in January.

Reagan had never been a "policy wonk," driven to master the details of governmenta affairs. He preferred to articulate broad, powerful themes and let others fill in the blanks.

At the least, Iran-contra called into question the president's easygoing management style, which some had previously cited as a source of his strength. Perhaps more important, Reagan's embrace of the Iranian arms sales seemed to make a mockery of his rock-ribbed opposition to terrorism. For the public, that may have been the most disturbing aspect of the entire affair.

Despite mounting evidence to the contrary, Reagan doggedly insisted that the weapons shipments to Iran were not part of a deal to win freedom for American hostages held by pro-Iranian Muslim fundamentalists in Lebanon.

During a speech November 13, Reagan had attacked what he called the "wildly speculative false stories about arms for hostages and alleged ransom payments." He concluded the televised address with this stern denial: "We did not—repeat, did not—trade weapons or anything else for hostages, nor will we."

It was only after weeks of increasing criticism that the president conceded that "mistakes were made" in the Iran dealings. In a prime time speech a few months later, Reagan said, a bit ruefully, that, in fact, weapons had been transferred to secure the hostages' freedom.

The arms gambit itself, however well-intentioned, had been an embarrassing failure. The Iranian initiative had succeeded in winning freedom for three of six American hostages held by pro-Iran factions, at a cost of more than 2,000 U.S.-made missiles. In the meantime, the same factions had seized three more American hostages.

By early December, the political damage inflicted by the revelations was becoming painfully apparent. Polls showed Reagan's approval rating plunging twenty percentage points in a month. One poll showed that people preferred the way President Jimmy Carter had handled Iran. It had been Carter's inability to gain freedom for U.S. hostages in Iran seven years earlier that helped pave the way for Reagan's sweeping victory in 1980.

The burning, twofold question about the diversion—what did the president know and when did he know it—bore echoes of Watergate. Newspapers had a field day exposing each twist and turn in the growing scandal. It was disclosed that North and Fawn Hall, his secretary, busily shredded documents and erased computer files even as Meese's Justice Department deputies conducted their inquiry.

But it soon became clear that Iran-contra was not to be a revival of the long-running drama that gripped the country in 1973 and 1974 and ended with the resignation of a president. Reagan, unlike the Watergate-weakened Richard M. Nixon, still enjoyed a substantial reservoir of popular goodwill. The policies undertaken in the president's name might have skirted the law and been incompetently managed, but no one was accusing Reagan of political corruption.

The president earned credit by moving to investigate the shenanigans of his NSC aides and to bring some supervision to his administration's foreign policy. He named a three-person panel—led by former Texas Republican senator John G. Tower and including former Maine Democratic senator Edmund S. Muskie and ex-national security adviser Brent Scowcroft—to review the case. Under pressure from Congress, Reagan also acceded to the appointment of an independent counsel, a rangy Oklahoma Republican named Lawrence E. Walsh, to investigate for possible criminal wrongdoing.

A commission consisting of former senators Edmund Muskie and John Tower and retired general Brent Scowcroft (from left) painted a devastating picture of an out-of-touch president and out-of-control staff members.

To replace Poindexter, the president named Frank G. Carlucci, a pillar of Washington's foreign policy establishment. Control over Iran policy was entrusted to Secretary of State George P. Shultz, who had publicly denounced the arms-for-hostages scheme.

In Congress, Democrats in the House and Senate moved quickly to establish select committees that would begin investigating the scandal when the new Congress convened in January. But even the lame-duck 99th Congress made preliminary probes into the controversy. In December 1986, the House Foreign Affairs Committee invited North, an earnest-looking Marine, and Poindexter, his owlish superior, to appear. Both declined to testify, invoking their protection against self-incrimination under the Fifth Amendment to the Constitution.

The nationally televised appearance by Iran-contra's central protagonists, while unproductive, foreshadowed some of the challenges facing the select committees, which would begin their probe in 1987. The biggest was how to handle North, who was already on his way to becoming a national phenomenon.

North arrived at the packed committee hearing in full Marine regalia, his uniform adorned with combat medals earned in the Vietnam war. The low-key, pipe-smoking Poindexter, by contrast, was attired in civilian clothes.

In a moment of high drama, North bit his lip as he told Indiana Democrat Lee H. Hamilton: "There isn't anyone in the world who wants this story out more than I do." But he "respectfully and regretfully" declined to tell that story.

Lawmakers normally disdain witnesses who "take the Fifth," but in this case they heaped praise on the forty-three-year-old Marine, who many felt was being "scapegoated" by the White House. "Col. North has acted in the best interest of the country," declared Daniel A. Mica, D-Fla.

Tom Lantos, D-Calif., a Hungarian-born anticommunist with a flair for public relations, went Mica one better, saying it would be a privilege to contribute to North's defense fund "as my colleagues and hundreds of thousands Americans will want to do."

The special review board set up by Reagan, which came to be known as the Tower Commission, quietly continued its inquiry throughout the winter. In its lengthy report, released February 26, 1987, the Tower Commission presented a devastating portrait of an out-of-touch president and an out-of-control NSC staff, which had taken over Iran and contra initiatives.

After a series of contradictory statements, an embarrassed Reagan told the board that he simply could not recall whether he had signed off on an August 1985 shipment of arms that had been made through Israel.

Drawing on thousands of computer messages that North was unable to erase, the panel documented how NSC aides stepped out of their traditional role as desk-bound policy analysts to become covert operators, wheeling and dealing with unscrupulous middlemen. "The result was a very unprofessional operation," the panel noted dryly.

Although it was not its central theme, the report touched on the contempt North and his comrades displayed toward Congress. The NSC aides, most of whom had served in the military, blamed Congress for endlessly litigating the question of whether to aid the contras. North, who clearly preferred action to talk, focused narrowly on the mission of keeping the guerrillas supplied—despite the political and legal risks.

White House Chief of Staff Donald T. Regan, who resigned under pressure after the Tower board blamed him for allowing "chaos" to descend on the administration, recalled a telling comment by Poindexter on why he did not stay on top of North's activities. " 'I really didn't want to know,' Regan quotes Poindexter as saying. " 'I was so damned mad at [House Speaker] Tip O'Neill for the way he was dragging the contras around, I didn't want to know what, if anything, was going on.' "

The Tower Commission's inquiry set the stage for climactic hearings by the select committees, which began May 5, 1987. For nine weeks, the public watched as a parade of witnesses gave testimony that ranged from the disturbing to the bizarre.

Hall, North's devoted secretary, recounted how she stuffed incriminating documents in her clothes and boots to smuggle them out of the Old Executive Office Building; Elliott Abrams, a cocksure State Department official, described a Keystone Kops scheme in which he solicited a $10 million contribution for the contras only to have it mistakenly wired to the wrong Swiss bank account; ex-military men recruited by North for his covert actions testified how they supplied the contras on a wing and a prayer.

The televised hearings also turned North, the supposed fall guy, into a folk hero. To get North and Poindexter to tell their stories in public, the committees had to offer them limited immunity. That decision ultimately led appeals courts to throw out criminal convictions of the two men for obstruction of Congress and other charges.

There was no Watergate-style denouement. In the end, lawmakers and the American people could never agree on whether Iran-contra represented a frightening power grab by an ideologically motivated cabal in the government, or a murky set of overseas dealings in which it was difficult to tell the good guys from the bad guys.

The U.S. Constitution calls for the election of a Speaker of the House of Representatives in Article I, Section 2, well before it mentions the election of a president. However, only a handful of Speakers have had the clout and control to rival the president as a political force. One such was Henry Clay of Kentucky, who stoked the fires for the War of 1812 and later became known as "the Great Compromiser" for his efforts to resolve the question of slavery.

But if Clay entered the pantheon of American heroes, other strong Speakers were reviled. Thomas Brackett Reed of Maine, a Republican Speaker who ruled the House in the 1890s, was autocratic enough to be dubbed "Czar Reed." A decade later, the power of the Speakership reached its baroque phase under Joseph G. Cannon of Illinois. An Old Guard Republican, "Uncle Joe" so abused his office that GOP progressives eventually joined the Democrats in revolt against him in March 1910.

After Cannon's overthrow, power in the House was exercised by committee chairmen who owed their positions to seniority and at times held them for decades. The authority and independence of this baronage had resulted from the dethroning of one Speaker and thereafter served to restrain the power of the office. Now and then there arose a man—most notably Democratic Speaker Sam Rayburn of Texas—who was able to move the House through personal influence and skillful orchestration. But even Rayburn knew his limits.

After Rayburn's death in 1961, the Democrats elected a series of relatively weak Speakers. The last of these was Thomas P. "Tip" O'Neill, an affable man of enormous charm who only occasionally could knit his party's factions together. O'Neill retired in 1987, and the Speakership passed to Jim Wright of Texas, who had waited impatiently for it for a decade as majority leader.

Wright's political roots were sunk in rural Texas populism and a ritual obeisance to the oil and gas industry. His congressional finishing school had been the Public Works Committee, where he learned how members in both parties could be brought to see reason by the judicious application of federal spending in their districts.

Wright was determined to restore power to the Speakership. Working closely with Tony Coelho of California, his tough majority whip, Wright compiled a near-perfect record in floor votes in the 100th Congress (1987-1989). On one occasion, a budget vote was held open for more than fifteen minutes while Wright's minions searched the halls for a member they could cajole into switching his vote so that Wright could prevail.

Wright even challenged President Reagan for the lead in conducting foreign policy, holding talks on his own initiative with representatives of the Nicaraguan government. With Reagan's energy and command in question in the 100th Congress (1987-1988), Wright's ambition and assurance became the dynamic force not just for the Hill but for Washington policy in general. But his heyday was destined to be brief.

= 1989 =

A Speaker's Downfall

Stephen Gettinger

Congress convened on January 3, 1989, ready to greet a new president, George Bush, and largely ignore him. The Senate also had a new majority leader in Democrat George J. Mitchell of Maine, but the towering figure in Washington was the House Speaker, Democrat Jim Wright of Texas.

In his first two years as Speaker, Wright had muscled past a lame-duck President Ronald Reagan to create a record for the 100th Congress on Medicare, welfare, and crime legislation that drew comparisons to the Great Society Congress of 1964-1965. For himself, Wright had carved out a role in foreign policy and agenda-setting that brought comparisons to Henry Clay in the early 1800s.

Within a month, however, "Foley for Speaker" buttons would sprout on lapels in the Capitol, a reference to Majority Leader Thomas S. Foley of Washington, Wright's No. 2 man. By June, that fantasy would have been fulfilled.

The inspiration for the buttons was Wright's mishandling of a congressional pay raise, a seemingly small matter of great sensitivity for members and, as it turned out, for their constituents.

An outside commission had recommended a 51 percent increase from $89,500 to $135,000, to take effect February 8, if Congress did not vote to cancel it. Wright's strategy, devised in concert with Republican leaders, was to avoid a vote. It had worked in 1987, and the fallout had been manageable.

But this time the public was aroused. The size of the raise, coming after years of increasing federal budget deficits, stirred outrage. Radio talk show hosts flailed the issue, urging citizens to flood the Capitol with tea bags to symbolize a latter-day Boston tea party.

Having lost control of the issue, Wright tried to recover by adopting new strategies. But he failed to consult his allies first. He launched a survey intended to show that it was members, not Wright alone, who wanted to avoid a vote. That just made members look like hypocrites. Then he tried a last-minute plan to cut the raise to 30 percent. "He's always going off on his own, the Lone Ranger," muttered one Democratic whip. After weeks of disarray, 108 Democrats deserted on an important procedural vote, and the pay raise evaporated February 7.

That afternoon, Wright called his sister Mary in one of his lachrymose moods: "I have no power, no base of operations," he moaned.

Wright's problem at base was that he was not well-liked—not by the liberals who dominated the Democratic Caucus (who remembered his vote against the Civil Rights Act of 1964 and his support of the Vietnam War), and not by southern conservatives, who increasingly felt he used his power to muffle them. The Republicans—utter victims of his agenda, his tactics, and his ambition—liked him least of all.

"If they think they do not like me, it is because they do not know me," read a slip of paper Wright kept in his pocket for years. After

135

R. MICHAEL JENKINS

Jim Wright, flanked by House Democratic leaders at a Capitol news conference on April 13, 1989, vows to fight for his reputation as the House ethics committee prepared to release formal charges against him.

thirty-four years in Congress, he was most feared by colleagues who knew him best, and he often ate breakfast alone in the members' dining room. Something of the oil industry, his legislative pet, clung to him: the slippery smile, the eyebrows tall as drilling-rigs, the vaporous rhetoric.

For all this, however, Wright might have survived had there not been another problem just below the surface. No one quite knew how seriously to take it, but a broad-ranging inquiry into Wright's business affairs had been under way since June 1988. The Committee on Standards of Official Conduct was questioning his investments and his boosting of home-state ventures.

Probers were particularly interested in a vanity book, *Reflections of a Public Man,* published by a hometown supporter. Book royalties were exempt from House limits on outside income, but these looked fishy: Wright made $3.25 on every $5.95 sale, and most copies were bought in bulk by lobbyists and supporters. The committee also was looking into benefits from Mallightco, an investment vehicle for Wright and his wife together with a Fort Worth business partner, George Mallick, and his wife.

To conduct the inquiry, the committee had hired an ambitious, slashing litigator from Chicago, Richard J. Phelan. But the real instigator of the investigation was a Republican firebrand with a knack for getting under Democrats' skin, Newt Gingrich of Georgia. In the summer of 1987, Gingrich had told John M. Barry, a journalist writing a book about Wright, that he was scrutinizing the Speaker's background to find a way to bring him down. "He's from Texas. He's been in politics over 30 years. An aggressive investigator with subpoena powers might find something."

A former college history instructor, Gingrich drew the power comparison to Henry Clay and then developed a mantra, "Jim Wright is the most corrupt Speaker in the 20th century." (The competition was weak: rumors had circulated about John Nance Garner's drinking and ties to railroads in the 1930s and Thomas P. O'Neill Jr.'s association with a Korean lobbyist in the 1970s, but these had not amounted to much.)

In April 1987 Gingrich had assigned his aide Karen Van Brocklin to search the media for any smudges on Wright's past. She and her boss plied reporters with tips and clips. On their own, major newspapers and Wright's hometown newspaper, the Fort Worth *Star-Telegram*, published articles questioning Wright's finances and ties to banking and oil interests. In May 1988 the self-styled citizens' watchdog group Common Cause called for an inquiry. Eight days later, Gingrich filed a formal ethics complaint against Wright, citing as evidence a sheaf of news articles.

Wright's response showed that Gingrich had indeed gotten under his skin: "My views of him are somewhat similar to those of a fire hydrant toward a dog."

On February 21, 1989, Phelan delivered his 476-page report to the committee. Only twelve copies were made, one for each member of the committee, and they were to be read only in the committee's offices. The panel's mission was to decide whether there was "reason to believe" that House rules had been broken, and, if so, to draw up formal charges akin to an indictment.

Despite the secrecy, word filtered out that Phelan had offered a flinty-eyed look at the web of favors and sloppy practices that characterized Texas politics. For almost three weeks, the committee—the only one in the House evenly split between the parties, giving Republicans a veto over the outcome—listened as Phelan walked them through his evidence.

Phelan gave a harsh reading, at one point denouncing Mallightco as "an artifice, a sham, a conduit to provide the Speaker and his wife with . . . cash dividends and salaries and apartments and condominiums and loans." Sitting an arm's length away, Wright's attorney, William C. Oldaker, offered a formalistic rebuttal, arguing the rules of evidence rather than the facts.

Wright kept up a brave front. "After all this is resolved, I'll be stronger than ever." But it was his nemesis, Gingrich, who was gaining stature. On March 22, he vaulted to the position of heir-apparent to the Republican leader's job by winning a two-vote victory to replace Dick Cheney of Wyoming, who was moving to the Bush Cabinet.

Inside the committee room, members pondered the evidence. The big questions concerned whether Mallick had an interest in specific legislation and whether Wright's wife, Betty, really worked for her $18,000 salary from Mallightco, plus her use of a car and a condo. Phelan said she could not prove that she did. He declared that Mallick's business ventures were so intertwined with Texas thrift failures and with the development of the Fort Worth stockyards, both pet causes of Wright's, that it did not matter whether they ever discussed the issues.

Republicans emphasized that the standard of proof was low at this stage and that Phelan had given the panel plenty of "reason to believe" that the matter should proceed to a formal, public hearing. The pivotal committee vote came on the question of whether Mallick had an interest in legislation. If the panel found that he was merely a friend, even a sycophantic one, then the major charges would fall into the minor category of improper reporting.

But when the roll was called, the Republicans were joined by two Democrats: Chester G. Atkins of Massachusetts and Bernard J. Dwyer of New Jersey, both of whom had won their appointments to the Appropriations Committee on the basis of party loyalty. The room fell still.

In a speech that ran the emotional gamut from tears to rage, Wright told a packed House chamber he would re-sign "as a propitiation for all of this season of bad will that has grown up among us."

With this bipartisan turn against the Speaker, the panel had crossed into uncharted territory.

On April 13, as rumors spread throughout the Capitol that two Democrats had jumped ship, Wright called a news conference. Surrounded by a wall of stone-faced colleagues, he vowed to fight, choking up with tears when defending his wife. "Whether I'm Speaker of the House . . . is not important," he said. "More important to me than any of that is my personal reputation, my personal honor."

More than 300 reporters packed a hearing room and spilled into the hallway of the Rayburn Building on Monday, April 17, as the ethics committee released its formal charges. It had dismissed almost all of Gingrich's specific accusations, but found sixty-nine possible violations in associated areas and vowed to continue investigating Wright's lucrative involvement in an oil well. His book, it said, was part of an "overall scheme to evade the House outside earned income limits." Mallick, it declared, had given him improper gifts to the tune of $145,000 over ten years.

The next day, Wright released a statement headlined "Betty Wright Worked!" detailing how she had screened prospective investments. He told a closed meeting of the Democratic Caucus that while he would not cling desperately to his office, he wanted a chance to clear his name. Colleagues came out vowing to fight for him, although Ways and Means Chairman Dan Rostenkowski of Illinois muttered, "I wouldn't bet on the steel stomach of some of these members." And indeed, no news conferences or advertisements to defend Wright ever materialized.

A siege mentality gripped the House, with little business transacted on the floor. Wright canceled most news briefings and skulked through the Capitol to avoid reporters. On May 4 the *Washington Post* unearthed a sixteen-year-old story about how Wright's top aide, John P. Mack, had beaten and stabbed a young woman. After serving more than two years in prison, Mack had been paroled to a filing job in Wright's office through a relative's connection. Mack soon resigned, but Charles Wilson, a

Texas Democrat who was one of Wright's chief defenders, said the story provided the coup de grace. "It was something everybody could relate to, and it gave the idea that we are living in an environment of lawlessness and violence."

Wright hired a more aggressive team of lawyers that included Democratic elder statesman Clark M. Clifford, and they began to attack both Phelan's facts and interpretation before the committee. But it was too late.

"The charges against Wright were small potatoes," wrote political scientist Ronald M. Peters Jr. in *The American Speakership*. But they had "come to symbolize a kind of petty profiteering inconsistent with the dignity of the office of speaker."

On May 17 a group of Wright supporters privately discussed the possibility of his resigning—then leaked the story of their meeting to the press. The next day, Philip R. Sharp, a mild-mannered former political science professor from Indiana, became the first Democrat to declare publicly that Wright should quit.

In a strategy session that morning, Wright's new lawyer asked him, "What do you really want, Jim?" Wright replied, "I want to preserve my reputation, as much as that is possible. I want to leave with some degree of dignity."

Wright's last hope for his reputation rested on a televised hearing May 23, where his lawyer argued that the charges should be dismissed. But Atkins and Dwyer were unmoved.

The leadership met for the last time May 24 at 3:30, with Majority Leader Thomas S. Foley and Whip Tony Coelho vowing loyalty. But within two days, Coelho was out of the leadership, beating Wright to the punch by announcing his own resignation in the face of controversy over a "junk bond" investment.

"Political deaths are a lot like real deaths," mourned Pat Williams, D-Mont. "There's a great deal of heavy emotion in the Congress right now."

Wright spent the long Memorial Day weekend in seclusion with Betty at a cabin in Virginia's Shenandoah Valley. As the House straggled back to work, word spread that Wright would address the chamber. The floor was packed.

At 4 p.m. sharp, Wright pushed open the door, strode to the podium, and asked for an hour to speak "on a question of personal privilege." The next hour was vintage Wright, with florid oratory carrying him from tears to rage. He defended his wife, sitting above him in the gallery, waved a copy of his book, and pleaded for an end to "this period of mindless cannibalism," with Gingrich sitting impassively in front of him.

Near the end, Wright bowed his head and offered his resignation as "total payment for the anger and hostility we feel toward each other." With a quiet, oddly casual voice, he said, "Let me give you back this job you gave me as a propitiation for all of this season of bad will that has grown up among us. Give it back to you."

He stayed in the Speakership for a week and in the Congress for a month, wrapping up loose ends. His place in history was secure—not as the new Henry Clay, but as the first Speaker to be forced out of office by scandal.

It can be argued that, in times of peace, the most important issue in Washington is taxes. The one-term presidency of George Bush offers a case in point.

Bush had hoped to win the Republican nomination in 1988 by virtue of being Ronald Reagan's vice president. As it turned out, he also needed an issue on which to focus. He settled on taxes, and the issue brought his campaign success. Bush won the New Hampshire primary in part because he signed an antitax pledge and ran television ads noting that Bob Dole, the Senate Republican leader, had refused to sign the same pledge. In August, with polls showing him behind the Democratic nominee, Gov. Michael S. Dukakis of Massachusetts, Bush roused the Republican National Convention to roars of approval when he vowed: "Read my lips, no new taxes."

Shortly after moving into the Oval Office in 1989, Bush declared that his highest domestic priority would be cutting the tax on capital gains—the profits made on the sale of stocks, bonds, real estate, and other forms of investment. The tax cut was popular among business-oriented Democrats in the House. It won a bipartisan majority first in the Ways and Means Committee and then, despite furious opposition from the Democratic leadership, on the House floor. The idea had the backing of most of the Senate, too, but the majority leader, George J. Mitchell, held together just enough Democratic votes on a procedural question to deny Bush a floor vote on the tax cut itself.

The capital gains defeat in the fall of 1989 was a kind of bookend on Bush's first year in the White House, which had begun with the Senate rejecting his nomination of former senator John Tower of Texas to be secretary of defense. With these two rebuffs, the Senate let the new president know it was taking no orders from the White House.

The following year, a slowing economy forced the president and congressional leaders back to the bargaining table to find a way to meet the deficit-reduction targets of the Gramm-Rudman law, which had been passed in 1985 and amended in 1987. As early as March, Bush indicated that he was ready to move in the Democrats' direction if it would mean a multiyear deal that spared him the annual budget wrangle. By summer, with deficit projections growing worse, the president felt even greater urgency. And in August, the Iraqi invasion of Kuwait made Bush all the more determined to reach a budget agreement so as to concentrate on the crisis abroad.

Bush's strategy presumed that the Democrats in Congress were the principal obstacle to his attempt to build a record of achievement. Some centrist Democrats were glad to meet the president halfway, while more partisan Democrats saw cooperation with the president as a two-edged sword. "If we get a budget agreement," one Democratic senator said in 1990, "we get George Bush re-elected."

In the long run, however, Bush found his greatest difficulty in dealing with the recalcitrant elements of his own party. For many Republicans elected in the Reagan era—particularly in the election of 1984—no issue mattered so much as taxes.

= 1990 =

"Read My Lips. . ."

Ronald D. Elving

On Tuesday morning June 26, 1990, President George Bush had breakfast at the White House with his top three economic policy aides and the top three leaders of the Democratic majority in Congress. At issue was the lack of progress in budget negotiations between the legislative and executive branches and between the rival parties that controlled them.

House Speaker Thomas S. Foley of Washington told Bush that the Democrats were about to quit the "budget summit" talks that Bush had convened in May. Their view was that meaningful deficit reduction could not be achieved through spending cuts alone.

The budget talks had begun only after Bush agreed there would be "no preconditions." Democrats had taken that phrase as a tacit agreement to discuss taxes. But after two months of talks, administration officials such as Chief of Staff John H. Sununu were still invoking Bush's renowned speech line from the 1988 Republican convention: "Read my lips: No new taxes."

So, Foley was saying, it was time to get serious. Was Bush prepared to cross his own line in the sand or not?

Bush said he was. Sununu huddled in a side room with Treasury Secretary Nicholas F. Brady and Budget Director Richard G. Darman to draft a statement, which they handed to Bush. It said controlling the deficit would require not only spending restraint but also "tax revenue increases." The president handed it to Foley.

The Speaker then repaired to another side room with his seconds, House Majority Leader Richard A. Gephardt of Missouri and Senate Majority Leader George J. Mitchell of Maine. They rewrote the third-person statement to put it all in the president's mouth, starting with the words "it is clear to me."

Bush accepted the changes and told his press secretary, Marlin Fitzwater, to "put it out." Fitzwater had the statement tacked to a bulletin board in the White House press briefing room. But the low-key treatment only delayed the inevitable grilling. Was the president backing off the no-new-taxes pledge he had made in 1988? The president, Fitzwater allowed, had "said the right thing then, and he's saying the right thing now."

Sununu insisted that the statement only indicated a willingness to continue talking. House Republican Whip Newt Gingrich of Georgia noted that "new revenues" might result from something as unobjectionable as a cut in the capital gains tax, which would stimulate taxable transactions.

But few were mollified. Two of the three television networks showed clips of Bush making his 1988 "read my lips" pledge on the evening news that night. Rep. Robert S. Walker, R-Pa., quickly gathered the signatures of eighty-nine colleagues in a letter of indignant protest. Any form of tax increase was, the letter said, simply "unacceptable." Conservatives in the Senate were scarcely happier: eighteen of them had

Democratic "summit" participants, from left, Reps. Leon Panetta, William H. Gray III, Tom Foley, and Richard Gephardt and Sens. George Mitchell and Wyche Fowler, believed the budget could not be balanced with spending cuts alone.

written a stern letter of warning to Bush in May protesting the "no preconditions" basis of the summit.

Indeed, no issue united as many elements of the Republican Party in that summer of 1990 as the tax issue. Global communism was collapsing, and the social issues that were swelling party ranks in some states were proving divisive in others. Nothing made Republicans more sure of themselves than their opposition to taxes, and Bush's antitax rhetoric in 1988 had been a key to conservative support for his election.

Yet from another perspective, the only thing shocking about Bush's acceptance of the Democrats' terms was the time it had taken him to come around. The deficit, which had shrunk to the $150-billion-per-year range in fiscal 1987-1989, was growing again. In fiscal 1990 it would reach $220 billion, nearly tying the record set in fiscal 1986, because of a slowing economy and an ever-greater drain on resources for entitlements such as Medicare and Medicaid.

The ability to respond to all this was complicated by the Gramm-Rudman antideficit law,

enacted in 1985 and revised in 1987. The law, named for its principal Republican cosponsors in the Senate, Phil Gramm of Texas and Warren B. Rudman of New Hampshire, set limits on the deficit that were to diminish each year until the budget was balanced in fiscal 1993.

For years, the White House and Congress had conspired to meet these shrinking targets by means of accounting legerdemain; had they not done so, automatic across-the-board spending cuts would have kicked in. But in fiscal 1991, the Gramm-Rudman limit would be just $74 billion. The cleverest sleight of hand would fall far short.

The Democrat-controlled House and Senate virtually ignored Bush's own first attempt at a budget that year. They also had trouble adopting budget resolutions of their own, and when they finally did so they could not reconcile the significant differences between them. In the meantime, the economic picture continued to darken.

Given these facts, many in the administration (and even some Republicans on the Hill) saw a capitulation on taxes as inevitable. The party

On the administration side, Richard G. Darman, Nicholas Brady, John Sununu, Robert Michel, and Newt Gingrich sought a way to combat rising deficits and an economic slowdown without increasing taxes.

pragmatists were now asking how much real spending reduction Bush could exact in exchange for his tax concession and how the deal could be sweetened to make it palatable to Republicans.

The president held a news conference to proclaim his priorities. He wanted to reduce the deficit so as to continue economic expansion and employment, he said. "I knew I'd catch some flak on this decision," he said. "But I've got to do what I think is right."

That only fueled the fire on the antitax right. Rep. Duncan Hunter, R-Calif., spoke for many Republicans when he said that Bush "gave away the crown jewel of his campaign promise to bring the Democrats to the table."

Before Bush's conversion on taxes, it had been the Democrats who stalled in the budget talks. Thereafter, it was the Republicans who seemed to dig in their heels. Rather than retreat, the Democratic leaders held a news conference July 11 to say the new tax revenues would have to make the tax code itself more progressive. Mitchell said he thought the top in-

come tax rate should rise from 28 percent to 33 percent as a tradeoff for a capital gains tax cut. Gingrich labeled this "arrogant and outrageous." A week later, the House Republican Conference adopted a resolution of its own members opposing taxes as a means of reducing the deficit. "Which Republican Party are we supposed to be negotiating with?" asked Sen. Wyche Fowler Jr., D-Ga.

In mid-July, Darman's shop released numbers pointing toward a deficit so high that Gramm-Rudman would require automatic spending cuts of about $100 billion in fiscal 1991. House Budget Committee Chairman Leon E. Panetta, D-Calif., called the figure "a fire alarm in the middle of the night," but instead the number had more of a numbing effect on all concerned.

With little movement on either side, the summit was adjourned for a month, beginning August 3. When the negotiators returned, the world had changed. A new set of circumstances had arisen to overshadow the process. Just before the recess, Iraqi strongman Saddam Hussein had invaded and overrun his oil-rich neighbor, Kuwait. Bush had immediately responded by deploying an army to defend other territory on the Persian Gulf and by organizing the United Nations denunciation of the invasion.

Bush was now focused on the foreign challenge, and he directed his designees in the summit talks to expedite an agreement. The negotiators sat down again September 7 and agreed again to seek $50 billion in cuts for fiscal 1991 and $500 billion over five years. Reflecting the mood of crisis, a core group of negotiators moved into the officers' club at Andrews Air Force Base. They struggled there through September 17, while back on the Hill the rank and file of both parties grew increasingly restive. Gingrich had laid down a marker of his own, saying there should be a tax cut for families, a lower tax on capital gains, and various other incentives for business. His package, scored to cost the Treasury $134 billion over five years, would stimulate the economy and ameliorate the deficit, he said.

Many Republicans wore bright yellow "Junk the Summit" buttons on the House floor. Rep. Tom DeLay, R-Texas, announced that one group of House Republicans had a no-new-tax budget all set for a vote on the floor. For their part, Democrats talked of sending a budget of their own to Bush just before the November midterm elections.

The negotiators felt the heat but could not seem to find their way to a solution. The atmosphere turned brackish over personal slights, real or perceived, until Robert C. Byrd of West Virginia, the Senate's president pro tempore and chairman of its Appropriations Committee, administered a tongue lashing to Sununu. It seemed to clear the air, and the talks got moving again.

On Sunday, September 30, the day before the start of the new fiscal year, Bush held a Rose Garden ceremony with the summiteers to announce an agreement. The deal would trim nearly $500 billion over five years and would establish a new structure for the budget process (one that would, in effect, end the charade of meeting Gramm-Rudman targets).

But the deal fell $10 billion short of the stated goal of reducing the fiscal 1991 deficit by $50 billion. And it bristled with spikes to irritate members of both parties. Many Democrats were stunned by the proposed increases in Medicare patients' share of their costs, as well as at the impact on middle- and lower-income brackets of the largely regressive taxes in the package (including an increase of 10 cents per gallon in the gasoline tax). These new levies were only somewhat balanced by higher marginal taxes on upper-income taxpayers.

Republicans, meanwhile, were opposed to tax increases of any kind and disappointed that they were not offset by a cut in the tax on capital gains. Moreover, the Pentagon was in for $67.2 billion in cuts in the plan's first three years, the entirety of the decrease in discretionary spending.

"Very few people want to vote for it, so we've got a lot of heavy lifting to do," conceded Gramm, who had been among the Senate's GOP negotiators. The president and the Democratic leaders applied the pressure, saying a vote against the deal was a vote for chaos or for Gramm-Rudman cuts.

Both sides had long since agreed that any deal would have to be approved by a majority of each party in each chamber. In the end, when the House voted on the Friday night of October 5, the deal could not muster a majority of either party. Just 71 Republicans voted with their president to adopt the budget resolution and put the summit deal in place, while 105 opposed him. Among Democrats, 108 stood with the leadership, while 149 did not. Nearly half the Democratic committee chairmen voted no, as did Gingrich and most of the GOP whip organization. The chamber briefly filled with the cheers of the victorious rebels. But as the noise died away, the realization struck home that something else would now need to be done.

To tide the government over while attempting to sell the budget deal in the House, the president and congressional leaders had agreed to a continuing resolution, or CR (a stopgap measure in lieu of appropriations bills). But this so-called CR was to last less than a week. On the night the budget failed, House leaders slapped together a new CR that Bush vetoed the following morning. The House failed to override, and during the long Columbus Day weekend the government closed museums and prepared for a broader shutdown Tuesday, October 9.

But the Democratic-controlled Congress worked frantically through the weekend and adopted a new budget resolution more to its own liking. Among other things, it restored the authority of individual committees to make decisions on spending priorities. Bush then signed a continuing resolution to reopen the government.

No sooner had he done so than the House Democrats, no longer seeking majorities on either side of the aisle, put together a budget-reconciliation bill (written to give the budget resolution the force of law) with an aggressive "tax equity" theme. Among the new taxes on the wealthy was a higher top tax rate on income, a surtax on millionaires, and a phaseout of the personal exemption for the well-to-do.

But most of this went by the board in conference with the Senate, where Bob Dole and a different set of rules forced some measure of bipartisanship. The Senate version had virtually none of the soak-the-rich provisions of the House plan, and it retained a gasoline tax and other revenue sources from the September 30 deal with Bush.

In the end, the conference between the House and Senate dropped the more egregious facets of both revenue plans. They conferees agreed on a new top tax rate of 31 percent, with capital gains to be taxed at no more than 28 percent.

Bush signed it into law on November 5, after Congress had adjourned and gone home. Terming the creature before him "the largest deficit-reduction package in history," Bush asserted that 70 percent of the deficit reduction was achieved by spending cuts.

It was the tax-increase portion of the deal that continued to reverberate in politics that fall and beyond, costing the Republicans eight seats in the House and one in the Senate in 1990. However, the disillusionment that would weaken Bush's reelection drive in 1992 also strengthened the House GOP's young Turks, who reasserted their claim on Gingrich and their party's future.

A s 1991 began, the latest Middle East crisis overshadowed all government business in Washington. Five months after his invasion of Kuwait, Iraqi leader Saddam Hussein had not retreated. The United States had issued an ultimatum to him and marshaled an enormous force in the Persian Gulf region, primarily in Saudi Arabia. Initially dispatched to defend the Saudis and their critical oil fields, the U.S. buildup in the region continued until it had assumed the scale needed to liberate Kuwait and invade Iraq.

Congress watched with admiration as President George Bush maneuvered the United Nations and other multinational organizations to support his moves. But anxiety ran high at the suggestion of a ground war against Hussein's highly regarded army. In January both chambers staged a lengthy and lucid debate on the impending war and then voted approval of the president's policy. Although war was not declared, the procedure amounted to the first formal congressional support for war making since 1941.

The war itself was almost anticlimactic. After days of massive air raids on military installations in Iraq, U.S. ground forces attacked and swiftly encircled the overmatched Iraqi army. Operation Desert Storm not only liberated Kuwait but also crushed Hussein's offensive capabilities for the foreseeable future.

In the summer of 1991, there would be more good news on the international front. Reformists in Moscow triumphed when an August coup led by communist hardliners and military officers collapsed. Mikhail Gorbachev, the Communist Party chairman who had ushered in the era of glasnost and perestroika, gave way to Boris Yeltsin, the president of the Russian Republic and the first freely elected leader in Russia's thousand-year history. The cold war, the defining idea of the decades following World War II, had finally come to an end.

Despite the glow of good news from these foreign fronts, the president and Congress seemed unable to make a fresh start. Bush spoke of an "Operation Domestic Storm" to stimulate the slowing economy, but any talk of tax cuts brought partisan bickering. In addition, the budget deal of 1990 had made funding scarce for programs of any kind. Much of the summer was lost in a partisan wrangle over a modest extension of unemployment benefits.

Complicating Bush's relations with the Hill was a vacancy on the Supreme Court, created by the retirement in June of Thurgood Marshall, the first black justice. Bush had appointed another African American, Clarence Thomas, a strong conservative with a contentious political history. By so doing, Bush stirred the ghost of a confirmation fight four years earlier, when Democrats had used racial issues to outmaneuver President Ronald Reagan and deny confirmation to his appointee Robert H. Bork.

Hill vs. Thomas

Rhodes Cook

In October 1991 the names of Clarence Thomas and Anita F. Hill became inextricably bound in a Capitol Hill drama that was larger than the individuals involved and destined to resonate far beyond Washington.

At stake was a lifetime seat on the highest court in the country. Under scrutiny were the president's methods of selecting Supreme Court nominees and the Senate's means of confirming them. At issue were the explosive subject of sexual harassment on the job and, beyond that, the relationship between men and women in society at large.

Appearing separately before the Senate Judiciary Committee, Hill and Thomas, accuser and accused, delivered some of the most extraordinary public testimony ever offered to a congressional committee.

The two shared similar backgrounds of poverty and prejudice, overcoming adversity to build successful and highly respected careers. Yet here they were, blaming each other for devastating wrongs. Both spoke convincingly and with great emotion, and both told their stories to a huge national television audience.

The explosive confrontation began Friday, October 11, in the historic Senate Caucus Room with a moving declaration of innocence by Thomas. But for the next seven hours, Hill, an African American law professor at the University of Oklahoma, meticulously recounted her story of how Thomas humiliated her with lewd comments and unwanted advances when he was her boss at the Education Department and the Equal Employment Opportunity Commission (EEOC) in the early 1980s.

After nightfall and throughout the next day, an angry Thomas was back with his own accusations. "This is a circus, it's a national disgrace, and from my standpoint as a black American," he said, "it's a high-tech lynching for an uppity black who in any way deigns to think for himself."

Thomas said the message was "that unless you kowtow to an old order, this is what will happen to you. You will be lynched, destroyed—caricatured by a committee of the U.S. Senate rather than hung from a tree."

Yet even before the volatile issues of sex and race were introduced, Thomas's nomination had been a partisan, high-stakes contest. His appointment to the Court by President George Bush was expected to complete the realignment to the right that began when President Ronald Reagan made his first appointment, Justice Sandra Day O'Connor, in 1981. A decade later, O'Connor had become a moderate swing vote pushed to the center by more conservative subsequent appointees. And there were only two justices left who could be considered liberals—Harry A. Blackmun and John Paul Stevens (both Republican appointees from the 1970s).

Many in the Democratic-controlled Congress were feeling the pressure of being sandwiched between a Republican president and an in-

PHOTOS BY R. MICHAEL JENKINS

Clarence Thomas seemed about to clear the final hurdle to confirmation until Anita Hill publicly leveled sexual harassment charges that riveted the nation in October 1991.

creasingly conservative court. Against this backdrop, the process of confirming justices "has taken on the trappings of a political campaign," said Senate Majority Leader George J. Mitchell, D-Maine.

Bush knew from the outset that Thomas would face a rougher ride than David H. Souter, the New Hampshire judge who was confirmed by a vote of 90-9 the previous fall.

Unlike Souter, who was virtually unknown outside his home state, Thomas was an established—and controversial—figure in Washington. He had been confirmed by the Senate in March 1990 for a seat on the U.S. Court of Appeals for the District of Columbia Circuit after serving nine years in political appointments under Presidents Reagan and Bush, including the chairmanship of the EEOC.

When Bush had nominated him for the appeals court, the move was widely viewed as a preliminary to a future Supreme Court appointment. That appointment was not long in coming. When the eighty-two-year-old Thurgood Marshall announced his retirement in June 1991,

Bush quickly chose Thomas to take his place. Like Marshall, Thomas was black. But Marshall, the first black to sit on the Supreme Court, was a civil rights pioneer and steadfast liberal. Thomas was a conservative who had opposed affirmative action and other efforts to redress past discrimination through group preferences.

Introducing his new Supreme Court nominee July 1 at his vacation home in Kennebunkport, Maine, Bush hailed Thomas as "a fiercely independent thinker with an excellent legal mind." He was, said Bush, "a model for all Americans."

Thomas had two major assets as he entered the confirmation process. One was his appealing personal story, from his upbringing in the poverty of rural Pin Point, Georgia, to a position of national influence. "As a child I could not dare dream that I would ever see the Supreme Court," said Thomas, "not to mention be nominated to it."

Equally important to Thomas was the support of an influential Senate patron: Republican John C. Danforth of Missouri. Following graduation from the Yale Law School in 1974, Thomas landed a job with Danforth in the Missouri attorney general's office. Several years later, Thomas followed Danforth to Washington as a legislative assistant in his Senate office.

Danforth shepherded Thomas around the Senate in the weeks before the Judiciary Committee hearings, a contrast with the experience of Robert H. Bork, whose failed nomination to the Supreme Court in 1987 lacked a Senate guardian.

Like Bork, however, Thomas had a long and troublesome paper trail. He had written dozens of articles and testified repeatedly before Congress as head of the EEOC. Thomas had disparaged affirmative action, faulted Congress as meddlesome, and hinted that he opposed abortion. Thomas joked that unlike Souter, who was dubbed the "stealth" candidate, he was more like "Bigfoot."

Yet in five days of testimony before the Judiciary Committee that began September 10, Thomas tempered many of his earlier views and even divorced himself from some. Since becoming a federal appeals judge, Thomas said, he had purged himself of many opinions so that he could look at any dispute impartially.

Democrats looked on with mounting frustration as Thomas refused to be "Borked" or baited into detailing views that might cost him confirmation. "The vanishing views of Judge Thomas have become a major issue in these hearings," said Democratic senator Edward M. Kennedy of Massachusetts.

But Thomas's GOP supporters responded that Democrats, by engineering Bork's defeat, had caused subsequent nominees to watch what they said. "They have made the process into the process it has become," said Republican senator Orrin G. Hatch of Utah.

Still, Democratic frustration with Thomas guaranteed that the Judiciary Committee vote would be close. And when the committee voted

September 27 on Thomas's nomination, it split 7-7. All six Republicans plus Democratic senator Dennis DeConcini of Arizona voted to report the nomination favorably. The other seven Democrats opposed it. Following the deadlock, the panel voted to send Thomas's name to the full Senate without recommendation.

There, Thomas's prospects appeared much brighter. A leading opponent, Senator Howard M. Metzenbaum, D-Ohio, conceded there was only a "very slim chance" Thomas would be defeated. Danforth predicted his protege's majority would be in the sixties when the vote was scheduled to take place October 8.

But just when Thomas and his supporters thought their battle had been won, Hill's allegations of sexual harassment suddenly surfaced. Hill had made her charges weeks earlier to the Judiciary Committee, but had not gone public until October 5, after reporters for the Long Island paper *Newsday* and for National Public Radio were leaked word of her complaint.

Republicans railed against this disclosure and demanded that the person responsible for the leak be found (although no one ever was). In any event, questions about the fairness of the process were quickly overwhelmed by the nature of the allegations.

They not only raised fundamental questions about Thomas's character, but also struck many as an indictment of the Senate as a sexist old boys' club. "What disturbs me as much as the allegations themselves is that the Senate does not appear to take the charge of sexual harassment seriously," said Democratic senator Barbara A. Mikulski of Maryland.

Throughout the Senate, members were stunned as Hill's allegations became front-page news. A *Washington Post*-ABC News Poll October 7 found that 87 percent of those questioned had already heard about the charges, and 63 percent said that if they were true Thomas should not be confirmed.

Sens. Orrin G. Hatch, Strom Thurmond, and Joseph R. Biden Jr., during the October 11, 1991, Judiciary Committee hearing at which Hill aired her charges and Thomas defended himself.

The following day, seven Democratic female House members marched across the Capitol and tried to crash the Senate Democrats' weekly policy luncheon to, in the words of Rep. Patricia Schroeder of Colorado, "demand justice."

Meanwhile, Judiciary Committee Chairman Joseph R. Biden Jr., D-Del., was forced on the defensive. He maintained that his committee "didn't screw up" in not telling the rest of the Senate about Hill's charges. Biden asserted that Hill's original request for confidentiality had led him to tell only panel members.

Danforth joined with other Republicans in describing the allegations as character assassination and last-minute mudslinging. In an impassioned speech to the Senate, he told his colleagues that Thomas had told him: "They have taken from me what I have worked 43 years to create . . . my reputation."

Danforth was initially hopeful that the vote on Thomas would go ahead as scheduled at 6 p.m., October 8. But the ground was quickly shifting. With Thomas's character in question,

many Democrats who had announced their support suddenly became swing votes again. These senators said they were not ready to oppose Thomas but wanted a delay so new hearings could be held.

Six o'clock came and went as Senate leaders discussed what to do next. Shortly after 8 p.m., Majority Leader Mitchell and Senate Minority Leader Bob Dole, R-Kan., came to the floor to recite an agreed-upon script of unanimous-consent requests that postponed the vote on Thomas for one week, allowing time for hearings to be held on Hill's allegations.

When the hearings resumed October 11, Thomas was the first to testify. It was the first time he had spoken in public to defend himself, and he drew a poignant picture of a man wrongly accused, his reputation in shreds and his family destroyed. He said that his mother had been confined to her bed, crying.

The nominee "categorically" denied that he had ever harassed Hill, or indeed, even tried to date her. "I have not said or done the things that

Anita Hill has alleged," he insisted. "This is not American. This is Kafkaesque."

In her testimony that followed, Hill portrayed a much different relationship. She said that early on, Thomas tried to ask her out socially. She said she declined because she believed it would corrupt their professional dealings. Under questioning, she detailed the nature of the alleged harassment—sexually oriented conversations initiated by Thomas that she often found embarrassing and humiliating. She said they occurred mostly in his office and when the two were alone.

Under a somewhat strained line of questioning from Republican senator Arlen Specter of Pennsylvania, Hill said she believed she had a healthy social life and no unusual romantic fantasies about Thomas or other men. She dismissed questions from Democratic senator Howell Heflin of Alabama about whether she was "a scorned woman" or "a zealot civil rights believer . . . [who thinks] progress will be turned back if Clarence Thomas goes on the court."

She also said she did not have a martyr complex and did not intend to write a book about her ordeal. "I have nothing to gain here," she said later.

The conflicting testimony left senators in the difficult position of deciding who was telling the truth. "You clearly have to say one of them is lying," said Democratic senator Herb Kohl of Wisconsin. "That's pretty stark." But committee Democrats, clearly unnerved by Thomas's injection of racism charges into the proceedings, made little effort to counterattack or defend Hill.

Kennedy, who was front and center in helping to sink Bork's nomination, might have been expected to take a similarly aggressive role against Thomas. But Kennedy, who had been criticized for a rather libertine personal life, let his colleagues ask the questions.

Leading Democrats were left to accusing Republicans of resorting to mudslinging and a cynical racial strategy to portray Thomas, rather than Hill, as a victim. Yet if that was the GOP strategy, it worked. By the close of the hearings, a majority of people polled—men and women, black and white—believed Thomas.

On October 15, a scant two days after the Thomas-Hill hearings had concluded, the long battle came to an end. The Senate voted 52-48 to confirm Thomas, the closest vote in favor of a Supreme Court nominee in more than a century.

Two Republicans, James M. Jeffords of Vermont and Bob Packwood of Oregon, voted against Thomas. Eleven Democrats, mostly southerners, voted for him.

Both sides estimated that Thomas lost about ten votes that he might have had before Anita Hill's allegations emerged. But in the end, most senators said Hill's charges and Thomas's defense were inconclusive, and only a handful actually changed their positions.

On October 23, Thomas took his oath as a justice of the Supreme Court. At forty-three, he became the youngest justice on the Court and only the second black to serve there.

Yet for women outraged by the outcome, the Thomas-Hill hearings served as catalyst. Women's issues began to appear on the political radar screen, and the following year a record number of women were elected to Congress. "If the class of 1974 is the Watergate class," said Democratic consultant Ann F. Lewis on the eve of the 1992 elections, "this could be called the Anita Hill class."

After the highlight of the Persian Gulf War debate and the low point of the Hill-Thomas controversy, the 101st Congress settled into a pattern of standoff that came to be called gridlock—a traffic term that connotes a collision of conflicting directions and uncompromising wills.

Congress was increasingly distracted by the debacle of the House of Representatives bank. A report by the General Accounting Office in 1991 had revealed that hundreds of members had routinely overdrawn their accounts at this in-house financial institution, in effect writing themselves interest-free loans on future paychecks. No money had been lost, but the incident proved a potent metaphor for congressional profligacy, and for the tendency of the powerful to live by a different set of rules.

The spring of 1992 also brought a new presidential election season. President George Bush was dogged throughout the primaries by conservative commentator Patrick J. Buchanan, who never won a primary but drew as much as 37 percent of the vote in pivotal states such as New Hampshire and Georgia. On the Democratic side, the best-known potential candidates gave up on the race in 1991, believing Bush to be unbeatable. The nomination went to Gov. Bill Clinton of Arkansas, who survived allegations of womanizing and draft evasion to win on the first ballot.

Clinton was aided that fall by the sluggish economy and a Bush campaign that still seemed unable to believe it was in trouble. Texas billionaire Ross Perot, a mercurial businessman, launched an independent candidacy in the spring and temporarily flirted with the lead in opinion polls. In July he abruptly terminated his candidacy, only to re-enter the race in the fall. Perot attracted 19 percent of the popular vote—the largest vote share for a third-option candidate since Theodore Roosevelt split the Republican vote with William H. Taft in 1912 and elected Woodrow Wilson. In 1992 the incumbent president once again suffered from the three-way split: Clinton was elected with just 43 percent of the popular vote.

In the congressional elections, Democrats retained control of both chambers. But the House bank scandal took its toll on House members, contributing to a record number of retirements and the biggest freshman class (110 members) since 1948. The 103d Congress opened with high expectations for renewed cooperation between the branches. A symbolic end to gridlock was celebrated when Clinton signed the Family and Medical Leave Act, which Bush had twice vetoed. But the administration failed to push through a jobs bill in the spring of 1993 and nearly failed to win approval of its budget, which had higher taxes on gasoline and the top income brackets.

In the course of two years, the Democrats would also pass two rounds of gun control and two major trade agreements, as well as a national service program. But the centerpiece of the Clinton agenda, an overhaul of the nation's health care system, would not even reach the floor in either chamber.

= 1994 =

An Era Comes to a Close

Holly Idelson

It was time to take a chance. In August 1994, deep in the second session of the 103d Congress, Speaker Thomas S. Foley, D-Wash., had been stalling action on a massive and controversial crime bill until he had 218 votes to prevail on the floor. His vote count had grown, then had begun to shrink. So he needed to act fast.

The vote was set for August 11 on the procedural motion that would determine the fate of the $33 billion package, with all its new police officers, prison beds, gun control, and death penalties.

Lobbyists worked the corridors outside the chamber; party whips scrambled and counted. Foley himself made a rare personal plea from the well of the chamber. Administration officials were also on hand, wooing a cluster of moderate Republicans who supported the bill. Such brinkmanship had enabled President Bill Clinton to prevail before, but within the first minutes of this vote the signs pointed toward a different outcome.

Several Republicans thought to be undecided cast early "nay" votes, and Democrats began defecting in droves. With defeat inevitable, the leadership released several reluctant supporters, and Foley watched the final numbers go up on the electronic tally board: 210-225. Members milled on the floor—some jubilant, others furious or simply dazed.

For several moments, Majority Leader Richard A. Gephardt of Missouri stood silent at the microphone, as if at a loss for words. His nine terms in the House had covered nearly half his party's forty-year reign in the majority. Yet nothing had quite prepared him for that moment. In the next few minutes, Minority Whip Newt Gingrich, R-Ga., won recognition to speak. Restraining his glee, the No. 2 Republican in the House hierarchy assured Democratic leaders that all was not lost and offered to instruct them in refashioning the bill to his party's satisfaction.

The 1994 crime bill turned out to be salvageable. Pivotal House Republicans would badger and bargain until the Democrats made some changes in the bill. That effort resuscitated it in the House and provided the momentum to surmount the last hurdles in the Senate. But while the result was a legislative victory for Clinton and the Democrats, it was hardly the tour de force they had envisioned in early 1993. The bill finally signed into law in September 1994 was tarnished. And voters would hear as much about its controversy as about its achievements.

These frustrations were due in part to the resistance displayed throughout the process by Republicans who were discomfited by the prospect of a Democratic victory on what was once a GOP issue. But the bill's bumpy ride through Congress also revealed much about Democratic congressional rule.

Internal divisions slowed the bill for months and muddled its purposes. Policy splits were at

Majority Leader Gephardt, caught a few votes short on the floor, had no immediate fallback strategy on August 11 to revive the crime legislation.

times papered over with money, leaving the legislation vulnerable to charges of pork-barrel bloat and incoherence. And in the endgame, House Democrats also erred by trying to muscle the bill through without significant GOP input—a strategy that would come back to haunt them.

Congress had twice come close to passing major crime legislation under President George Bush, but both efforts ultimately foundered on partisan disputes. After ousting Bush, Clinton delegated the specific design of a Democratic approach to the relevant Hill chairmen: Joseph R. Biden Jr., D-Del., of Senate Judiciary, and his House counterpart, Jack Brooks, D-Texas. Biden and Brooks tried to take a legislative shortcut and drew on many of the compromises hammered out in the failed 1992 crime bill: curbs on death row appeals, new federal death

penalties, restrictions on handgun purchases, and money for new prisons and police.

"The American people have waited long enough," Clinton declared at the Rose Garden sendoff for the bill. "They want more police on the street and fewer guns." But minutes later, Rep. John Conyers Jr., D-Mich., stood in the White House driveway to sound an early alarm. Conyers and some of his African American colleagues wanted to focus on crime prevention, rather than on punishment after the fact. "Without the Congressional Black Caucus signing off on this legislation, it is not going anywhere," Conyers said. "Period."

The Democrats also needed a strategy for passing two forms of controversial gun restrictions: a waiting period for handgun purchases (known as the Brady bill) and a ban on certain "assault weapons." Party strategists were divided over whether to seek separate votes on these measures or to include one or both in the overall crime bill.

In the Senate, Biden bypassed formal committee action and took his version of the crime bill to the floor in early November 1993. But it quickly bogged down, as Senate Republicans insisted on more money for prison construction. In an increasingly tight budget, finding money for any ambitious new federal spending was not easy. And a move to accommodate conservatives in this regard would almost certainly provoke parallel demands from liberals interested in crime prevention and alternatives to incarceration.

Deliverance came November 4, when word filtered down about a grand deal brokered by Biden and the ranking Republican on Judiciary, Orrin G. Hatch of Utah, with the aid of GOP Senate Leader Bob Dole of Kansas and Appropriations Chairman Robert C. Byrd, D-W.Va.

The deal was built on Byrd's willingness to let the crime bill sponsors snatch all of the anticipated savings from the planned elimination of 252,000 federal jobs. This "found money" amounted to about $22 billion over five years— enough to cover the president's cops-on-the-beat initiative, prison construction, and a $1.8 billion package of programs to combat violence against women. Rather than choose among competing crime-fighting strategies, the senators proposed to embrace them all. It was called the toughest crime bill ever. But the new spending level was about twice as high as in the original bill, generating some private doubts.

The 95-4 vote for passage also belied widespread unease about the inclusion of a ban on certain semiautomatic, assault-style weapons. Sen. Dianne Feinstein, D-Calif., offered the ban as an amendment and saw it survive a tense 49-51 vote to kill it. Many senators still expected the ban would die in the House, where gun rights and the powerful National Rifle Association (NRA) had long held sway. The Brady bill, meanwhile, moving on a separate track, was passed by the Senate and sent to the president for his signature in the final hours of the 1993 session.

In the House, Judiciary Chairman Brooks began with a comprehensive bill that was comparable to the Senate measure. But he was quickly stymied in his own committee by discontented conservatives and liberals alike. Brooks then extracted several of the most popular proposals— including grants for police hiring and drug treatment for prison inmates—and sent five of them to the floor as free-standing bills.

That strategy may have worked under different circumstances. But once the Senate had weighed in with its behemoth in late 1993, House members were determined to respond in kind and in scale. That meant another trip in early 1994 through Brooks' Judiciary Committee, where House liberals and the Black Caucus were at their strongest.

Charles E. Schumer, D-N.Y., the chairman of Judiciary's Subcommittee on Crime, had been trying to balance punishment and prevention to sustain a winning coalition of votes. Given the expanded death penalty and other punitive measures in the bill, Schumer needed a sweetener for liberals, and he found it in the form of crime prevention grants—about $7 billion worth. The formula worked in committee, and it appeared to be working on the House floor as well, once an amendment also had added billions more for prison construction. The House passed a $28 billion crime bill.

Then the House turned to the explosive issue of assault weapons as a separate issue. Brooks, a longstanding gun rights champion, had thought he had this matter contained. As recently as 1991, the House had defeated a similar measure handily. But the Senate vote had lent momentum to the cause, and public opinion polls were moving votes as well. When a vote was held May 5, Brooks and the gun lobby lost. Suddenly, both chambers were on their way to the crime bill conference with a majority vote for the assault-weapons ban on record.

Brooks, a blunt-spoken Texan first elected in 1952, was a loyal Democrat but an autocratic chairman with an appetite for getting his way. Although he would eventually relent and leave the gun ban in the bill, he chafed at being forced to violate his principles and endanger his own reelection.

At the same time, members of the Black Caucus were fighting to preserve language in the House version of the bill that would let prisoners challenge their sentences on the grounds of racial bias. The provision was considered a deal-breaker in the Senate, and the black lawmakers eventually lost. But their efforts, along with those of gun rights advocates, helped to bog down conference proceedings for weeks.

Conference committees are often an exercise in power politics, but even by normal standards the crime bill negotiations were a display of majority muscle. Brooks kept Republican negotiators shut out of the final deal-making—in some cases literally—although Biden did allow one emissary from the enemy's camp to monitor the final, late-night talks.

Democrats shrugged off the protests and prepared to forge ahead, even as House leadership whip counts came up at least twenty votes short. That gap dwindled when some black lawmakers relented and agreed at least to let the report come to the floor. But many Democrats opposed to the gun ban refused to budge.

It did not help matters that word had gotten out about $10 million earmarked for a crime research center at Lamar University in Brooks's district. This was nearly the only such plum tucked into the massive bill, but it helped confirm the perception that the bill was laden with pork for important Democrats and so stirred indignation within the GOP. Adding to the mis-

trust, the full text of the bill was kept under wraps for days and filed just one hour before the Rules Committee took up the legislation on the evening of August 10.

Suddenly, the once-invincible crime bill was in real peril. The Democratic leadership decided to go ahead, hoping the pressure of the moment would tip votes their way. The administration hoped that about three dozen moderate Republicans would stand with the bill, and some were so inclined. But Gingrich was urging the same group to stand with the party.

The day of the vote, even Minority Leader Robert Michel, R-Ill., normally a mild-mannered, consensus-minded lawmaker, exhorted Republicans to send the Democrats a message. "How many times have we been had on our side of the aisle by the rules of this House?" he thundered, as the years of insult and legislative impotence suddenly found their voice.

The crucial vote came not on the bill itself, but on the rule to bring it to the floor. Only eleven Republicans voted for the rule, and they were more than countered by fifty-eight Democratic defectors. What followed was near chaos. "There is no Plan B," said a morose Schumer. Democratic leaders sequestered themselves that same night but broke up soon after without a plan of action. One of the leaders, Barbara B. Kennelly, D-Conn., emerged near tears, blaming the defeat on the gun rights lobby.

Foley and Gephardt were ready to abandon the gun ban. But Clinton and some of the Senate Democrats balked, forcing the House leaders to switch to a bipartisan coalition strategy based on winning over more of the gun-control Republicans.

The price of GOP votes was going up. "There is less and less willingness to [settle for] cosmetic changes," Gingrich said August 18. "With every passing day more people are showing up and saying 'Hey, I found another thing that's dumb in the bill.'"

Democrats charged the GOP was really fighting the gun ban, but Republicans found plenty of other ammunition in a bill they assailed as larded with wasteful, ill-conceived prevention programs and soft on tougher anticrime measures.

Yet the Republicans were a little like the dog who, having caught the car, did not know what to do with it. Exultant at the Democrats' defeat, Gingrich nonetheless encouraged GOP moderates to negotiate. He seemed wary of the political ramifications of killing the bill outright. The Democrats prevailed, but only after turning the Capitol into a kind of legislative bazaar with multiple bargains to mollify swing Republicans.

In the end, the parties agreed to trim $3.3 billion in spending, to add provisions for tracking convicted sex offenders after prison, and, to no one's surprise, to deep-six Brooks' $10 million earmark—hardly a major rewrite.

The revised conference report got through, 235-195, on a rare Sunday vote August 21. Sixty-four Democrats deserted their leadership to vote no—a slightly larger number than had rebelled August 11—but forty-six Republicans supported the revised version. On the Senate side, some of the House's insurrectionist spirit had seeped in. Dole, who had helped craft the $22 billion Senate crime bill, ripped the $30 billion model as "an over-hyped, multibillion-dollar boondoggle that emphasized social theory over law enforcement." But Senate Democrats were more unified in support of the bill, their Republican colleagues less unified against it. So after a few days of debate, the Senate cleared the report by a vote of 61 to 38.

The Democrats could be said to have finished on top. But they went home exhausted and in some cases embittered, having squandered the time and energy that might have gone for a final legislative sally on health care reform, the centerpiece of the Clinton program.

Some Democrats would wield the crime bill as a trophy in the fall elections. Many others would have it used as a bludgeon against them, especially in rural, southern, and western districts, where gun owners were aroused.

Republicans were on the march nearly everywhere that fall, campaigning against the ways of Washington and the majority Democrats in Congress. They were pushing an agenda they called the "Contract with America," which had its own approach to crime. And when the 104th Congress convened the following January, Gingrich would be the first Republican Speaker in four decades.

Epilogue

Shortly after the crime bill mess and the official death of the health-care overhaul in 1992, jubilant Republicans met on the steps of the Capitol's West Front to celebrate and sign a document. It was called the Contract with America, and it had been in the making for several years under the aegis of GOP House Whip Newt Gingrich and several like-minded colleagues.

The contract's ten planks were a compendium of dozens of policy changes from the sweeping (a balanced budget amendment to the Constitution) to the detailed (new penalties for purveyors of child pornography). Each item had been pollster-tested with target groups, and each item had won approval from more than 60 percent of those surveyed.

Virtually every Republican running for the House that fall, challenger and incumbent alike, signed the contract. It said that if they won the majority in the House they would bring every component item to the floor for a vote within 100 days. It was an implausibly immodest promise, taken seriously only by those who thought the Republicans might actually gain the forty seats net they needed for control.

In fact, they gained fifty-two seats net in what was the most successful Republican House election since 1946, when the party had also seized both chambers of Congress during a Democratic presidency.

It was not a bad year for Republicans in the Senate, either. The GOP won all of the vacant seats, protected all their incumbents, and knocked off two Democratic incumbents, including Jim Sasser of Tennessee, who was about to become his party's leader. It was the first time ever that a class of elected Senate freshmen did not include even one Democrat.

But the real glory of that Election Day was reserved for the long-suffering House Republicans. After forty years in the political wilderness, the Republicans entered the promised land with rejoicing. They elected Gingrich, the firebrand ex-professor from Georgia, to be the first GOP Speaker since Joe Martin of Massachusetts nearly two generations earlier. They also elected two other southerners, Dick Armey and Tom DeLay of Texas, to be the majority leader and majority whip, respectively. As recently as the 1970s there had been almost no Republicans at all—much less in leadership roles—from either Georgia or Texas.

But if the Republican Party seemed to be southernized, it was because the South finally had been Republicanized. In 1994 the party of Lincoln won its first majority of southern governorships, southern Senate seats, and southern House seats since Reconstruction.

The long hegemony of Democrats on the Hill had ended. And with their increasing power in the southern states, the Republicans needed less than an even split in House and Senate races in the rest of the country to maintain that control for some time to come.

Index